Catholic High Schools

Catholic High Schools

Facing the New Realities

JAMES L. HEFT, S.M.

OXFORD
UNIVERSITY PRESS

OXFORD
UNIVERSITY PRESS

Oxford University Press, Inc., publishes works that further
Oxford University's objective of excellence
in research, scholarship, and education.

Oxford New York
Auckland Cape Town Dar es Salaam Hong Kong Karachi
Kuala Lumpur Madrid Melbourne Mexico City Nairobi
New Delhi Shanghai Taipei Toronto

With offices in
Argentina Austria Brazil Chile Czech Republic France Greece
Guatemala Hungary Italy Japan Poland Portugal Singa pore
South Korea Switzerland Thailand Turkey Ukraine Vietnam

Published by Oxford University Press, Inc.
198 Madison Avenue, New York, New York 10016

www.oup.com

Library of Congress Cataloging-in-Publication Data
Heft, James.
Catholic high schools : facing the new realities / James L. Heft.
p. cm.
Includes bibliographical references and index.
ISBN 978-0-19-979665-6 (hardcover : alk. paper)
1. Catholic high schools—United States—History.
2. Catholic high schools—United States—Administration. I. Title.
LC501.H42 2011
371.071'2—dc22 2010042457

3 5 7 9 8 6 4

Printed in the United States of America
on acid-free paper

To Hazel and Berl,
beloved parents,
who before Vatican II
raised my four siblings and me
as Ecumenical Catholics.

Contents

Acknowledgments

TODAY, THE 30TH of March 2010, the media reported the death of Jaime Escalante, the gifted high school teacher of mathematics and calculus who was made famous by the 1988 film, *Stand and Deliver.* Shortly after the film came out, I went to see it. I remember vividly how I began to cry toward the end of the film, when Escalante's East LA Hispanic students, accused of cheating, retook their exams and proved that they were excellent students. Escalante was a great teacher—the kind of teacher that I, too, have always wanted to be.

For the most part, great teachers and friends have made this book possible, beginning with my parents, the Ursuline sisters who taught me while I was in grade school, and then, while in high school, the Marianists. Ever since my life was transformed in high school, I have understood the potential that good Catholic high schools have for making a significant difference in the lives of adolescents. I especially remember two of my teachers from high school. First, the young layman, Jack Doyle, a graduate of Notre Dame, my English teacher for two years, who died suddenly in a car accident not long after he had been engaged to be married. I also remember Brother Philip Eichner, S.M., now Father Eichner and still a close friend, my gifted Latin teacher for three years (and still teaching Latin while president of a high school on Long Island) who has continued to teach me much more than Latin. There were also professors in both undergraduate and graduate classes who exemplified for me what it meant to teach and inspire. To all of them, I am grateful.

Over the years, Michael Guerra and then Sister Mary Fran Taymans, S.N.D., (Sisters of Notre Dame) kindly invited me to speak to Catholic high school leaders and teachers gathered at the annual convention of the National Catholic Education Association. It was Sr. Mary Fran who encouraged me to put together some of these talks and publish them as a book. I accepted her invitation and, instead of putting together already published essays, I set myself to writing as coherent an argument as I could about the unique mission and importance of Catholic high schools today.

Several people in particular have read all or part of the manuscript as it slowly evolved. Bishop John Cummins, Michael Guerra and Dr. Merritt Hemenway read some very early drafts of chapters and made helpful suggestions. Mark Edwards, a professor of the History of Christianity at the Harvard Divinity School, then president of St. Olaf College and now has returned to the HDS as Senior Advisor to the Dean, read earlier drafts and made invaluable suggestions, including one that I seek a publisher that would insure a broad readership since, he assured me, many people, and not just Catholics, would find some value in what I have written. Una Cadegan, once a student of mine at the University of Dayton and now a professor of American Studies there, read the entire manuscript more than once and helped me improve it greatly. Nicholas Hedgpeth, a student of mine at the University of Southern California and also a graduate of a Catholic high school, read and commented on all the chapters and helped me track down some references. Fr. Eichner found the time to comment on many of these chapters, often pointing out the practical realities of leading an excellent Catholic high school. I am also indebted to the three anonymous reviewers of the manuscript solicited by Oxford, especially the lengthy and detailed one that helped me sharpen my focus and overall argument. To all of them, I am deeply grateful. I am grateful to Dr. Donald Wigal for the careful and thoughtful way that he indexed this book. Whatever lack of insight and understanding that undoubtedly appears throughout the book is due only to my own biases and limitations.

James L. Heft, S.M.
March 30, 2010
University of Southern California

Catholic High Schools

I

Conditions For Success

Introduction

In the spring 2007 issue of *Education Next*, Peter Meyer, the former news editor of *Life* magazine, after taking a brief look at the history of Catholic schools, concluded that they were in serious trouble:

> Not only are the nuns and priests now gone, but so too is a Catholic culture that for 100 years produced nuns and priests with faithful regularity. Of course, the debate as to whether the demise of Catholic didacticism and marshal order has been good or bad still roils Church waters. But the fact remains that the American Catholic school system isn't what it used to be.[1]

Meyer's terse description echoes the analyses of many observers of Catholic primary and secondary education in the United States. Despite the call of the bishops to rally around the schools, many Catholics, including those who themselves have benefited from a Catholic education, express a persistent ambivalence about the value of Catholic schools.

This book makes three arguments. First, Catholic schools have an enduring value which deserves greater support from parents, pastors, religious and the public sector. Second, the value of Catholic schools, so dependent in the past on the services and pedagogical skills of thousands of religious sisters, brothers and priests, can be sustained by dedicated, justly compensated and appropriately educated lay leaders. And third, since Catholic culture has weakened dramatically over the last fifty years, Catholic educators must address critically the dominant culture that shapes so much of the way students—indeed, not just students, but many educators themselves—think today.

Catholic schools need confident and competent leadership that not only communicates the Catholic tradition to young people, but also generates the financial support that will continue this great educational project. Without vision, all institutions eventually fail. Without vision, Catholic schools have and

---

1. "Can Catholic Schools Be Saved?" in *Education Next*, Spring 2007, p. 17.

will continue to perish. Money follows vision. Ambivalence about the vision that sustains Catholic schools eventually weakens the resolve needed to ensure their future.

The Author's Aim and Audience

Had I been able some thirty-five years ago to convince my Marianist religious superiors, I would have spent not just three years but the rest of my religious life teaching in Catholic high schools. In retrospect, they were right to tell me then to finish my doctoral studies and move on to teaching at the university level, where I have been ever since. Nevertheless, since then, I have been invited frequently to speak about Catholic high schools at the annual conventions of the National Catholic Education Association. I have also been invited to speak throughout the country at many high school faculty in-service days. Though my doctoral studies were in medieval history and theology, and though I have taught college and graduate courses in contemporary theology and ethics, and served in several capacities as a university administrator, I have always retained a deep interest in seeing Catholic high schools thrive.

In this book I have tried to bring together my thoughts on the current situation of Catholic high schools and to make a compelling and realistic argument for their importance and future. While I make use of many studies and scholarly works, I am not addressing scholars in this book. Rather, I envision as my readers those actually involved in leading, teaching and supporting Catholic schools—that is, administrators, teachers, parents, board members, bishops and those few religious and priests who continue this great tradition of educating youth in Catholic schools. Besides educational research, I have drawn freely from many of the classics in Catholic tradition: from Augustine to Aquinas, from Newman to Herbert McCabe, as well as from other authors such as Judith Viorst, Grace Davie and C. S. Lewis.

The three years that I taught in Catholic high schools were enough to convince me of their critical importance. Adolescents go through extraordinary changes during their high school years. It is, I believe, a privilege to teach and accompany them during these years, and especially do so in a setting—a Catholic high school—which is carefully designed to deepen their faith as they deepen their understanding and appreciation of the riches of literature, the sweep and lessons of history, and the wonders of science. The high school years provide an excellent opportunity to help adolescents enhance their skills in oral and written communication, skills that can all too easily atrophy in our oral, musical and media culture. Such opportunities make Catholic schools, in the words of the US bishops in 2005, "the most effective means available to the Church for the education of children and young people."[2]

The Closing of Catholic Schools: Some Statistics

Despite the bishops' ringing 2005 endorsement, Catholic schools continue to close at an alarming rate. The bishops noted, in that same endorsement, that although the Church had opened more than 400 new schools since 1990, it had closed 850, most of which were in urban and inner-city locations. And while 2,500 Catholic schools have waiting lists, almost all of these schools are located in the suburbs. The leadership and staffing of Catholic schools has changed dramatically: over 95 percent of the principals and teachers are now lay people. By contrast, in 1967 nearly 60 percent of teachers in urban schools were priests and religious.[3]

At the beginning of 2009, the leadership of the Brooklyn diocese, which has 1.5 million Catholics, announced that they would close or merge fourteen schools. Since 2002, that diocese has closed nearly 40 percent of its elementary schools. The archdiocese of New York has closed fifteen of its schools, with more to come. In 2005, a commission appointed by the then cardinal archbishop of Washington, D.C., James Hickey, told him that he should close twelve of his sixteen struggling inner-city grade schools.[4] The cardinal did not accept their recommendation and boldly stated, "Closing schools in not an option." Four years later, Hickey's successor, Archbishop Donald Wuerl, concluded that the commission was right after all. Wuerl hopes that charter schools will be a better alternative to public schools, but states they are not an adequate alternative to Catholic schools. In September of 2008, Wuerl turned seven of his Catholic schools into government-supported charter schools, with 97 percent of the parents' approval.

The extent of the decline in Catholic education is best understood by going back fifty years. In the archdiocese of Philadelphia, Cardinal Dougherty High School had 6,000 students, and the Most Blessed Sacrament elementary school

---

2. The United States Conference of Catholic Bishops Committee on Education, "Renewing our Commitment to Catholic Elementary and Secondary Schools in the Third Millennium," issued in June of 2005, published in *Catholic Education: A Journal of Inquiry and Practice* Vol. 9, No. 3, (March 2006), p. 267. The bishops' quotation was drawn from their 1973 statement on Catholic schools, "To Teach as Jesus Did."

3. Unless otherwise indicated, the statistics in this chapter are drawn from an article by David Gibson, "Keep the Doors of Hope Open," in *The Tablet*, Vol. 263, Issue 8792 (May 16, 2009), pp. S4–S5.

4. Meyer, "Can Catholic Schools be Saved?" p. 19.

connected to it had 3,800 students. In fact, I remember visiting my newly married oldest sister in 1959 in Philadelphia, where I went to a dance at Cardinal Dougherty High School; the huge gymnasium was literally wall-to-wall young people, squeezed together so tightly that if anyone danced, everyone around them did as well. The number of Catholic schools and the students attending them continued to grow until they reached their peak in 1965; since then, there has been a steady decline in both, with a slight but brief uptick in the early 1990s. In 1965, 5.6 million students attended Catholic schools (10,931 elementary and 2,465 secondary). By 2005, only 2.4 million students attended Catholic schools (6,574 elementary and 1,225 secondary).[5] Philadelphia's Most Blessed Sacrament elementary school closed in 1994, and Cardinal Dougherty closed in 2010.[6]

While part of this decline is due to smaller Catholic families, that alone does not warrant the rapid decline in the number of schools, especially given the number of Catholic immigrants with large families. Despite the large influx of Catholic immigrants, especially in the southwest, schools continue to close, and the numbers of students continue to decline. These statistics are alarming. Most authors point to money as the main problem—lay principals must raise tuition to pay lay teachers appropriate salaries which makes most Catholic schools, especially those in poorer neighborhoods, inaccessible to low-income families. Too few authors, however, point to the need for a clearer vision of the mission of Catholic schools, one that provides a compelling alternative not only to public schools, but more recently to the rapidly growing number of charter schools.[7]

Finances have been, no doubt, one of the major problems facing the leaders of Catholic schools. But there have been other problems, some less on the surface and more deeply lodged in their quality of leadership and clarity of vision. The distinctive vision of a school needs to be embraced by the faculty, staff and parents. Students will absorb it by osmosis, and though they may be limited in their ability to articulate it, most will treasure it all of their lives. Serious doubts about the value of Catholics schools began to crop up just at a time when they were at their numerical peak. Some leading Catholics began to question openly the value of Catholic schools. Their questions about Catholic education were joined to many other questions that churned in the turbulent and hopeful waters already stirred by the many issues raised at the Second Vatican Council.

---

5. *America* magazine editorial, "Loss and Gain," September 19, 2005, p. 5.

6. John J. DiIulio, Jr., "The Five M's," *America,* November 9, 2009, p. 9.

7. Meyer, "Can Catholic Schools be Saved?" p. 17. Meyer quotes Fr. Ronald Nuzzi, director of Notre Dame University's Alliance for Catholic Schools, who believes that charter schools are the greatest threat to Catholic schools.

Vatican II and the Ambivalence Over Catholic Schools

Most American Catholics welcomed the teachings of Vatican Council II (1962–1965). It promised more active participation in the Eucharistic liturgy; more shared authority in the Church; a greater openness to dialogue with Protestants and members of other religions; and most important, especially for liberal Catholics, a real "opening of the windows" of the Church. At least among a number of influential Catholics, like the then young Dan Callahan, Vatican II supported the already existing feeling that the older institutional forms of the preconciliar church needed root and branch reform.

The catechetical movement, which gained great momentum in the 1950s, began to explore ways of handing on the faith outside of the school setting. In 1964, when almost half of all Catholic children attended Catholic grade schools, Mary Perkins Ryan challenged the quality and necessity of Catholic schools. In her book, *Are Parochial Schools the Answer? Catholic Education in the Light of the Council*, she argued that, besides their other drawbacks, parochial schools were not the best means for providing religious education, which she believed was their fundamental purpose. She did not stop at criticizing the quality of Catholic grade schools, but included also Catholic high schools and colleges. She warned that "if a young person receives his whole education under Catholic auspices, he suffers the disadvantages of a hothouse atmosphere almost from the cradle to maturity." As an active member of the 1950s liturgical movement, she argued that Catholics should be formed first and primarily through the liturgy rather than through classroom instruction. By 1972 however, not ten years after attacking Catholic schools, she underwent something of a change of heart. In a new book, *We're All in This Together*, she admits that her 1964 reliance on liturgy alone was "astonishingly naïve." But not all Catholics came to the same realization.[8]

During the first half of the twentieth century, members of male religious orders—Jesuits, Dominicans, Franciscans, Marianists and Christian brothers—enjoyed greater freedom from the direct control of bishops than did the sisters. These mainly teaching communities of men, like the sisters, grew rapidly in numbers, especially after World War II. They staffed many Catholic high schools, mostly single-sex schools, some co-ed. These religious men and women led these institutions and populated their faculty and staff. They required little financial support, often no more than that which covered the cost of their room and board. By the mid-1960s, enrollments in Catholic schools constituted 87 percent of all students not enrolled in public schools and 12 percent of all pupils in the United States.

---

8. Mary Perkins Ryan, *We're All in this Together: Options in the Education of Catholics* (New York: Holt, Rinehart and Winston, 1972).

But not long after 1965, things began visibly to unravel. Religious sisters and brothers serving in these schools began to leave the classroom in great numbers, and sometimes also left their religious orders and even the Church. As lay persons began to replace them in the classrooms and in the administration, costs rose sharply. In 1965, religious women, many involved in primary education, numbered as high as 180,000; now their number is closer to 60,000 and their average age is well above 70. Instead of nearly half of young Catholics in Catholic grade schools, now only about 15 percent are there.[9]

Despite this grim picture of decline, researchers have published in the 1970s and 1980s studies that document the impressive educational achievements of Catholic schools.[10] On average, they reported, Catholic schools operated at a considerably lower per-pupil cost than public schools. With few exceptions, Catholic schools maintained open admission policies and increased their minority enrollment from 11 percent in 1970 to 23 percent in 1989. In 2004–05, the percentage of minority enrollment increased to at least 27 percent; of these, 13.6 percent were not Catholic. The student dropout rate stood at one-fourth of those students in public schools. Moreover, research showed that students in Catholic schools, especially minority students, attained significantly higher achievement scores than did their counterparts in comparable public schools. In an important 1989 interview, James S. Coleman, a Protestant sociologist at the University of Chicago who studied close to 60,000 high schools across the nation, came to the conclusion that

> ...on the whole, Catholic high schools educate students better than public schools do. Catholic high school students score higher in academic tests, especially in math and English; they attend college 20 to 30 percent more; and they succeed in college more often than public school students with similar backgrounds. Public high school students also drop out of high school four times more often than Catholic school students.[11]

Catholic sociologist Fr. Andrew Greeley, one of the very few scholars who since the 1960s constantly pointed out the importance of Catholic schools, has also measured, along with other researchers like Coleman, a strong correlation

9. Maurice Timothy Reidy, "Needed: The Vision Thing: Rethinking the Mission of Catholic Primary Schools," in *Commonweal*, April 9, 2004, p. 15.

10. See, for example, "Why Catholic Schools Outperform all Others," an interview with James S. Coleman, in *U.S. Catholic*, July 1989, pp. 6–12.

11. Ibid.

between attendance at Catholic schools for more than eight years and attendance at Sunday mass, activity in the parish, belief in life after death and opposition to abortion.[12]

Current Ambivalence

Despite evidence of academic quality and effective religious education in Catholic schools, the great majority of Catholics today send their children to public schools. Some of them expect that a weekly one-hour religion class (often referred to as a CCD class, that is, a Confraternity of Christian Doctrine class) will transmit to their children the necessary religious education. Many parents do not continue to send their children to such classes, especially when they are in high school. Some of the typical reasons why Catholic parents choose public schools are well expressed by Michael McCauley. In an article published in 1998, he explained why he and his wife decided to send their five children to public schools. He attributed the decision ultimately to a "changing concept of what being a Catholic meant." He mentioned how Vatican II's document on *The Church in the Modern World* (*Gaudium et spes*) helped them both realize that to be a follower of Christ was not to be a separatist but rather "a leaven in the world made holy by creation." Thinking this way made them wonder why it had never occurred to them before to send their children to public schools. Perhaps it was because, between them, they could count thirty-three years of Catholic education. Perhaps, he wrote, it also had something to do with the fact that in Catholic schools they had felt "safe and comfortable." He wrote:

> The Catholic schools I attended had both nurtured the spirituality and reinforced the cultural fabric. The cultural benefits were a supportive community and a firm stance from which to view the world as it opened up to me. The costs were a limited experience of diverse cultures, values and viewpoints, a certain defensiveness against an unknown and perhaps hostile world, a tendency toward judgment and triumphalism.

McCauley wrote about how disturbed he became when he learned that the Catholic school received financial support from the parishes as well as from the archdiocese, while the majority of the Catholic children outside the schools (78 percent in 1987) received no resources for religious education and had no

---

12. Andrew Greeley, *The Catholic Myth: The Behavior and Beliefs of American Catholics* (New York: Charles Scribner's Sons, 1990), Chapter 8, "The Touchstone: Catholic Schools."

organized program for faith development—an unfortunate situation that still prevails in many parishes. He was especially incensed when, at the time of confirmation, parents of the Catholic school children, because they had formed a strong bond being together in school, sat together in Church and received the Sacrament together. This meant that CCD students sat on the other side of the aisle and received confirmation afterwards. He concluded that "one sometimes gets the impression that they (Catholic children who are not in Catholic schools) are more on the periphery of institutional concern than those in Catholic schools." But then, McCauley wondered whether he and his wife had done the right thing for their children:

> These are the many factors that led to and confirmed our choice of public schools. Strangely enough, we are not sure we have made the right decision. The supplementary education we had planned to do at home has come to very little in the rush of events. I fear the power of secular culture may overwhelm a Christian counter-culture that is weak from lack of nourishment. I wonder what is happening when my son is assigned the "pro" side of an abortion debate and he wants to do it so he will "learn all sides of the issue." Ironically, I wonder if I would have cared about the CCD program if I had not gone to Catholic schools.[13]

McCauley clearly expresses the ambivalent feelings that a good number of Catholics continue to have regarding the value of Catholic education. The reasons the McCauleys had for their ambivalence about Catholic schools are not the only reasons why the children of most Catholics are not in Catholic schools. For some Catholics, typically those who have not had the experience of Catholic education themselves, the importance of continuing education in the faith and the religious formation that can be gained through good Catholic schools does not appear that important. For still other Catholics, especially poor immigrants who have a desire to send their children to a Catholic school, the cost is prohibitive, especially if they have five children, as do the McCauleys.

Having fled the so-called Catholic ghetto of the 1950s, at least some suburban Catholics have since discovered that they are no match for the growing power of a secular and consumerist culture. Never themselves having gone to Catholic schools, they had little idea of what their children, now in public schools, might be missing. Despite the extensive empirical data on the quality

13. Michael McCauley, "A Catholic Choice for Public School," *America*, October 18, 1988.

and achievements of Catholic schools, the legacy of Mary Perkins Ryan seems to persist, at least among a good number of suburban Catholics. A growing number of Hispanics and many African Americans, who for obvious reasons strongly support Catholic schools in their inner-city locales, do not share the same ambivalence that more affluent white suburban Catholics have about the value of Catholic education.

Suburban parents are not the only ones who have doubts about the value of Catholic schools—so do some pastors. For example, one East Coast pastor explained that his parish had established a Faith Formation Center that offered religious education to 380 children in their Catholic school and a different program for 650 children who attended public schools. The parish hired a layman full time to serve as its youth and young-adult minister. When asked about the situation, the pastor explained that his parishioners had growing doubts about the wisdom of devoting nearly half of the $500,000 in non-tuition revenue each year to subsidize the school. "The question is whether you should bankrupt the church to bankroll the school," he was quoted as saying. "At some point," he continued, "you have to say enough is enough." This pastor is not alone in his thinking. Since the Second Vatican Council, more than one thousand new parishes have opened, but a much smaller number of Catholic schools were started during the same time period.[14]

Andrew Greeley has repeatedly written that since the Second Vatican Council too many pastors and bishops have simply decided to give up on Catholic schools. He thought they had been actually persuaded by the Mary Perkins Ryan thesis, despite the findings of researchers that CCD programs have not transmitted the faith effectively. In 1990 Greeley rendered this bleak assessment of the future of Catholic schools:

> I have no illusion that these data will reverse the decline of Catholic schools. Bishops will continue to think that they can't afford to build new ones. Suburban pastors will continue to believe that life is a lot simpler without a school to worry about. Those laity who imagine themselves to be independent-minded and sophisticated because they do not send their children to Catholic schools will continue to congratulate themselves on their own wisdom. The CCD 'movement' will continue to claim superior virtue for itself although none of the effects discussed in this chapter can be found for their programs. Catholic educators will continue to feel apologetic and perhaps even sorry for themselves. The implacable critics of

14. Bishop William McManus, "Building Support for Catholic Schools and Their Teachers," *Origins*, May 19, 1988, p. 12.

> Catholic education will ignore these findings as they have ignored all previous findings.[15]

In 1987, J. Stephen O'Brien published a study entitled *Mixed Messages: What Bishops and Priests Say about Catholic Schools.*[16] One of his most important findings was that while 99 percent of bishops thought Catholic schools afforded the best opportunity to realize the purpose of Catholic education, only 76 percent of pastors agreed. Ten years later, a study conducted by John Convey found that "the more removed in terms of distance the ministry of a priest is from the inner city, the less supportive he is of issues pertaining to supporting Catholic schools financially, including sharing of resources to help non-parishioners attend Catholic schools."[17]

Recently the University of Notre Dame's Alliance for Catholic Education set out to test these conclusions again. In a study published in 2008 entitled *Faith, Finances and the Future: The Notre Dame Study of U.S. Pastors,* the researchers interviewed over one thousand pastors who had responsibility for Catholic schools. The pastors reported as their two most pressing concerns finances and Catholic identity. In their summary, the authors of the study grouped as the pastors' first concern a "triumvirate of financial concerns": enrollment, financial management and affordability. The second major theme was Catholic identity, which ranked fifth out of a list of sixteen possible needs. Ranked near the bottom were faculty recruitment and retention, board management and alumni organizations. The authors of the study recommended that the identity question needed to take primacy.[18]

Even more telling were the responses reported in Appendix B of the study, which allowed for open-ended responses to questions. There it becomes clear that most pastors are wary about school boards; they make it clear that such boards should be only advisory, leaving all major decisions to the pastor. Many pastors were critical of parents who send their children to their schools but do not attend Sunday mass. More than a few pastors regretted that the money it took to maintain the school left little for the religious education of the majority of the children in their parish. In the words of one pastor:

---

15. Greeley, *The Catholic Myth*, p. 178.

16. Published in 1987 by the National Catholic Education Association, Washington D.C.

17. John J. Convey, "Factors Affecting the Views of Bishops and Priests about Catholic Schools," *Catholic Education: A Journal of Inquiry and Practice*, Vol. 2, No. 3 (March 1998), p. 260.

18. "This study leads us to hypothesize that it is the value proposition of Catholic education that has been lost, and that value proposition is highly theological in nature" (*The Notre Dame Study of U.S. Pastors*), p. 55.

> In this day and age, with great public schools...I am hard pressed to understand the need of every parish trying to maintain a school. I have 1,400 children in Religious Education on Saturday morning. But I have limited resources to provide greater assistance to them because we spend so much on the school for 280 students.[19]

It would seem, then, that Mary Perkins Ryan's argument against Catholic schools continues to resonate among a number of pastors. Many pastors share the ambivalence over the value of Catholic schools that the laity express. They worry more about enrollment and finances than the mission of the Catholic school. And it would seem that the latest generation of seminarians share this ambivalence, but include as a reason for it their lack of confidence in the lay leadership of elementary schools.[20]

I concur with the authors of the Notre Dame study of pastors who state the most important need for Catholic schools is clarity about their distinctive religious and educational mission. Certainly, finances are also a critical problem in many schools, especially those in urban and inner-city areas. But today vision and leadership, I will argue, are the most important factors for the future of Catholic schools. Money follows vision. Without vision, the scripture states, the people perish. Without vision, schools also, eventually, perish.

Unlike Catholics in the nineteenth century for whom the compelling reason for maintaining Catholic schools was the hostile Protestant culture, Catholics today, along with Protestants, face a largely secular and consumerist culture, a culture that can be indifferent and even toxic to all religious traditions. How is a Catholic community that by and large is more educated and more affluent, and, perhaps now, also more secular than Catholics of earlier generations, to recapture a conviction about the importance of Catholic schools? How well do Catholic educators understand the prevailing culture of the United States, its strengths and weaknesses? In this new era, how might teachers and administrators understand their roles—roles which differ from those their counterparts played one hundred years ago? Are there credible alternatives to Catholic schools for the religious education and formation of Catholic youth? To begin to answer these questions, we shall proceed in several steps.

Chapter 2 weaves several threads together—especially historical, cultural and legal—to explain the current situation of Catholic high schools. The third

---

19. *The Notre Dame Study of U.S. Pastors*, p. 74.

20. In a 2004 survey of 67 seminarians, the author concluded that although seminarians "have a clear vision of their own pertinent school leadership abilities, skills and knowledge... it appears that [they] question the abilities, skills and knowledge of other professionals working in the schools" (cited in the *Notre Dame Study*, p. 11).

chapter delineates five characteristics of contemporary American culture, giving special attention to three which have the greatest impact on youth. Chapter 4 describes the distinctive mission of a Catholic school and argues that, because of that distinctive mission, a Catholic school has major advantages over public schools. Chapters 5 and 6 are devoted to leadership in Catholic high schools and focus respectively on its theological and then moral dimensions. Chapter 7 evaluates many recent studies on today's adolescents and describes the students who come to Catholic high schools today. Chapter 8 looks at the critically important role of those who daily occupy the front lines, the teachers, and argues that their recruitment and formation is every bit as important as that of the leaders of the school. Chapter 9 examines financial issues and alternative models of high schools. Chapter 10 briefly restates my main arguments in the light of the preceding chapters. Chapter 11, an Epilogue, provides a description of many of the parents of the students who are now, or could be, in Catholic high schools. I have entitled this reflection, "Post-Deferential Parents," to emphasize that the days of obligating parents, by whatever means, to send their children to Catholic schools are over. Unless we couple strong religious formation with excellent academic formation, many parents will seek superior public schools.

2

Historical Developments

Introduction

This chapter examines several historical and cultural developments necessary for understanding the current challenges that face educators in today's Catholic schools. During the colonial period religion and education were seamlessly woven together. By the middle and late nineteenth century, however, waves of immigrants posed new threats to Americans who thought that the greatest need was to "Americanize" the "unwashed" immigrants. How else, they asked, to prepare them for intelligent citizenship in a democratic country? Many Americans, therefore, welcomed the common school movement, begun by Horace Mann (1796–1859), a Unitarian minister, who designed the schools to provide a common socialization for all citizens. Actually, Mann's educational program promoted a generic Protestantism, beginning with daily readings from the King James Bible. In response, the Catholic bishops felt they had to establish their own educational system.

But after a few decades, American society grew increasingly secular and threatened both Protestants and Catholics, evidenced in a series of legal decisions in the twentieth century which stripped religious practices from the public schools. At the beginning of the twentieth century, the high school movement gained great momentum, but had little affect on most Catholic high schools, that is, until the 1960s, when it became more and more difficult to sustain Catholic schools in the ways they had been sustained for most of the first half of the twentieth century.

It is this multifaceted and fascinating story of the historical forces and cultural changes that affected Catholic education, especially Catholic high schools, that this chapter tells.

The Importance of Historical Understanding

For interpretative purposes, historians divide their narratives into historical periods that sometimes reveal as much about themselves and their presuppositions as they do about their narratives. For example, eighteenth century European historians, feeling the growing power of the sciences and the power of reason separated from faith, did not hesitate to name their own period of history as the "Enlightenment," and describe the earlier periods when the Church exercised great influence as the "dark" and "middle" ages.

In a less self-revealing practice of naming historical periods, historians of Catholicism in the United States have also divided their narratives into distinct periods. For example, John Tracy Ellis, the late dean of Catholic historians, divided his classic 1955 history of Catholicism in the United States along the following lines: "The Church in Colonial America 1492–1790," "Catholics as Citizens, 1790–1852," "Civil War and Immigration 1852–1908," and "Recent American Catholicism 1908–1956."[1] In 1987, Patrick Carey used the titles of "Enlightenment Catholicism" (1784–1842), "Romantic Catholicism" (1830–1888), "Americanism and Modernism" (1880–1910), and "Neo-Thomism and Catholic Culture" (1920–1960). In 1996, David O'Brien wrote about the republican, the immigrant and the Americanist periods.[2] At the outset of this chapter, the important point here is not the differences in the ways these particular historians have named successive periods of the history of American Catholics, nor even what those divisions might reveal about the perspectives of the authors themselves. Rather, the point is to underscore what should be obvious, but is too often forgotten: that from the beginning of the history of the United States to the present, extensive changes have marked and shaped the cultural and religious environment of Catholics. For those who think of the Catholic Church as forever the same, *semper idem*, a careful study of history proves otherwise.[3]

Only in the eighteenth and nineteenth centuries did scholars begin to focus not just on changes in history, but also on the meaning of historical change in the life of the Church. It was in the middle of the nineteenth century that a gifted religious thinker, John Henry Newman, who converted in 1845 from the Church of England to the Roman Catholic Church, addressed in an extended and systematic way what has come to be referred to as the "development of dogma." Newman wrote about the difficulty of how the Catholic Church of his day could legitimately claim to be the Church of the Apostles, despite the obvious and major changes it had undergone since the apostolic age. At the very same time, he also wrote about continuities in Catholicism, such as centralized authority, core dogmatic teachings, and sacramental practices that can be traced to the earliest centuries of Christianity. He explained that dogmas don't change, but they do develop.

---

1. John Tracy Ellis, *American Catholicism* (Chicago: University of Chicago Press, 1956).

2. Patrick Carey, *American Catholic Religious Thought* (New York: Paulist Press, 1987), pp. 3–70; and David O'Brien, *Public Catholicism: American Catholics and Public Life, 1787–1987* (Maryknoll, NY: Orbis Books, 1996).

3. See for example John T. Noonan's study, *A Church that Can and Cannot Change* (Notre Dame, IN: Univ. of Notre Dame Press, 2005), where he focuses on the issues of slavery, religious freedom, and the indissolubility of marriage.

As stated in chapter 1 of this book, there are both continuities and discontinuities in the short history of Catholic high schools in the United States. The fundamental mission of Catholic schools, primary or secondary, forms a principle of continuity. Since the foundation of Catholic schools in the United States, there have been two major changes: First, the shift in modern culture from a dominantly Protestant culture to greater pluralism and secularization in the late nineteenth century; second, the exodus of many religious brothers and sisters from the schools and the dramatic increase in the lay leadership in the latter twentieth century. The triple focus of this book—mission, culture and laity—will appear repeatedly through the following chapters: the shape of contemporary culture, the distinctive mission of a Catholic school, and the type of leadership Catholic schools need today. This chapter describes the dynamic evolution of Catholic education first in a dominantly Protestant and often blatantly anti-Catholic environment and then in an environment that grows increasingly secular and opposed to religious schools being conduits of religious education and formation. Understanding these developments makes possible a better grasp of the challenges contemporary culture poses for Catholic educators, the focus of the next chapter.

American History and Religious Education

It would not be an exaggeration to say that for the first several centuries, beginning with the establishment of the first colonies and continuing on through the revolutionary period, nearly all education in the country was run by religious groups for mainly religious purposes. In 1516, for example, a Spanish document instructed its missionaries in the New World—missionaries who, by the way, were paid by the state—to make sure that "each village... was to have its own school and Church, and... to see that each individual was taught and instructed... in the Catholic faith." A little over a century later, in 1642, the civil and church leaders of the English Massachusetts Bay Colony adopted the first compulsory school attendance law in order that the children would learn to "read and understand the principles of religion."[4] Until the beginning of the nineteenth century, the schools, customarily led by clergy, were primarily places of religious instruction with some "secular" subjects added. Almost all these schools were what today would be described as primary schools, not high schools.

4. William F. Davis, O.S.F.S., "Public Policy, Religion, and Education in the United States," in *Religion and Schooling in Contemporary America: Confronting our Cultural Pluralism*, eds. Thomas C. Hunt and James C. Carpenter (New York: Garland Publishing, 1997), p. 159.

Even at the time the United States was founded, the Constitution of the new Republic and the First Amendment of the Bill of Rights excluded the establishment of religion only on the federal level. In other words, it was quite possible for individual states to support a particular church, as some of them did. Thus, "public tax support for religious church-related schools continued and even increased until about 1820."[5] In those days, there was no clearly drawn line between what we now call public and private schools, nor was there a sharp division between church and state, especially on the state level. A few Catholic schools existed before then. The small number of Catholic "convent schools" and some Catholic grade schools in Louisiana and Florida created few problems in the seventeenth century, since most people then believed that all schools could be both religious in purpose and tax supported—which is precisely what people continued to believe until the early nineteenth century.

In the 1820s and 1830s, controversies, mainly between various Protestant groups, moved a group of civic and religious leaders to explore whether they might be able to create a single form of education for everyone. Horace Mann set out in his "common school" movement, concentrated as it was in the Northeast, to educate all citizens of the country for democracy. Mann's intentions were noble. He wanted to establish schools first in Massachusetts and then throughout the country—schools which were tax supported and met state standards for both curricula and teachers. He also deeply opposed slavery, arguing that to provide universal education required opposing slavery.[6] He tried to establish "common ground" with other Protestant believers. Therefore, the school had to embody a form of Protestantism with which all Protestants could agree—one which affirmed no divisive doctrines or unique religious practices. He wanted to create a school system that was "non-sectarian." Finally these schools were to teach *paideia,* that is, they were to promote moral ideals such as patriotism, responsible citizenship and democratic participation.[7] But the schools Mann created in Massachusetts turned out to be, in fact, not really "common," but commonly Protestant in ethos and practice—schools which required, for example, daily devotional readings of the King James Bible.

Once Catholics began to immigrate in great numbers to the Northeast, that is, once they began to live squarely in the midst of what was a settled Protestant

---

5. Davis, p. 160.

6. John T. McGreevy, *Catholicism and American Freedom* (New York: Norton and Company, 2003), p. 38.

7. Daniel Walker Howe, "Religion and Education in the Young Republic," in *Figures in the Carpet: Finding the Human Person in the American Past,* ed., Wilfred M. McClay (Grand Rapids, MI: Eerdmans, 2007), p. 400.

culture, tensions were bound to arise. Between 1821 and 1850, almost 2.5 million Europeans had immigrated to the United States, the majority of them from Ireland and Germany.[8] Several incidents in the 1830s and 1840s signaled a growing anti-Catholicism. The most famous of them was the burning of the Ursuline convent in Charlestown, Massachusetts, just across the Charles River from the city of Boston. Lyman Beecher, the president of the Protestant western seminary outpost in Cincinnati, Ohio, preached in Boston a series of three anti-Catholic sermons, the last of which was delivered August 10, 1834. Similar denunciations of Catholicism poured forth from other Protestant pulpits in the city. On the night of August 11, less than twenty-four hours after Beecher's sermon, a working-class mob burned the Ursuline convent to the ground. It is ironic that the school the sisters had been running enrolled a good number of the daughters of wealthy Unitarians of Boston.[9]

In the fall of that same year, 1834, Samuel F. B. Morse (the inventor of the Code, as well as the telegraph) published a series of anti-Catholic articles in the New York *Observer* entitled "A Foreign Conspiracy against the Liberties of the United States." He claimed that the pope, along with the embattled Catholic monarchies of the Old World, was plotting to have great numbers of Catholics invade the United States in order to oppose the liberties enjoyed by American Protestants. The recently restored Jesuits, according to Morse, were orchestrating this grand take-over scheme. So popular was Morse's series of articles that he wrote another series the next year for the New York *Journal of Commerce*. He entitled that series the "Imminent Dangers to the Free Institutions of the United States."[10]

Gathered at the Fourth Provincial Council of Baltimore in 1840, Catholic leaders had already begun to complain about the hostile attitude their children encountered in some of these "common" schools. John McGreevy begins his book, *Catholicism and American Freedom*,[11] with a description of a dramatic confrontation that took place March 7, 1859, when a Catholic boy, named Thomas Whall, enrolled in a common school refused to read the King James Version of

---

8. See Thomas Hunt's short but informative article, "Catholic Schools: Yesterday, Today and Tomorrow," *The Journal of Research on Christian Education*, Vol. 14, No. 2 (Fall 2005), pp. 161–176. The information on the immigrant population came from the *Report on the Population of the United States at the Eleventh Census*, 1890, Vol. 1, part 1 (1890), Washington D.C., p. 163.

9. Mark S. Massa, S.J., *Anti-Catholicism in America: the Last Acceptable Prejudice* (New York: Crossroads, 2003), pp. 24–25.

10. Massa, pp. 23–24.

11. McGreevy, *Catholicism and American Freedom*, pp. 7–15.

the Ten Commandments. At that time, the law required that all students in these schools read the commandments out loud in class. The teacher beat Thomas' hands with a rattan stick until they bled. Within a few days, front-page articles about the incident appeared in the Boston papers. Soon the incident became a national story—a phenomenon made possible, ironically, by Samuel F. B. Morse's telegraph. School officials and many Protestants who supported the common school movement became even more convinced that Catholicism was a foreign religion that would destroy the democracy on which their country had been founded. But Catholics weren't the only ones who found the common schools inhospitable. Evangelical Protestants also found the type of religion being taught in these schools—a nondenominational Protestantism—not sufficiently biblical and doctrinal. And for still different religious reasons, the small Jewish community in the Northeast also felt unwelcome in the common schools.

In summary, from the beginning of the arrival of immigrants from Europe in America until the beginning of the nineteenth century, religious schooling included the teaching of religion, according to one's own tradition and denomination. Protestants who desired to overcome their internal squabbles and prepare the young to participate in a democratic society founded the common school movement, but seemed oblivious to how such schools would alienate Catholics and more conservative Protestants. In effect, Horace Mann's common schools required all students, regardless of their religious tradition, to accept a generic Protestantism that turned out to be anti-Catholic. Catholics understandably found that unacceptable.

The Bishops: Catholic Education in a Protestant Land

By the time they met in 1884 for the Third Plenary Council of Baltimore, the Catholic bishops faced several problems that had become more pronounced since the end of the Civil War: the rights of priests, the treatment and care of immigrants, and the pastoral care of Indian and black Catholics. But that Council is most famous because it was there that the bishops decided to require every parish to establish its own school. They knew they needed an alternative to the common schools. A quarter of all the decrees of the 1884 Council had to do with Catholic education.[12]

---

12. Patrick Carey, *Catholics in America: A History* (Westport, CT: Praeger Publishers, 2004), p. 54. They also passed legislation having to do with seminaries and called for the writing of a Catholic catechism, which became known as the Baltimore Catechism which underwent many editions and was eventually published in a nationally standardized form in the early 1940s. The Baltimore Catechism remained influential until shortly after Vatican II.

A subchapter of the Council's main document on schools bore the title of the "absolute necessity for parochial schools." It began with a clear urgent statement: "If ever in any age, then surely in this our age, the Church of God and the Spirit of the world are in a certain wondrous and bitter conflict over the education of youth." The bishops continued: "Under the influence of those most ruinous movements of indifferentism, naturalism and materialism," the world had drifted away from religious truth and adopted a purely secular outlook on the meaning and purpose of life.[13] The bishops continued to worry about the Protestant emphasis in the public schools. The German Catholics in the upper Midwest wanted schools in which they could instruct their children in their mother tongue, a cultural heritage that for them embodied their Catholic identity. Irish Catholics in the Northeast, already native speakers of English, did not feel the same need for Catholic schools. But most of the Catholic bishops, living as they did in the midst of Protestant America, believed that they faced a danger greater than any they had previously encountered. Whether German or English speakers, the Catholics of the United States, the bishops argued, needed their own primary schools.

The bishops did not mince words: they stated clearly and forcefully that the preservation of the faith was most important, and that Catholic schools were the best means to do so. Where the bishops remained divided, however, was whether to *require* Catholic parents to send their children to Catholic schools under the explicit threat of refusing them absolution in confession. The bishops voted 37 to 32 not to require, under pain of sin, parents to send their children to Catholic schools. Rome responded to the bishops' report of their vote by warning them that they were being too strict.[14] Despite the determination of the bishops to have every parish establish a school, no more than half the parishes ever did. But by 1900, 44 percent of the parishes had Catholic schools—no small achievement in sixteen years by a mainly immigrant Church.

The success of the bishops' efforts was in no small part due to the contributions of many congregations of women religious. From the time of the Third Plenary Council of Baltimore in 1884 to the Second Vatican Council in the early 1960s, Catholic schools represented an extraordinary commitment on the part of most bishops and a large number of Catholics. Even though Catholic schools never enrolled even half of the Catholic children in the country, they became by far the country's largest system of private religious education. Given the poverty

13. Philip Gleason, *Keeping the Faith: American Catholicism, Past and Present* (Notre Dame, IN: University of Notre Dame Press, 1987), p. 119.

14. Gleason, p. 132.

of most Catholics then, private religious education would have been inaccessible without the enormous contribution of women's religious orders. In 1830, only about five hundred women religious representing twelve religious orders served in the United States. They provided many services, especially teaching in Catholic primary schools. By 1870, that number had grown to over two thousand religious women, both immigrants and native born, who served in schools and hospitals and orphanages. The women in these orders, according to Patrick Carey, offered young women an opportunity to live the religious life in community and in the service of immigrants and pioneers:

> They (these sisters) were an essential part of the church's missionary efforts and an integral part of the institutional means of care and hope. Their social and educational activism was frequently combined with a contemplative quasi-monastic lifestyle (i.e., seclusion in communal convent living, celibacy, retreat from the materialism and acquisitiveness of American life) that made them signs of contradiction in society. They were generally under Episcopal and/or clerical supervision and control, yet they were independent, self-confident builders of the institutions that served the church and society.[15]

Though most of the sisters were solidly behind Catholic education, a few bishops remained ambivalent about Catholic schools. Deep differences between them and the rest of the bishops became public by the 1890s when Bishop John Ireland of St. Paul Minnesota led an effort to cooperate with public schools. He thought it was acceptable to have Catholics enroll in public schools as long as they were allowed time to attend religious instruction. The controversy became so bitter and public that Leo XIII intervened. Conservative bishops took the high ground and argued that Catholic schools were the best means of passing on the faith; anything less, they claimed, would endanger the faith of Catholic youth. Ireland and those bishops who agreed with him saw some value in public schools, believing that in fact they transmitted a form of civic virtue upon which Catholicism could build. In other words, these bishops saw the nonsectarian form of Protestant Christianity not so much as anti-Catholic but as sub-Catholic, to which they could add through separate religious instruction the necessary Catholic specifics. Part of Ireland's liberal movement manifested itself in other ways which, taken together, erupted at the turn of the century in what came to be known as the Americanist Crisis. Episcopal appointments subsequent

---

15. Carey, *Catholics in America*, p. 35.

to Leo XIII's 1899 encyclical, *Testem benevolentiae*, an encyclical which raised the alarm about the dangers of trying to reconcile the faith with modern civilization, solidified support for Catholic schools that lasted until the post–World War II period.

The Separation of Church and State Hardens: Legal Challenges

The leaders of Catholic schools worked hard to preserve their mission and keep their independence. They had ample motivation to do so: a pan-Protestantism in the public schools and an increasing secularism in the larger culture. But they also faced legal challenges, most of which during the first half of the twentieth century dealt with Catholic grade schools. However, these very decisions typically were then applied to Catholic high schools, since the courts began to make an ever sharper distinction between, on the one hand, primary and secondary religious schools, and on the other hand religious colleges and universities. The former were dedicated, the courts assumed, to socializing their students in the religious traditions that totally suffused their atmosphere and directed their mission, while the latter permitted only a loose connection with their respective religious tradition, forbad all proselytism and left plenty of room for diversity of thought and critical thinking. (I will say more about the development of Catholic high schools later in this chapter.)

One of the landmark cases of the twentieth century challenged the very legitimacy of the existence of Catholic schools. The case arose in Oregon where in the 1920s anti-Catholicism was especially strong. The influence of the Ku Klux Klan, then at its peak, targeted Catholics as enemies of the country. One of its leaders, Grand Dragon Fred Gifford, called immigrants "mongrel hordes" who needed to "be Americanized. Failing that, deportation is the only remedy."[16] The Klan was the most active supporter of a ballot initiative, the Oregon Compulsory Education Act, passed in 1922. It required all children from the ages of eight to sixteen to attend public schools. The Sisters of the Holy Names of Jesus and Mary, joined by the Hill Military Academy, both incorporated in the state of Oregon, challenged the constitutionality of the statute, which was to go into effect in 1926. The case eventually made its way to the US Supreme Court (*Pierce v. Society of Sisters*, 1925) which declared the statute unconstitutional and established the right of Catholic and other private schools to exist. It affirmed the right of parents to send

16. Libby Sternberg, "An Anti-Catholic Law's Troubling Legacy," in *The Catalyst*, November 2007, p. 8.

their children to such schools. The legal team for the sisters argued that public education, which had existed only since the 1840s, was an infant when compared to the long history of private schools. They had existed for centuries.

Even though the case was finally decided on the sisters' Fourteenth Amendment right to own property (the schools were their source of livelihood), the language of the Court's decision enshrined a principle of the Catholic understanding of the priority of the family over the state: "A child is not the mere creature of the State; those who nurture him and direct his destiny have the right, coupled with the high duty, to recognize and prepare him for additional obligations."[17] Whether those who preferred private schools could expect the state to provide financial support in part or *in toto* continues to be debated to today.[18]

However, a very important legal principle in the United States had been established. Parents, rather than the state, were recognized as exercising primary responsibility for the education of their children. No doubt by 1928, various political movements and revolutions in Europe and Russia underscored for all Americans, Catholic or not, that the state should not have absolute control over all aspects of education.

The fact that the extraordinary 1944 GI Bill covered tuition for the veterans of World War II, whether they went to a Catholic college or not, raised the question as to why federal aid could not also be extended to Catholic schools. The *Everson v. Board of Education of Ewing Township* case took that very question all the way to the US Supreme Court in 1947, where it was decided on an interpretation of the Establishment Clause to the First Amendment. The Court's decision also introduced the "child benefit test," which reappeared in subsequent cases. That test addressed questions concerning public funds assisting children attending religious nonpublic schools. A statute had been passed in New Jersey that allowed local school boards to reimburse parents with public funds so that they could transport their children to and from any nonprofit schools. A New Jersey taxpayer challenged the law and argued that it violated the Establishment Clause since it provided support to church schools. In a five-to-four decision, the Supreme Court decided in favor of the statute arguing that it served a public purpose by paying the bus fare of all students who were required by law to attend

17. See Mary Angela Shaughnessy, S.C.N., "Pierce v. Society of Sisters," eds. Thomas C. Hunt, Ellis A. Joseph, and Ronald J. Nuzzi, *Catholic Schools in the United States: An Encyclopedia* (Westport, CT: Greenwood Publishing Group Inc., 2004), Vol. II, pp. 508–509.

18. For a thorough historical overview of the situation of public and private education during this period, see Douglas J. Slawson, *The Department of Education Battle, 1918–1932* (Notre Dame, IN: Univ. of Notre Dame Press, 2005).

school, some of whom attended religious schools. Moreover, the aid did not go to the schools but to the parents.[19]

Legal decisions about aid to Catholic schools continued to zigzag back and forth[20] on the question of whether tax dollars should be used to give any support to faith-based schools. After World War II many of the legal decisions on this question show no settled consensus on how to interpret the First Amendment. For example, in 1948 the US Supreme Court struck down an Illinois statute that permitted a local school board to provide released time for religious instruction held in the public school during regular school time; the instruction was to be provided by a local religious council representing the various faiths. The decision of the Supreme Court, *McCollum v. Board of Education*, ruled that the Illinois law violated the constitutional principle of the separation of church and state. Four years later, however, the Supreme Court upheld a New York educational law that allowed the city public schools, with the written permission of the parents, to permit students to be released from school so that they could attend religious instruction elsewhere. Those who challenged the law claimed that it was no different than the 1948 case. But the Court disagreed and said no student was forced to attend religious instruction and that none of the religious instruction took place in the public school.[21] Jesuit scholar John Courtney Murray believed that the *McCollum* decision embodied hostility to religion, whereas the *Zorach* case struck a better balance. Murray observed that, originally, the First Amendment "simply forbids preferential aid to one religion and consequently permits non-preferential aid to all religions."[22] Nevertheless, the courts continue to have difficulty in deciding what the First Amendment means "simply."

Besides the *Pierce v. Society of Sisters* decision, a second Supreme Court decision nearly forty years later sharpened the contrast between religious and public schools. In 1963, the US Supreme Court in the *School District of Abington*

---

19. See Charles J. Russo, "Everson v. Board of Education of Ewing Township," in *Encyclopedia*, Vol. I, pp. 285–287.

20. Noah Feldman, a professor of law, recently commented that "the Supreme Court, with its confused and confusing doctrine on the establishment clause, has not provided the guidance to resolve these problems [the teaching of religion in public schools in an ever more religiously diverse society]" ("Universal Faith," *The New York Times Magazine*, August 26, 2007), p. 13.

21. Mary Angela Shaughnessy, SCN, McCollum v. Board of Education, *Encyclopedia*, Vol. II, pp. 424–425; and "Zorach v. Clauson," also in Vol. II, pp. 700–701, by the same author. However, in a concurring opinion, Justice Robert Black stated, "One can hardly respect the system of education that would leave the student wholly ignorant of the currents of religious thought that move the world society for . . . which he is being prepared" ("The Case for Teaching the Bible," *Time Magazine*, April 2, 2007), p. 42.

22. John Courtney Murray, S.J., *We Hold These Truths* (Doubleday: Image Books, 1960), p. 149.

Township v. Schempp case ruled that Bible-reading and other religious devotions were unconstitutional for all public schools.[23] The key issue was whether Bible reading constituted "sectarian instruction." Already in the late 1940s, John Courtney Murray had warned the leaders of both public and Catholic schools that the greatest danger facing the nation's schools was a growing secularism in the wider culture. The 1963 *Abington* decision proved that Murray's worry was not groundless. One of the ironies about the debate over the proper interpretation of the separation of church and state and the funding of private religious schools is that Catholic and conservative Protestant opposition to the teaching of religion other than their own contributed to the eventual secularization of all public education. In other words, sharp disagreements over which version of Christianity should be taught has led many to conclude, unfortunately, that no version should be taught.

Until the beginning of the twentieth century, Catholic parochial schools (which, until the twentieth century, were primarily grade schools) began to find themselves required not just to defend their right to be religious schools, but to demonstrate also a "secular" purpose. Leaders of the Catholic schools believed that their schools served not just a religious purpose but also the common good; they educated students to be not just disciples but also good citizens. Therefore, they argued, these schools should be recipients of public funds. In the view of advocates for public funding for Catholic schools, the terms "public" and "private" caused multiple misunderstandings. This common terminology suggested a false dichotomy between what was public and what was private. Opponents of Catholic schools argued that they could not serve the common good since they were "sectarian" and divisive, authoritarian rather than democratic. Moreover, if tax monies were "public" monies, then they should never be used to support "private" endeavors. Embedded in the terms used in this debate were false dichotomies that made it nearly impossible for most civic leaders and mainline Protestants to imagine how tax dollars might legitimately be used to support religious schools.

Subsequent legal decisions revolved around the Establishment Clause and directly affected the financial resources on which Catholic schools could count. In 1968, the Supreme Court decided in *Board of Education of Central School*

---

23. Thomas C. Hunt, "The Edgerton Bible Decision: The End of an Era," *The Catholic Historical Review* LXVII, 4 (October 1981), p. 589. The *Schempp* decision, however, made an exception for the academic study of religion. Justice Tom Clark wrote: "Nothing we have said here indicates that such [secular] study of the Bible or of religion, when presented objectively as part of a secular program of education, may not be effected consistently with the First Amendment" (*Time*, April 2, 2007, p. 42). The distinction between the "objective" teaching *about* religion and the teaching *of* religion is difficult to make in practice. More on this later.

District No. 1 v. Allen in favor of a New York statute that required public school boards to purchase and loan textbooks for secular instruction of all students, grades 7–12, living within district boundaries, regardless of whether they attended public or private schools. Drawing on the *Everson* case, the court saw no problem if a state offered assistance to all its citizens; moreover, relying on the child benefit test, the court noted that the benefit was going directly to the parents and their children, not to the schools. The decision argued that religious schools serve both a religious and secular purpose.[24]

Not long afterward, in 1971, the *Lemon v. Kurtzman* case involved a Rhode Island statute that authorized paying teachers of secular subjects a salary supplement in private elementary schools. The Supreme Court ruled that the statute violated the Establishment Clause. The Court's ruling also established the so-called three-prong "Lemon test" to determine the constitutionality of financial aid to religious schools: "(1) the statute or aid must have a secular purpose; (2) the statute or aid can neither promote nor hinder religion; and (3) the statute or aid cannot foster excessive government entanglement with religion."[25]

Two other legal decisions bring the debates over public aid to private schools up to the most recent voucher controversies. In the 1997 *Agostini v. Felton* case, a divided Supreme Court decided 5 to 4, drawing again on the child benefit test, to reverse an earlier decision (the 1985 *Aguilar* case). The Court's decision permitted on-site delivery of remedial forms of education for under-privileged students attending religious schools. Addressing the Lemon test, the Court concluded that there was no governmental indoctrination, that no distinction of recipients was made on the basis of religion, and that there was no excessive entanglement.[26] In the second case, *Zelman v. Simmons-Harris*, the Supreme Court decided in 2002 in a 5 to 4 decision that a voucher program in Cleveland, Ohio was constitutional since it gave vouchers directly to poor inner-city parents whose only educational alternative were failing public schools. In other words, the statute acted with true "secular purpose" that neither inhibited nor advanced religious purposes.[27]

All of these decisions draw upon that critically important 1925 case. Once the decision was made then that private and religious schools had a right to exist,

---

24. Charles J. Russo, "Board of Education of Central School District No. 1 v. Allen," in *Encyclopedia*, Vol. 1, pp. 75–76.

25. Mary Angela Shaughnessy, SCN, "Lemon v. Kurtzman," in *Encyclopedia*, Vol. I, pp. 406–408.

26. Charles J. Russo, "Agostini v. Felton," in *Encyclopedia*, Vol. 1, pp. 33–34.

27. Charles J. Russo, "Zelman v. Simmons-Harris," in *Encyclopedia*, Vol. II, pp. 697–698.

those educational institutions had to face the next question: how to finance their existence. Ever since 1925, Catholic educators who have sought public funds for their "secular" purposes have been tempted to stress the secular character of the education they offered. Few leaders of Catholic schools would have felt the need to stress their "nonsectarian" character if they had thought that the lines of separation between church and state were so sharply drawn by the courts as to exclude any hope for support.

Throughout the twentieth century, regulations for the accrediting of both public and private schools increased. Moving from the 1920s, when that Oregon statute challenged the very right of Catholic schools to exist, through the 1960s when Supreme Court decisions prevented public schools from advancing religion through Bible reading, on into the '80s and '90s when a variety of legal decisions affecting financial aid based on different understandings of the secular and religious purposes of religious schools—all of these decisions continue to affect Catholic schools, not just in their understanding of their twofold mission of forming disciples and citizens, but also in their understanding of how secular they might legitimately be. Without some secular characteristics, there would be no chance to receive any financial aid from the state.

In summary then, to understand the history of Catholic schools in the twentieth century, attention must be paid to a series of legal decisions by both state and federal courts, including the Supreme Court. Secondly, the cultural setting of Catholic schools gradually changed from the public ("common") schools being a vehicle for Protestant socialization to becoming secular institutions.

Another important and extensive educational development of the twentieth century was the rapid growth of high schools, the main focus of this book. We need, therefore, to look at the growth and mission of Catholic high schools.

The High School Movement

It was not until 1821 in Boston that the first public high school was established. Until then, a few private high schools prepared a small group of mainly young men for college. By 1870, about 50,000 students attended 500 public high schools. By 1900, 6,000 public high schools enrolled over 500,000 students, about 8.5 percent of eligible youth, but only 6.3 percent of the enrolled ever graduated.[28] The private high schools of the nineteenth century prepared young men to enter college. Toward the end of the nineteenth century, when huge

28. Ernest L. Boyer, *High School: A Report on Secondary Education in America* (Harper and Row, 1983), p. 49.

numbers of immigrants began to flow into the United States, educational leaders, noticing the differences in the academic standards of the nation's high schools, began debating their purposes: Were they primarily aimed at preparing youth for college or for the work force? Or was their purpose to teach all youth, whatever their differing academic abilities, how to be American citizens? Throughout the twentieth century, these different visions of the purpose of a high school education vied with one other, until one of them prevailed. The leaders of Catholic high schools watched this debate from the sidelines, content to draw instead upon a largely agreed upon understanding of the mission of Catholic education: education in the faith through a common academic curriculum.

In 1892 Charles W. Eliot, the president of Harvard University, led a committee that wanted to restrict the high school curriculum to a set of rigorous courses that would prepare students for a smooth transition to elite colleges. His "Committee of Ten," as it was known, recommended the study of Latin and Greek, mathematics and several "modern" subjects: "English, foreign languages, natural history, physical science, geography, history, civil government, and political economy."[29] In other words, the curriculum remained the same for both those students who would go on to college and those who would enter the work force upon graduation. All students were to take college prep courses.

The other vision of education, promoted by G. Stanley Hall, a psychologist and president of Clark University, attacked as "elitist" the recommendations of the Eliot committee, claiming that most high school students were "a great army of incapables . . . who should be in schools for dullards or subnormal children."[30] A Commission on the Reorganization of Secondary Education, dominated by professionals in the new field of education, published in 1918 its report calling for, in more tactful language than Hall's, a differentiated high school curriculum adapted to the abilities of the students—an approach that came to be known as the "child-centered" theory of learning. They assumed that most high school students were less intelligent than earlier generations of students, and that as a consequence it was harmful to expect them all to follow a college prep curriculum. Many of the reformers who made up the Progressive movement took this view. Chief among the progressives was the very influential philosopher John Dewey, who believed in the education of the "whole student." Unfortunately, a number of progressive educational leaders, unlike Dewey, overlooked completely

---

29. Boyer, p. 49.

30. Jeffrey Mirel, "The Traditional High School," in *Education Next*, Winter 2006, p. 15.

the value of academic rigor and a traditional curriculum.[31] The progressives, however, won: before 1920, high schools offered only about 40 different subjects, but by 1940 they taught as many as 274 different subjects, only 59 of which were the traditional academic subjects.[32]

The number of young people attending high schools continued to grow. The depression and laws against child labor made it more natural that many adolescents went to high school. By 1930, over 4.4 million or 47 percent of their age group had enrolled. By 1950, 5.7 million or 67 percent of the age group were enrolled. The transition of high school education from an elite to a mass education movement was by then complete.[33] As a supporter of this transition, James B. Conant, a scientist and former president of Harvard, promoted in the 1950s and 1960s the idea of a comprehensive high school. He argued in 1967 that large high schools (with enrollments of between 750 and 2,000 students) were best equipped to accomplish three goals: "First, to provide a general education for all the future citizens; second, to provide good elective programs for those who wish to use their acquired skills immediately after graduation; third, to provide satisfactory programs for those whose vocation will depend on their subsequent education in a college or university."[34] Moreover, Conant believed that mixing together students who took advanced placement courses with those who took vocational courses would encourage a democratic spirit essential for Americans.

By the 1980s, when the economy was growing and a higher percentage of high school students were preparing to go to college, various reform movements tried to return public high schools to a college prep academic focus. These movements often focused on increasing the rigor of the academic programs. In 1983, for example, the Ronald Regan presidency issued *A Nation at Risk*. Then in 2001, the George W. Bush presidency passed the No Child Left Behind Act. The Act called in vain for standardized testing on the federal level since each state sets and enforces its own educational standards. These standards vary greatly, and their enforcement is uneven. As a consequence, any national reform again was thwarted. Courses with little academic content have continued to proliferate. And the public seems to be pleased. In a survey conducted in 2005, 73 percent of Americans opposed

31. For example, in 1939, a certain Charles Prosser saw value only in "useful" subjects. Prosser confidently asserted: "On all these counts, business arithmetic is superior to plane or solid geometry; learning ways of keeping physically fit, to the study of French; learning the techniques of selecting an occupation, to the study of algebra; simple science of everyday life, to geology, simple business English to Elizabethan Classics" (cited by Boyer, p. 51).

32. Thomas Toch, *High Schools on a Human Scale* (Beacon Press, Boston; 2003), p. 3.

33. Boyer, pp. 52–54.

34. James B. Conant, *The Comprehensive High School* (McGraw-Hill; New York, 1967), p.23.

making college prep courses the norm; they favored instead "career/technical education" to equip students who don't go to college with "real-world needs."[35]

Recently, the Bill Gates Foundation devoted a generous portion of its considerable funds to reforming high schools. Following upon Boyer's 1983 study, the Gates Foundation believed that large comprehensive schools created impersonal places where it was difficult to have close relationships between faculty and students. These large schools, many "drab, cinderblock fortresses," spawned big bureaucracies.[36] In 2000, the Gates Foundation began to fund smaller schools (no more than 400 students) in which students were expected to take demanding courses to prepare them for the knowledge economy (thus, no technical/shop courses). Smaller schools, they concluded, would permit closer relationships between students and faculty and create an environment in which students could be better motivated to become active learners. They also believed that smaller schools would allow for a stronger sense of shared mission on the part of the faculty and administration. While it is too soon for any definitive studies of the success of the Gates initiative, early reports are promising.

In summary, by the middle of the twentieth century, the push for mass education at the high school level had triumphed over an "elitist" model. Nonacademic courses proliferated, overall academic performance declined, and efforts at reform have had little success. How were Catholic high schools affected by all these developments in the public sector?

For much of the first half of the twentieth century, Catholic high schools stood, as we have said, mostly on the sidelines. However, the leaders of Catholics schools knew that they needed to compete professionally with the public schools. During the first half of the twentieth century, the government began to establish accrediting agencies. Consequently, the graduates of any school, public or private, that was not accredited were at a distinct disadvantage, especially if they wished to go on to good high schools and colleges. While the proponents of the elitist model of the high school curriculum and the progressives agreed on little, they both recommended the adoption of some standardization. For example, they agreed that classes should be of a prescribed length; that is, they would last a set time that constituted a "unit," fourteen to sixteen of which were necessary to complete if a student was to graduate from high school. As one school leader concluded:

> Thus the unit-credit system came to define both the structure and the meaning of a high school education: a rigid schedule of subjects and

35. Chester Finn Jr., "Things Are Falling Apart," in *Education Next,* Winter 2006, p. 31.

36. Toch, *High Schools,* p. 9.

> classes, an emphasis on time served rather than amount learned, and a belief that once a student obtained the required number of graduation credits, his high school education was complete.[37]

Under the force of law and the need to be accredited, Catholic schools, especially the high schools, embraced professionalism and became somewhat "Americanized." Patrick Carey states that instead of becoming vehicles for complete separatism from the dominantly Protestant and secular culture, Catholic schools began to adopt some forms of professionalism with the hope of being recognized as better schools.[38]

Some of the largest Catholic high schools, located mainly in the Northeast, adopted a tracking system that put their brightest students in advanced placement courses, the less talented in college prep courses, and the least talented in vocational courses. But the lack of federal funds limited severely the variety of courses they could offer. As a consequence, most Catholic high schools have focused on traditional subjects, not only during the glory days of the Progressive movement, but right up to the present. In 1993 one of the most widely read and acclaimed studies of Catholic high schools, building on the research done by Coleman and Greeley, reported that they "manage simultaneously to achieve relatively high levels of student learning, distribute this learning more equitably with regard to race and class than in the public sector, and sustain high levels of teacher commitment and student engagement."[39]

The authors of the 1993 study singled out four foundational characteristics that account for the extraordinary success of Catholic high schools: "a delimited technical core, communal organization, decentralized governance, and an inspirational ideology." By a delimited technical core, the authors meant that these

---

37. Barney Brawer, "Carnegie Units: Defining a High School Education," in *Education Next* (Winter 2006), p. 16; this article is part of a forum entitled "The American High School: Can it be Saved?"

38. Carey, *Catholics in America*, p. 82. Carey, a careful historian, may have overstated the intent of Catholic educators when he writes: "Many Catholic educators, like their counterparts in the public school system, began to worship at the shrine of scientific efficiency, believing that standardization, professionalism, state certification of teachers and bureaucratic centralization were the means for improving education" (p. 82). See also Slawson, who describes the "administrative progressives" of that time who "sought to replace the decentralized decision making of local school boards composed of lay people with centralized, bureaucratic, top-down direction by professional educators, chosen by a corporate board of directors selected in citywide elections.... Thus, education was to be 'taken out of politics' by removing it from the contentiousness of local boards and entrusting it to the hands of an objective professional" (p. 3).

39. Anthony Bryk, Valerie Lee and Peter Holland, *Catholic Schools and the Common Good* (Harvard University Press, 1993), p. 297.

schools offered a single core curriculum, regardless of whether the students intended to go to college. They offered few electives. Each student, whatever his or her ability, is expected to make academic progress. The schools' communal organization rests on three practices: a wide array of co-curricular activities that bring students and faculty face-to- face; an extended role for teachers, encouraging them to be more collegial and more than subject experts confined to the classroom; and a shared moral tone that respects the dignity of each person. Decentralized government simply points out that there really isn't a "Catholic school system," but rather a very loose federation of schools where decision making is largely local. And finally, the authors note that Catholic schools benefit from an inspirational ideology that draws freely upon the principles of Christian personalism and subsidiarity. They reported that the former, personalism, encouraged the humane treatment of everyone in the school, students as well as faculty, while the latter, subsidiarity, respected the genuine competencies of the principal, faculty and staff, and softened the centralization impersonality of a highly bureaucratic approach to organization.[40]

Since 1985, the National Catholic Education Association has been systematically collecting data on Catholic high schools. Their 2007 study offers an informative overview of the current situation of Catholic high schools. The average student population from 1993 to 2006 remained between 540 and 580 (though 12 percent of these schools have enrollments of less than 200 students and face special financial difficulties). About 40 percent are sponsored by dioceses, 40 percent by religious communities, and the remaining are either connected to a parish or sponsored by a private corporation. Over 60 percent are co-ed, 21 percent are all female and 17 percent are all male. Nearly two-thirds of school leaders are laypersons, and the remaining third religious and priests. 95 percent of the high schools have boards (usually about 15 persons) with slightly more than half functioning in only an advisory capacity. In those schools sponsored by religious orders and private corporations, the board actually makes policy. In recent years, a significant number of these schools have appointed people for advancement, in public relations and as alumni/ae and to raise money in addition to tuition. 75 percent of the schools have endowments, the average size of which is about 3.5 million dollars.

The report also includes some ongoing concerns, including the salaries of teachers (the report does not provide comparisons with the salaries teachers make in public schools), especially in high schools sponsored by dioceses. Moreover,

---

40. Bryk et al., *Catholic Schools and the Common Good,* pp. 297–304. The authors also make observations, somewhat questionable, about their vision of Catholicism and religious education most appropriate for the post-Vatican II era. We will return to their vision and these issues in our chapter on the mission of Catholic high schools.

25 percent of teachers leave after two years, and 46 percent after three to five years. Principals rarely serve longer than five years. Despite a number of court cases that permit private and religious schools access to some public funds, the high schools in this study report that only 2 percent of their income is derived from federal, state and local public sources.[41]

Despite the good news about Catholic high schools documented by researchers such as James Coleman, Andrew Greeley and Anthony Bryk and his colleagues, both Catholic grade schools and high schools continue to close, as recounted in the introduction to this book, at an alarming rate. Certainly, finances are a significant challenge, especially for diocesan schools in urban and inner-city areas. But, as stated, there is also a continuing ambivalence about the value of maintaining these schools. That ambivalence began to grow after World War II and especially after Vatican II. Few things sap the resolve of those responsible for Catholic education than ambivalence about their value and mission.

Ambivalence and Questioning

In 1884 the bishops of the United States called for the establishment of Catholic schools to protect Catholic children against the public schools, which then still breathed a Protestant atmosphere. Toward the end of that century, the bishops also sensed a second major threat that would grow only stronger in the twentieth century: secularism. As long as Catholic schools could count on having large numbers of priests and religious as teachers, they remained affordable. And as long as they could count on the support of parents who trusted in the vision of education that prevailed in the majority of these institutions, they remained relatively insulated from the dominant forces of the wider culture, including the competing visions—elitist and progressive—of the purpose of a high school education. That relative isolation from public education did not mean, however, that they were not challenged several times by various legal threats, as we have seen. But after World War II, things began to change: first for the majority of the Catholic community in the United States, and then, in the mid 1960s, for the religious and priests who had founded and led the vast majority of these schools. In the 1950s, Catholic veterans of the war, funded generously by the federal government's GI Bill, began entering in unprecedented numbers the ranks of college graduates. More and more Catholics moved to the suburbs, and many, along with religious and priests, began to have questions about the need for Catholic schools. By that time, many Catholics

41. *Dollars and $ense: Catholic High School and their Finances*, Secondary Schools Department of the National Catholic Education Association: Executive Summary Report (Washington, DC, 2007).

were beginning to feel very much at home in mainstream American culture. They had entered for the first time the middle and upper-middle classes, most evidently during the 1950s through the 1980s in the Northeast and Midwest.[42]

While it would be difficult to prove a strong correlation between the "liberal" movements of Catholics in American culture and the weakening of a commitment to Catholic schools, those Catholics who expressed the desire to break out of the Catholic "ghetto" rarely endorsed Catholic schools. One influential critic of the Catholic ghetto was John Tracy Ellis. The 1955 issue of *Thought*, a Jesuit journal of theology and culture, carried Ellis' essay, "American Catholics and the Intellectual Life," an article, in the opinion of another prominent American Church historian, that "provoked a greater reaction than any other piece of comparable length in the history of American Catholicism."[43] Ellis argued that the lack of intellectual achievement among Catholics was due in part to their refusal to learn from elite educational institutions, most of them by then secular. He complained that isolated Catholic institutions dedicated themselves more to fielding winning athletic teams than fostering excellent scholarship. The elite universities—unlike the academically undistinguished Catholic colleges and universities—knew how to foster scholarship, and the best of them didn't care, Ellis explained, much about inter-college athletics.

"Liberal" Catholics began to write about dropping the "siege mentality," and of becoming active participants in the wider American culture. By 1965, several Catholics confidently moved into the secular world determined to leave their mark, although hardly sure of what that mark would be. That same year, the already mentioned Catholic layman and Harvard graduate Daniel Callahan, who edited and introduced a collection of autobiographical essays by young Catholic intellectuals, *Generation of the Third Eye*, spoke of his generation as one "cut loose from many of its roots, from the nurture of old traditions," and one that "looks constantly into itself." Having graduated from Catholic colleges, many of these young Catholics went off to prestigious secular graduate schools in search of a new "more mature" Catholicism. Their search, as we shall see later, hardly resulted in an unqualified success.[44] Only fifty years after Leo XIII's warning about efforts

---

42. For an interpretation of movement away from the mainstream into a more conscious Catholic identity among some younger Catholics today, see William Portier's "Here Come the Catholic Evangelicals," *Communio* 31 (Spring 2004).

43. Gleason, p. 72.

44. See James T. Fisher, "Young American Catholics: Who are They and What do They Want?" in *Commonweal*, November 23, 2001, pp. 9–12. Fisher cites Callahan's description of his generation as looking into itself, and as a consequence, in Callahan's own words, was "thus partially paralyzed." (Daniel Callahan, *Third Eye* [New York: Sheed and Ward, 1965]), p. 13.

to reconcile the faith with modernity, a number of prominent American Catholics were leading just such an effort.

Conclusion

Before the Second Vatican Council, the Catholic community was able, certainly not without some difficulty, to lead and fund their schools. Large numbers of religious sisters and brothers and priests staffed and led these schools. Developments after Vatican II put the stability and future of Catholic schools in question, not just because of the exodus of many of the religious men and women and the subsequent escalation of the cost of a Catholic education, but because Catholic institutions—not just schools but also the Church itself—became the object of more extensive criticism. Many Catholics wondered where the Church was going and what they should believe. One close observer of the Catholic community after Vatican II entitled his book, *A People Adrift*.[45] Taken together, these changes created a two-tiered challenge for Catholic schools. First, they created impoverished inner-city schools, typically grade schools, populated by growing numbers of non-Catholic students. The parents of these children nonetheless desired an alternative to the failing inner-city public schools. Second, a growing number of affluent suburban Catholics who had access to good suburban public schools became less convinced of the importance of sending their children to Catholic schools. In the inner city where finances were more scarce, there was a desperate need for Catholic schools; in (oops, leave as is) where families could afford Catholic schools, there was less conviction about their importance.

One of the major forces contributing to the difficulty of sustaining a clear and compelling vision for Catholic high schools still needs to be explored. That force is the pervasive power of the larger culture, made all the more influential by the simultaneous dissolution of the Catholic subculture. Our next chapter explores the major characteristics of contemporary culture in the United States and their effect on Catholic education.

---

45. See Peter Steinfels, *A People Adrift: The Crisis of the Roman Catholic Church in America* (Simon & Schuster; 2003). See especially chapter four, "Catholic Institutions and Catholic Identity."

3

American Culture and Religion

Introduction

To be effective, educators need to understand the culture that forms not only their students, but also themselves. Later, I will devote an entire chapter to recent literature that attempts to describe the adolescents of today. This chapter explores the culture that all too often has more influence on the thinking and habits of adolescents than the Catholic culture and its traditions. There are, of course, good things in our culture—but there are also harmful trends. It is important to see how a number of the dominant trends in the culture cuts both ways; that is, from one angle, they are quite positive and to be celebrated, but from another they can be detrimental, even toxic, especially to a faith tradition such as Catholicism.

The last chapter showed how the legal questions that affected Catholic schools turned in large part on interpretations of what judges thought the separation of church and state required. Ironically, the growing religious diversity of the United States actually contributed to the secularization of the public schools. In the first half of the nineteenth century, Protestantism dominated the culture and the public schools. But after the Civil War, when large numbers of Catholic immigrants came to the United States, the culture began to change. Secularism and materialism become more powerful forces. In the twentieth century, the United States became the most powerful economic and military force in the world. By the beginning of the twenty-first century, however, the geopolitical situation has changed: both India and China are rising economic powers, the Soviet Union, which no longer exists, is diminished both in size and influence, and Europe is working to consolidate its economic power as an Economic Union. The United States can no longer be accurately described as Protestant, even though 80 percent of the population still identifies itself as Christian.

The cultural and religious tapestry of the United States is complex. Though more secular and pluralistic than ever,[1] this country continues to nourish a wide variety of religious movements. Despite efforts among mainline Protestants and

1. See John Coleman's review of Robert Wuthnow's *America and the Challenges of Religious Diversity* (Princeton, NJ: Princeton University Press, 2004) in *America*, October 10, 2005, p. 33.

Catholics to come closer together, religious divisions among them remain, especially on abortion, homosexuality and the role of women in the Church. Some Christians are very conservative and others quite liberal, but despite the media stories, most religious people are moderate and stand mostly in the middle. Some believers are affluent, many are middle class, and too many are poor. This chapter sketches the larger complex story of American culture and its effect on religious belief and practice. In the next chapter, I will clarify how people involved in Catholic education, and in particular, Catholic high schools, might best understand their mission in the context of contemporary US culture.

Five Currents in American Culture

In the last chapter, I described how the early English speaking settlers in the Northeast sought religious freedom for themselves, a search that was eventually redefined in the Bill of Rights under the First Amendment. I also wrote about the challenges Catholics faced in raising their children—challenges presented by Protestantism and then also by secularism. It is time now to sketch a contemporary portrait of the culture in the United States. For many reasons, this is not an easy task. To mention only one, a geographical reason, the culture in the Northeast is hardly the same as that in the South. The culture in the Northwest of the country is quite different from the Southwest. The textures of Catholicism on the two coasts differ. As one moves northwest, one encounters less and less religious practice altogether. Despite these differences within the country, some generalizations, with qualifications, can be made. This chapter singles out five general themes in contemporary US culture that leaders of Catholic high schools need to understand. The first two are clearly historically rooted: the stress on individual and especially religious freedom, and then, as the different types of religious practices multiplied in the United States, the effort to privatize the expression of religion. The last three are recent cultural developments, ones that are especially influential today, particularly on the younger generation.

1. Individualism

Clearly visible since the beginning of the seventeenth century, the early settlers in the country wanted religious freedom. They wanted freedom from religious persecution, especially persecution waged by the countries which had established religions, such as those then in medieval and early modern Christian Europe, when the Catholic Church still opposed religious freedom. But the Catholic Church was not the only oppressor. The modern confessional states that rose up after the Reformation waged their own persecutions, sometimes one form of

Protestantism against another, and both against Catholicism. It should be no surprise then that the colonists of Rhode Island, Maryland, Virginia and Pennsylvania made it clear that religious freedom, defined in a variety of ways, would constitute one of the cornerstones of the way they wanted to live.

Too much of a good thing—such as freedom from religious persecution—can become a bad thing. Coupled with the need to create one's own livelihood and build a new country, religious freedom led to an exaggerated emphasis on individual freedom. The rapid growth of capitalism in the second half of the nineteenth century transformed the emphasis on individual rights into an intense individualism. The theme of the rugged and righteous individual locked in a struggle against an evil society and corrupt institutions has become in our time a staple of movies, from the classic 1950 film, *High Noon*, to the many unmemorable action movies, beginning with Sylvester Stallone in the 1970s, right through to Arnold Schwarzenegger, Mel Gibson and Bruce Willis. The theme is the same: one good person alone against a corrupt system. It is within this culture of exaggerated individualism that "freedom" and "choice" become the mantras for every program and political movement that wants to succeed. But when too great a stress is put on individual freedom, people have a difficult time forming and building communities.

This lack of community is a very serious problem in American culture. Perhaps more than any other powerful culture-shaping force, modern capitalism, with its cultivation of consumerist behaviors, has effectively shifted peoples' practices and relationships away from tradition and shared experience. Robert Putnam's widely read article, "Bowling Alone," documents the significant decrease over the past two decades in political and civic participation—in religious groups, neighborhood organizations and, as the title suggests, in bowling leagues. Among the causes of this trend toward social disengagement, Putnam lists the many millions of women who, despite lower wages than men, have moved out of the home and into paid employment. Moreover, he points to the increase in the number of divorces and the decrease in the number of children, both of which have had a negative impact on social engagement since "married, middle-class parents are generally more socially involved than other people."[2]

Putnam's thesis has not gone unchallenged. For example, Thomas Rotolo, using data from the General Social Survey (1974–1994) has argued that although aggregate voluntary association participation decreased from 1974 to 1984, participation increased in the later half of that same time period.[3] Another critic has argued that people watch more TV because they are exhausted from the extended

2. Robert Putnam, "Bowling Alone: America's Declining Social Capital," in *Journal of Democracy* 6:1 (1995), p. 75.

3. Thomas Rotolo, "Trends in Voluntary Association Participation: A Research Note," in *Nonprofit and Voluntary Sector Quarterly* 28:2 (1999), pp. 199–212.

work week, thus making TV not the cause of disengagement, but the consequence of overwork.[4] Perhaps some people watch TV simply out of boredom, having found nothing more worthwhile to do with their time. Whatever the explanation, close family ties and strong neighborhood communities are rarer today than in the past. As the social philosopher Michael Walzer explains:

> Weakness is a general feature of associational life in America today. Unions, churches, interest groups, ethnic organizations, political parties and sects, societies for self-improvement and good works, local philanthropies, neighborhood clubs and cooperatives, religious sodalities, brotherhoods and sisterhoods: this American civil society is wonderfully multitudinous. Most associations, however, are precariously established, skimpily funded, and always at risk. They have less reach and holding power than once they did.[5]

As a consequence of weakened organizations, most people feel isolated, even within their own families, from an experience of community with others. Siding with Walzer and Putnam is Robert Wuthnow, the Princeton sociologist of religion, who describes just how tenuous are the relationships that characterize even those groups formed for the mutual support of their members:

> The kind of community [these small groups] create is quite different from the communities in which people have lived in the past. These communities are more fluid and more concerned with the emotional states of the individual.... The communities they create are seldom frail. People are cared for. They help one another. They share their intimate problems.... But in another sense small groups may not be fostering community as effectively as many of their proponents would like. Some small groups merely provide occasions for individuals to focus on themselves in the presence of others. The social contract binding members together asserts only the weakest of obligations. Come if you have time. Talk if you feel like it. Respect everyone's opinion. Never criticize. Leave quietly if you become dissatisfied.... We can imagine that [these small groups] really substitute for families, neighborhoods, and broader community attachments that may demand lifelong commitments, when, in fact, they do not.[6]

---

4. J. Schor, *The Overworked American: The Unexpected Decline of Leisure* (New York: Basic Books, 1991).

5. Michael Walzer, "Multiculturalism and Individualism," in *Dissent* (Spring, 1994), p. 187.

6. Robert Wuthnow, *Sharing the Journey: Support Groups and America's New Question for Community* (New York: The Free Press, 1994), pp. 3–6.

Excessive individualism, however, does not aptly characterize an increasingly influential group of Americans located mainly in the Southwest. The rapidly growing number of Hispanics, three-quarters of whom are Catholics, has a strong sense of community which is strengthened by their distinct ethnicity and Spanish language. A strong sense of community clearly sets them apart from most of the rest of the citizens who, as Robert Bellah has argued, have adopted the individualism that "lies at the very core of American culture."[7] Theologian Roberto Goizueta supports this sociological description of Hispanics and illustrates it through the example of how Hispanics view the relationship between Jesus and Mary. Instead of seeing Mary as the autonomous questioning woman, as many feminists do, or Jesus as the strong individual man "for others," Goizueta says that Hispanics picture Mary as "the symbol of the preexistent, involuntary community which defines and constitutes the individual person we call Jesus." And since community is constitutive of the person, "then to know Mary, the mother of Jesus, *is* (at least partially) to know Jesus. Conversely, one *cannot* know Jesus without also knowing Mary."[8] It remains to be seen, however, whether Hispanics, and others who immigrate to the United States from more traditional cultures, will be able to maintain a strong sense of family and community as they become more and more assimilated into the larger culture.

It should be obvious that since Catholicism stresses community, a highly individualistic culture presents problems for Catholic teachers and religious leaders responsible for forming their students in that religious tradition. Moreover, the extent to which families are fragmented leaves adolescents less able to trust and be open to relationships with their peers and with God. Finally, weakened family structures leave adolescents even more vulnerable to secular culture. Instead of developing an interior spirit, a spirit of prayerfulness which presupposes an ability to welcome periods of silence and personal reflection, adolescents are inundated as never before through the media, personal electronic devices and games, and the cornucopia that floods into their bedrooms through the Internet—their personal capacity to be formed in the Catholic tradition has been greatly diminished.

So far, I've stressed the negative consequence of an exaggerated individualism. What is needed, of course, is a more balanced understanding of individual freedom and how it relates to one's responsibilities to be part of a community. In other words, what is needed is an emphasis on the individual that strengthens a community. After all, there are a number of good things that have come out of a greater emphasis on the individual. Take for example, the great emphasis in recent decades on human rights—one of the great achievements of modern civilization.

---

7. Robert Bellah et alia, *Habits of the Heart: Individualism and Commitment in American Life* (Berkeley: University of California Press, 1985).

8. Roberto Goizueta, *Caminemos con Jesus: Toward a Hispanic/Latino Theology of Accompaniment* (Maryknoll, NY: Orbis Books, 1955), p. 66.

The desire for freedom and human dignity, rooted in a religious vision that all people are God's children, fueled the civil rights movement. Another dramatic example of the desire for individual freedom and respect is the women's movement. It is hard to imagine even a hundred years ago that women and minors who had been sexually abused would be recognized then as real victims, as persons whose rights and dignity had been violated. Including women in the work force, especially during World War II, and then after the war, witnessing their entrance into higher education in ever increasing numbers, signaled that it was only a matter of time before they would find their own public voice. It wasn't so many decades before that neither black Americans nor women were considered legal persons. But the voices of women became more and more prominent. Pope John XXIII recognized as one of the great movements of the twentieth century the quest for the rights of women.[9] One has only to read John Paul II's 1988 apostolic letter, *Mulieris dignitatem* (*On the Dignity and Vocation of Women*) to realize not only that John XXIII had accurately pinpointed a powerful trend of our own times, one of the "signs of the times" that needed to be understood and interpreted in the light of the Gospel, but also that papal teaching on women has changed considerably over the years.[10] The movement for women's rights has hardly exhausted itself, nor has papal teaching said all that can and should be said about this modern movement.

From the founding of the colonies, most advocates of religious freedom in the United States were wary of Catholics. They were hesitant to extend such freedom to Catholics since at least officially the Catholic Church denied that very freedom to others—that is, until the Second Vatican Council. Most Catholics in the US, however, experienced and treasured that freedom, and their bishops worked hard to persuade the rest of the Church of its value. At the Second Vatican Council, the bishops of the world, with the American bishops in the lead, finally officially affirmed religious freedom as a right. Charles Taylor, the Catholic philosopher, argues that were it not for the Enlightenment's emphasis on individual rights, it is unlikely that the Catholic Church, two centuries later, would have dug deeply enough into its own rich religious and philosophical traditions to find the basis that would allow them to affirm those rights in our own time.[11]

---

9. Pope John XXIII, *Pacem in terris* (Vatican Publications), paragraph 41.

10. John Paul II, *Mulieris dignitatem* (Washington, DC: United States Catholic Conference, 1988). Of course, as is the case with any living tradition, issues continued to be debated. Thus, the opposition of the Vatican under John Paul II to the ordination of women has been sharply criticized by both men and women who see the exclusion of women from the priesthood as a denial of their dignity.

11. Charles Taylor, *A Catholic Modernity?: Charles Taylor's Marianist Award Lecture*, edited by James L. Heft, S.M., (New York: Oxford University Press, 1999), p. 18.

Closely connected with a greater respect for the individual is an expectation for greater integrity. While the case could easily be made that people have always demonstrated a lack of integrity, beginning with the dissimulations of Adam and Eve in the Garden of Eden, there seems to be less tolerance today for dishonesty—or at least more widespread media coverage of dishonesty. One need not point only, for example, to the difference between what reporters agreed to ignore about John F. Kennedy's philandering in comparison to the near obsession reporters had with William Clinton's sexual transgression with Monica Lewinsky. However, there seems to be less concern for transparency in the corporate and financial worlds than there is for transparency in individual's lives.

One also can detect today a greater sensitivity, admittedly hard to document precisely, to the search many people undertake to find their true calling. Many people today enjoy more choices than did their parents and grandparents. While some people can be paralyzed by an array of choices, others are able to discern more authentic ways to be their true selves.[12] The Lilly Endowment recently gave millions of dollars to nearly seventy mainly religious colleges and universities to support programs to assist highly talented students think theologically about their calling. The response from these colleges and universities went well beyond the expectations of the Endowment's officers. The program obviously had hit a nerve. A number of students on these campuses were in fact searching for more than a well-paying job. They wanted to find their vocation, something greater to which they felt they were called. In this positive sense, seeking one's calling is not an exercise in narcissism, but rather an effort to find greater meaning by serving the larger community.

These considerations about individualism leave us with a complex picture. In its exaggerated forms, individualism leads to the dissolution of communities. On the other hand, in a more balanced relationship with community, individualism has also contributed to the human rights movement and to the possibility that more people can find their calling in life. But the emphasis on the individual and freedom needs to be embedded in still another prominent dimension of our culture—the curious combination of a heightened secularism coupled with a growing religious pluralism.

2. From the One to the Many: Religious Pluralism

The United States was founded at a time when the major intellectuals of Europe were exploring themes that they would eventually describe as the Enlightenment.

12. Charles Taylor, *The Ethics of Authenticity* (Cambridge, MA: Harvard University Press, 1992).

The word, "enlightenment," is best understood as an umbrella term since there were several forms that the Enlightenment took. In fact, one scholar, Gertrude Himmelfarb, argued recently in her widely discussed book, *The Roads to Modernity: The British, French and American Enlightenments*,[13] that there were three enlightenments. While we do not need to go into the details of her thesis, widely debated since the book's appearance, most critics agree that she has put her finger on some important differences. For example, the French Enlightenment strongly endorsed a freedom *from* religion (which became even stronger in 1905, when the state aggressively separated itself from the Catholic Church). On the other hand, the American Enlightenment opposed an established church precisely so that there could be greater freedom *for* religion, that is, primarily for the various forms of Protestantism that had already taken root in the colonies. The British and American Enlightenments have more in common with each other than either has with the French Enlightenment, even though the British have retained an established Church.

But as different as these three Enlightenments have been, they all emphasized reason, which was related to faith in a variety of ways. The French Enlightenment set itself to "liberate" reason from the control of faith, establish the scientific method as the most reliable form of knowing—more reliable and objective than the knowledge that religious believers claim—and to limit any public expression of religion. The British and American Enlightenments drew upon a different tradition, one that did not oppose reason and faith, so much as celebrate reason as a vehicle for practicality and compromise in the political sphere. Reason, therefore, was not thought of as the opposite of faith or superior to it. As a consequence, various forms of faith had the freedom to function publicly without any of them being established for the entire country. This form of the separation of church and state made the practice of all religions voluntary. Religion was then less a culture into which one was born and more of a choice which a person needed to make freely. But since "religion" generally meant Protestantism, any other choice was thought to be unreasonable. Whether one's personal religious choice needed to be kept private, that is, practiced in such a way as to have no political content and public power, has come under sharp debate in recent years.[14]

13. Himmelfarb, *The Roads to Modernity* (New York: Vintage Books, 2004).

14. Different religious groups reacted in different ways to the secularists' efforts to privatize faith. Speaking of Europe, Peter Berger explains that religious believers were offered a bargain: "You are completely free to live by your religion in private, but keep it out of the public sphere." Religious groups responded differently to this bargain: "Protestants came to accept this bargain in most countries. Jews did so with considerable enthusiasm, because it afforded them protection and opportunity. The Catholic Church resisted the bargain for a long time, and still does in theory, but by and large it has been pushed to accept it in practice." Berger, Davie and Fokas, eds., *Religious America, Secular Europe?* (Ashgate Press, 2008), p. 130.

The legal structure that has supported these developments in the United States can be found in the First Amendment: "Congress shall make no law respecting an establishment of religion, or prohibiting the free exercise thereof. . . ."[15] This legal framework created the possibility for a more radical religious pluralism. Though such religious pluralism existed from the foundation of the United States, it began to be experienced first by Protestants in the 1830s, and then in the 1840s even more with the first large-scale influx of Irish and German Catholics. Up until then, most Americans believed that they were God's chosen Protestant people—that their country was and would be forever Protestant. But the firm Protestant grip on American culture began to loosen and continued to loosen over the next century, except for brief but strong periods of influence for fundamentalists in the 1920s and then evangelicals in the 1980s. The Protestants were hardly united amongst themselves and battled, from the beginning of the twentieth century, fiercely over biblical interpretation and doctrine:

> Protestants had battled with heretical movements such as Deists, Owenites, and Unitarians. Serious divisions were caused by the Civil War and the war on modernism (e.g., Darwinism, higher biblical criticism) with the "private party" of fundamentalism and the "public" party of liberalism.[16]

Instead of fighting mainly amongst themselves, Protestants began to fight with Catholics, beginning in the 1840s and then again in the 1880s and 1890s, when large numbers of immigrants, mostly Catholics, began to arrive in the United States, first from northern and then from southern Europe. All immigration was drastically curtailed from 1921 until well after World War II. A new surge of immigration, made possible by the Hart-Cellar Immigration Act of 1965, opened the door to immigrants who brought with them even more religiously diversity, including Asians, Latin Americans and Caribbeans. Most recently, Muslims, who in the United States today number more than Episcopalians, constitute, after the Pentecostals, the fastest growing religious group, a development that would surely have surprised the founders of the country. These developments would have shocked Horace Mann (the Unitarian who founded the common school movement in the 1840s) and his colleagues as well.

---

15. Significantly and perhaps unintentionally, Americans "are among the first people in history not to consider their religions as primarily shared and public" in William Portier, *Tradition and Incarnation* (New York: Paulist Press, 1994), p. 49.

16. E. V. Randall, "Culture, Religion and Education," eds. T. C. Hunt and J. C. Carper, *Religion and School in Contemporary America* (New York: Garland Publishing, 1997), p. 67.

Mann and his followers aren't the only ones who would be shocked by these developments. The European founders of sociology assumed, along with most sociologists of religion right up to the 1960s, that modernization would gradually bring about a decline in, and even the disappearance of, religion. It is very clear that in the United States and in most other parts of the world, except in Europe, religion has hardly disappeared. Most sociologists of religion now agree that modernization does not cause religion to decline. What characterizes modernization, however, is pluralism, and religious pluralism brings with it its own host of challenges and opportunities.[17]

Given the separation of church from the state and the growing religious pluralism, many US citizens debate what the proper role should be for religion in the nation, especially in its political life. A vocal minority has argued that religious groups should have no voice in the public square. Peter Berger has suggested that these people can be described as arguing for a "hard" version of separation, a version that grew rapidly after World War II. Secularists espouse this position; they want to keep all religion private. Vocal and organized proponents for a public role for religion argue instead for a soft view of separation: they expect the government to protect their freedom to argue publicly for their religious views but do not expect it to favor any one religion.[18] The previous chapter explained how the Supreme Court in 1963 declared unconstitutional in public schools all school-sponsored prayer and Bible reading. In 1973, the Supreme Court declared abortion a constitutional right. These decisions galvanized the religious right and conservatives in general, both of whom have pushed for more public roles for their religious beliefs. Secularists have vigorously opposed them. The conflict between them has been described as the latest version of the "culture wars" (more about the accuracy of that description later). Tensions continue to exist between secularists and religious conservatives about the public role of religion.

Despite these tensions over the exact nature of the separation of church and state, the United States has welcomed many religious traditions. A steady flow of immigrants increases religious pluralism. Whatever else one might say about the United States, one can say at least that a thousand religious flowers bloom. The expressions of religion differ from region to region, from the Northeast to the Southwest, from rural to urban and suburban settings, from within the various

17. There is a burgeoning literature on why the "secularization theory" is no longer valid. Two of the best sources are Jose Casanova's *Public Religions in the Modern World* (University of Chicago Press, 1994), and Berger's *Religious America, Secular Europe?* As to why it took sociologists so long to see what should have been obvious to them sooner, Berger, a sociologist, wrote: "... theories are the product of intellectuals, who mainly talk to each other and who, like everyone else, tend to see the world from their own point of view" (p. 10).

18. Berger et al., *Religious America, Secular Europe?*, p. 126.

levels of affluence and religious perspectives. Even more diverse are the expressions of our many religious cultures in the United States, where the terrain is uneven—mountainous in some areas, smooth valleys in others, carefully protected among the Amish, easily accessible through some TV evangelists, esoteric with some New Age forms, vibrant among some Pentecostals, deeply tied in with family and community among Hispanics and African Americans, deeply traditional in some synagogues, deeply divided over fault lines of biblical interpretation among many Christians, and highly visible in some mosques newly built along interstate highways.

As a country, then, the United States has moved from a time when it was populated mainly by Protestants to the present, when we see a greater religious pluralism. Some have tried to deny any public role for religion, but only with limited success. Despite efforts to privatize religion, the so-called secularization thesis—namely, that with the advent of modernization religion would disappear—has been proven false, at least in part.[19] Despite widespread religious pluralism, some segments of American society remain quite secular. Higher education and some of the major media outlets are highly secular and are pervaded by a prejudice against Catholics and Christian fundamentalists. Similar secularism characterizes elite cultural circles.[20]

If we now have religious pluralism and largely secular media, both combine to influence the transmission of an individual religious tradition to the next generation. They have exercised considerable influence on the way in which people, especially young people, think.

3. The Media Culture

The two profound trends in American culture described above—individualism and religious pluralism—affect all Americans. I now turn to descriptions of three other trends that especially affect youth. I shall describe the impact of media, the therapeutic shape that religious belief takes in a culture that stresses individual choice in the midst of religious pluralism, and the growing number of people who have been described as the "spiritual but not religious."

Under the heading of the "Technological Transformation of Leisure," Robert Putnam, a sociologist at Harvard, documents how technological trends have radically "privatized" and "individualized" the use of our leisure time. Studies since

---

19. See Peter L. Berger, "Protestantism and the Quest for Certainty," *The Christian Century* 115:23 (August 26, 1998), pp. 782–796; and Casanova, *Public Religions in the Modern World.*

20. See Mark S. Massa, S.J., *Anti-Catholicism in America: The Last Acceptable Prejudice* (New York: Crossroads, 2003). See also John McGreevy's "Thinking on One's Own: Catholicism in the American Intellectual Imagination, 1928–1960," *Journal of American History* 84 (1997).

the 1960s have demonstrated that the amount of time devoted to watching television "literally dwarfed all other changes in the ways that Americans spent their days and nights. Television has made our communities (or rather what we experience as our communities) wider and shallower. Rather than playing football on weekends, we watch other people play it half a continent away, or play virtual football on video game consoles. Rather than confide in close friends, we watch total strangers on TV discuss with Oprah astonishingly intimate matters."[21] And even though Americans now spend more actual time listening to classical music and to jazz, they do not do so in concert halls or small clubs. Through cassette tapes, compact discs, and most recently, the ubiquitous iPod and iPhone (I hesitate to name these devices, since within a decade many of them will be obsolete), people have their musical entertainment when they want, by themselves, and in just the order and at the time they prefer. Cable TV has made an immense selection of channels possible for "niche" audiences, and people with pay-TV order the film they wish to see when they want to see it. In summary, according to Putnam, technology, consumer culture and various social media are creating a huge gap between individual interests, which can now be met more easily and immediately, and the interests of the community, which appear to be less important and more distant.[22] As a consequence, the needs of the community suffer.

The late Walter Cronkite, looking back at his long and distinguished career as a news reporter on television, said that at one time the three major television network news broadcasts did their best to present as accurately as possible the news of the day. Given the recent arrival of literally hundreds of cable networks, those in the news business now compete with each other more than ever before for their audience share. Moreover, they interpret the news according to their political persuasions; now it is possible to find cable channels with "conservative" and "liberal" versions of the news. When people watch a cable channel that consistently promotes only one interpretation, they can easily believe that the version they watch actually informs them about the way things really are.

A second consequence of the annual ratings competition is the need to feature conflict, tragedies and scandals. Good news, except as feel-good "Sunday

---

21. Putnam, "Bowling Alone: America's Declining Social Capital," in *Journal of Democracy* 6:1 (1995), p. 75.

22. In an interview published in *Christian Century* (February 10, 2004), Putnam comments on subsequent research done with Lewis M. Feldstein and Don Cohen, *Better Together: Restoring the American Community* (New York: Simon and Schuster, 2003) which shows that people involved in religious communities are more likely than their secular counterparts to be involved in the life of the overall community. And while no substitute for face-to-face communication, the computer and the Internet can create at least some sense of community.

evening fillers" in the last minutes of a broadcast, rarely makes headlines. Stories of "major" conflicts dominate the news for several days and then, all of the sudden, disappear when another major controversy or tragedy, or natural disaster, will dominate for a while and then promptly disappear. Complex and multifaceted stories that have a long history seem to appear suddenly out of nowhere and are explained in simple black-and-white terms, often as a battle between liberals and conservatives, the Left and the Right, the forces of freedom against the oppressors. Such media coverage grossly oversimplifies reality.

In the print world, James Hunter's widely read *Culture Wars: The Struggle to Define America*, subtitled, *Making Sense of the Battles over the Family, Art, Education, Law and Politics*, exemplifies an overly simplified picture of what is happening in the United States.[23] There is no doubt that there are some people on each end of the spectrum who shout and capture the attention of the media; however, there are also many—indeed most—people in the middle whose views and significance are simply ignored. American Protestantism, for example, comes in many forms, not just liberal and conservative. Jacobsen and Trollinger argue persuasively that the notion of a Protestantism divided into two mutually exclusive and hostile camps collapses in face of the actual reality; namely, numerous Protestants and Protestant groups (e.g., Lutherans, Mennonites, Black Baptists and Methodists) who cannot be neatly forced into a liberal or a conservative party.[24] Moreover, the fact that the fault lines within American Protestantism are constantly shifting ensures that no single or simple bifurcated division of faith and its practices exists.[25]

The same can be said about American Catholics. Several years ago, Joseph Bernardin, then cardinal archbishop of Chicago, launched the "Common Ground" project. Motivated in part by his desire to overcome a polarization among Catholics that was exaggerated by the media, Bernardin wanted to bring together face-to-face those who had been arguing only through their writings and public statements. The official Common Ground statement begins: "Will the Catholic Church in the United States enter the new millennium as a Church

23. James D. Hunter, *Culture Wars* (New York: Basic Books, 1991).

24. Douglas Jacobsen and William Trollinger, eds., *Re-forming the Center: American Protestantism, 1900–Present* (Grand Rapids, MI: W. B. Eerdmans, 1998).

25. In his widely read book, *The Clash of Civilizations and the Remaking of the World Order* (New York: Simon and Schuster, 1998), Samuel Huntington presents a portrait of the looming conflict between the West and Islam that, in the view of many commentators, exaggerates not only the likelihood of an all-out confrontation, but also the differences between the two "civilizations." For a more careful reading of Huntingon's book see Daniel Madigan, S.J., "Catholicism and Islam: Dialogue in Difficult Times," in *Catholicism and Other World Religions,* James L. Heft, S.M., ed. (forthcoming, Oxford University Press).

of promise, augmented by the faith of rising generations and able to be a leavening force in our culture? Or will it become a church on the defensive torn by dissension and weakened in its core structures?" The negative public reactions to the Common Ground statement by high-ranking American prelates, including other cardinals, made it quite clear that real dissension did mark the Catholic community, beginning with some of its bishops. To find the same intensity of public disagreement among American bishops, one has to go back to the "Americanist Crisis" of the 1890s when liberal bishops like John Ireland of Minneapolis publicly disagreed with conservative bishops like Bernard McQuaid of Rochester, New York, not least about the value of Catholic schools.[26] Such sharp division among a few of the bishops showed up prominently again during the 1984, 2000 and 2004 presidential election campaigns concerning pro-choice Catholic politicians, and then again in the 2008 election about whether Catholics could vote for a pro-choice candidate.[27] Differences of opinion, sometimes deep among bishops, are not unusual. It is just that those differences are usually not as public as they have been in recent years.

At the time of the public disagreement among some bishops over the purposes and appropriateness of Bernardin's initiative, sociologist Andrew Greeley explained that while Catholics needed to overcome their fractious behavior, most Catholics actually continue to occupy a middle ground.[28] Greeley produced statistical evidence that supported a profile of the Catholic laity who were found to be largely in agreement on major issues of Church teaching and in a good relationship with their pastors—a general finding that remains true even after the most recent eruption of the sexual abuse crisis in 2002, and then again in 2010 and 2011, especially in Europe. Not just Catholics, but most Americans, who remain in the middle on most issues, are absent from media portrayals which lionize the Left and the Right. Peter Berger describes the actual situation well:

> Americans tend toward the center. Survey data, for example, show that on all the neuralgic "social issues," most Americans hold middle-of-the-road opinions. Thus most Americans do not like abortion, but would not want to make it illegal again—rather would impose more restrictions. Similarly most Americans do not particularly like homosexuality, and are ready to

---

26. Bishop Kenneth Untener, "How Bishops Talk," *America* (October 19, 1996), pp. 9–15.

27. James L. Heft, S.M., "US Catholics and the Presidential Election: Abortion and Proportionate Reasons," in *New Blackfriars: A Review* Vol. 86, No. 1993 (May 2005).

28. Andrew Greeley, "Polarized Catholics? Don't Believe Your Mail!" in *America*, February 22, 1997, pp. 11–15.

concede them all sorts of rights as long as they do not usurp the traditional meaning of Marriage.[29]

However, despite the tendency of people on the Left and Right to polarize debates, especially news organizations and the print media, it can't be denied that a country with considerable religious pluralism lends itself to controversy. And part of what adds to that confusion and controversy in the Catholic community are the wide array of journals and magazines that present very different and sometimes even opposite descriptions of the Church today.[30]

One of the consequences of the separation of church and state, the current degree of religious pluralism and the tendency of the media to exaggerate disagreements, is greater confusion about just what any one religious tradition actually teaches. When there are so many different religious arguments in the marketplace, it becomes impossible for one of them to claim absolute authority. Multiple and competing explanations abound. When an expert on television states something about a religious tradition that contradicts what is preached from the pulpit, who then should be believed, especially if one receives little instruction in the faith from the leaders of one's own congregation? Because of misinformation about and misunderstanding of their own religious tradition, some people switch denominations, even religions. Endlessly publicized disagreements and religious chatter, to say nothing of highly publicized scandals, can lead people simply to quit religious practices all together. The cumulative effect of media polarization and contradictory statements about what a specific religious tradition says or ought to say has the effect, in the long run, of actually trivializing religion's importance. Stephen Carter, a Yale law professor, struck a chord with his widely read book, *The Culture of Disbelief*, subtitled unambiguously *How American Law and Politics Trivialize Religious Devotion*.[31] Religion no longer is important. Given so many different "opinions," how can religion be anything other than a matter of opinion?

One of the most secular groups in the United States, many university professors, often do their work in such a way that religion, not a factor any longer in their lives, also ceases to be a part of their teaching and research. Stephen Carter, for example, showed how many writers portrayed Martin Luther King's vision for

29. Berger et al., *Religious America, Secular Europe*, p. 128.

30. In terms of Catholic publications, one thinks of the *National Catholic Reporter* and *Commonweal* on the liberal side, and *First Things* and *Our Sunday Visitor* on the conservative side. All four of these publications are, on the whole, responsibly liberal or conservative. More radical departures include *Crisis Magazine* on the Right and *Catholics for Free Choice* on the Left.

31. Stephen Carter, *The Culture of Disbelief* (New York: Basic Books; 1993).

racial equality as King's commitment to civil rights, but not also as King's Christian passion that all people, regardless of race, were God's children, and therefore should be treated with the dignity and respect due to them. Even before he was a civil rights leader, Carter writes, King was a minister of the Gospel. Had he not been such a dedicated religious believer, Carter argues, it is hard to imagine that King would have been the courageous civil rights leader that he was. But, contemporary historians and media commentators trivialized, if not completely ignored, King's religious roots and motivation.

In introducing these first three characteristics of contemporary culture in the United States, I mentioned that youth can be especially affected by the third characteristic, the media.[32] Most teenagers seem to get turned off by religious controversies. In fact, most of them seem to be much more interested in how the Internet can connect them with each other, perhaps to cope with the lack of community they experience at home and at church. We will look at this more closely in the chapter devoted to high school students.

4. Therapeutic: Non-Cognitive

Any religious tradition which makes truth claims, such as Catholicism and Islam, is not easily privatized. If religion is based on revelation, that is, if it offers a trans-human insight into how God expects people to live and worship, then it easily goes public. On the other hand, if religion can be reduced primarily to personal feelings and preferences (as that ubiquitous billboard sign of the 1950s recommended, "Attend the Church of your Choice"), it can more easily be something a person is free to "choose" because they find it "comfortable." Comfortable religions do not make demands on people, much less require them to proselytize others. In this sense, religion becomes therapeutic, that is, it is less about truth, which requires an intellectual dimension, and more about addressing one's personal needs.

It is not so much that American forms of religion are typically anti-intellectual; rather, they are more accurately described as a-intellectual—that is, understood to be not about truth, but about opinions and emotions. Cathleen Kaveny, a professor

---

32. Robert Barron, a popular author and theology professor at the Chicago Catholic seminary of Mundelein, began posting brief reflections on YouTube about movies, music and culture. He was bombarded with responses, especially to his video on atheism and Bill Maher's film, *Religulous*. He received hundreds of responses from young opponents of religion whom he described in four categories: scientism, ecclesial angelism, biblical fundamentalism and Marcionism. All the responses reflected little understanding of the history of Christianity and practically no understanding of Christian theology. See "Youtube Heresies: On Today's Virtual Areopagus," in *America,* May 25–June 1, 2009, pp. 21–23.

of law and theology at the University of Notre Dame, reports that both her conservative and liberal Catholic students "treat their intellects in an almost exclusively instrumental fashion." That is, the conservative students use their minds to defend the Church and the liberals to achieve worldly success—good grades for them means good jobs. Both groups, she believes, need to be shown how they can be "fully intellectually engaged in the exploration of their faith."[33]

Much of this de-intellectualizing of religion, of course, can be traced to the Enlightenment whose proponents, prominent among them Thomas Jefferson, thought of religion as inherently sectarian (read: divisive and therefore bad) and non-rational (read: irrational and therefore against reason). Jefferson concluded that religion should be kept in private if not disappear altogether, at least in its "supernatural" forms. According to thinkers like Jefferson, what all persons of goodwill possess and should use is reason, not faith. Everyone, they believed, including even the atheist, can be reasonable.[34] There is a problem, however, with this view. In the words of literary critic Terry Eagleton, the problem is that though we can perish because of religious extremism, reason alone "does not go down all the way. It is not wall to wall."[35] Somewhere deep down in people's lives, faith must function as well. Such an appeal to faith—actually for faith and reason—is hard for secularists to accept as credible, at least for themselves. I wish to argue that faith rightly understood welcomes the extensive use of reason, and therefore has cognitive elements. But this does not mean that the knowledge communicated through faith is the type of knowledge that can be scientifically proven. Picking up on an insight from Slavoj Zizek, Eagleton writes that the fundamentalist, who equates faith with provable knowledge, "is like the kind of neurotic who can't trust that he is loved, but in infantile spirit demands some irrefragable proof of the fact." In that sense, Eagleton writes that fundamentalists are not really believers, but rather "the mirror image of skeptics."[36]

The English and Scottish colonists who first came to America brought with them their particular understanding of the Enlightenment. The strict separation of church and state characteristic of the French Revolution did not take root in colonial America. The early American Christians worked through various positive ways of understanding a variety of relationships that might exist between reason and faith. Catholics and mainline Protestants never got rid of faith

---

33. Cathleen Kaveny, "Young Catholics: When Labels Don't Fit," in *Commonweal*, November 19, 2004, p. 20.

34. Robert Wilkens, *Remembering the Christian Past* (Grand Rapids, MI: W. B. Eerdmans, 1995).

35. Terry Eagleton, *Reason, Faith, and Revolution* (Yale University Press, 2009), p. 109.

36. Eagleton, p. 114.

in order to adopt reason alone.[37] More conservative Protestants stressed a literal acceptance of the Bible, but even they looked to biblical texts to help them understand their experience in the New World. It could be said that for nearly all the colonial Christians, reflecting on their personal experiences remained an important source for understanding their Christian life. The Puritan colonists in the 1630s, for example, felt compelled to demonstrate to their co-religionists of the Massachusetts Bay Colony that the Holy Spirit had in fact wrought a change in their hearts. This same tendency to link authentic religion to intense personal experiences extended itself to the larger population through the powerful first and second Great Awakenings.[38]

Secular Americans view religion not only as sectarian, but also as irrational. They tend to see religion as based on a body of assertions impossible to verify empirically. A growing number of believers have conceded ground to such critics. They have begun to think of faith as a "value" rather than as a truth. They think of religion as something good for them personally. Two authors, one a sociologist, Philip Rieff, and the other a philosopher, Alisdair MacIntyre, have written extensively about how religion, in the process of becoming private, has also become therapeutic and emotive.[39] These authors show how the content of religion changed from something that was thought to be true, to something that was considered to be personally valuable (that is, worthwhile not because it has value in and of itself, but because it is useful), and finally to something that is mainly therapeutic, that is, a value for an individual person's wholeness, well-being and self-realization. During

---

37. To every generalization of this sort, there are of course exceptions. Richard Mouw, a prominent evangelical and now professor and president of Fuller Theological Seminary in Pasadena California, wrote about a nineteenth century Methodist circuit rider who recalled how he had preached the Gospel with wondrous results without ever having any formal theological training: he declared that he and his friends "had preached the Gospel with more success and had more seals to their ministry" than all of those "sapient, downy D.D.'s in modern times who . . . are seeking presidencies or professorships in colleges, editorships, or any agencies that have a fat salary, and are trying to create newfangled institutions where good livings can be monopolized"—and all this "while millions of poor, dying sinners are thronging the way to hell without God, without Gospel" ("Fool-osophy," in *Christian Century,* March 24, 2009, p. 35). As both a professor and a president of a research institute, I take the warning of the circuit rider seriously, though I'd like to think that learning and true devotion are not mutually exclusive.

38. Nathan Hatch, *The Democratization of American Christianity* (New Haven, CT: Yale University Press, 1989).

39. Philip Rieff, *The Triumph of the Therapeutic: The Uses of Faith After Freud* (New York: Harper and Row, 1966), and *Fellow Travelers* (New York: Harper and Row, 1972). See also William F. Lynch, "Psychological Man," in *America*, November 25, 1967, pp. 635–637; and Thomas R. Cole, "The Uses of Faith After Rieff," in *Figures in the Carpet*, pp. 265–289. For Alisdair MacIntyre's critique, see *After Virtue* (Notre Dame, IN: Univ. of Notre Dame Press, 1981); and *Three Rival Versions of Moral Inquiry* (Notre Dame, IN: Univ. of Notre Dame Press, 1990).

this evolution, the priest, minister and rabbi have been replaced by the psychologist, the manager, and the therapist. The "emotivist," writes MacIntyre, "the peculiarly modern self... in acquiring sovereignty in its own realm lost its traditional boundaries provided by a social identity and a view of human life as ordered to a given end."[40] In other words, MacIntyre's emotivists determine the value of religion mainly on the grounds of how well it helps them find themselves and supports what they decide their lives are for, apart from any normative tradition.

Another rapidly growing suburban form of this subjective and a-intellectual approach to religion is the movement that separates "spirituality" from religion, especially when this separation removes a person from normative communal practices sustained by a historic religious tradition.[41] In the chapter on students, I will again discuss the therapeutic use of religion. Suffice it to note here that, Catholic educators need to grasp how deeply influenced their students are by this strong cultural trend that emphasizes seeking immediate and gratifying personal experience. Few students ask serious questions about what is true and trustworthy, or if they do, they really want to know what can be empirically verified. In its appropriate place—in chemistry and biology, for example—seeking what is empirically verifiable makes perfect sense. Therefore, Catholic educators need to respect, even celebrate the findings of dedicated scientists. At the same time, they need to explain to students that there are multiple ways of knowing, and not just the empirical way, that are reliable. In their book, *The Good Society*, Robert Bellah and his associates make five suggestions to enable schools in our society to be more "life-enabling," among which is their suggestion that educators today need to rediscover an "enlarged paradigm of knowledge, which recognizes the value of science but acknowledges that other ways of knowing have equal dignity."[42] For Catholic educators in particular, this "enlarged paradigm of knowledge" includes art, literature, rituals and practices of religious traditions which communicate religious and moral insight every bit as valuable as scientific knowledge.

5. Spiritual but Not Religious

Much has been written in recent years about the growing number of people, especially among the younger segment of the population, who can be described as

40. MacIntyre, *After Virtue*, p. 32.

41. See the study of the Vatican's Pontifical Council for Culture and Interreligious Dialogue, "Jesus Christ, the Bearer of the Water of Life: A Christian Reflection on the New Age," in *Origins*, Vol. 32, No. 35, February 13, 2003. I will return to this trend, the "I'm spiritual but not religious," later.

42. Robert Bellah et al, *The Good Society* (New York: Alfred A. Knopf, 1991), p. 177.

"spiritual but not religious." There is, however, little consensus on the significance of this movement. Some observers interpret it positively, others negatively, still others ambiguously. A closer look at the different evaluations of the movement shows that the movement, though not consciously expressed by high school students, can in its most positive forms indicate a spiritual hunger with which educators can work. On the other hand, building on the cultural transformation of religion into a form of personal therapy, this movement too easily degenerates into narcissism.

It is not easy to get a precise understanding of what is meant by "spiritual" and by "religious." Consider, for example, these widely divergent interpretations. The editor of the Jewish Reform magazine, *Tikkun*, describes spirituality as a lived experience which typically involves first, "a feeling of awe, wonder, and radical amazement in response to the universe." Moreover, he continues, spirituality recognizes the "ultimate Unity of All Being," and in that, the "sanctity" of every person. Furthermore, spirituality is a "deep trust that there is enough for all," and that the world is "filled with a conscious energy which transcends the categories and concepts" used to describe ordinary reality. By contrast, he describes religion as "various historical attempts to organize a set of doctrines, rituals, and specific practices which are supposed to be 'the right way to live.' "[43] *Tikkun*'s description of the difference between spirituality and religion may be caricatures of both, especially for people whose religious tradition has been a vibrant source of their spirituality.

A second interpretation of this phenomenon points to the way in which a number of adults today select from different religious traditions to form their own spirituality. In a thoughtful book aimed at persuading academics at secular universities to take the study of religion more seriously, Mark Edwards explains that people who left the religious traditions in which they have been raised often take with them practices they learned in their youth—practices like spiritual reading or meditation. Moreover, some of these same adults join new groups which support the practices that they have selected from their past.[44] Sociologist of religion Robert Wuthnow notes that there may be an advantage that spiritual practices have over the beliefs of traditional religions:

> If exposure to diverse religious teaching erodes the plausibility of particular beliefs, practices appear to be somewhat more resistant to such erosion

43. Michael Lerner, "Why Spirituality?" in *Tikkun*, Vol. 15, No. 2, March/April 2000, pp. 7–8.

44. Mark Edwards, *Religion on our Campuses* (Palgrave MacMillan, 2006), pp. 34–35.

> because they can be defended less as absolute truths and more as interchangeable activities through which people seek a common experience of the sacred.[45]

While I think both Edwards and Wuthnow accurately describe the habits of some adults who have been raised in a religious tradition with its communal beliefs and practices, I also think that many of the people who leave their religious communities to seek their own spiritual paths run several risks, including narcissism. Catholic theologian Lawrence Cunningham offers first a positive view of the movement when he suggests that such people are actually seeking a fulfilling religious experience without the constrictions and demands of a religious tradition. If the choice is beholding a spectacular sunset in the Rocky Mountains versus listening to a boring sermon, the choice for these seekers is easy: "spiritual means freedom and exaltation. Religion means rules, rote rituals and, well, religion." But Cunningham also describes the limits of this approach:

> Much spirituality (think of the preachments of such best-selling authors as Thomas Moore or Deepak Chopra) is highly narcissistic and not easily distinguishable from old self-improvement schemes and/or the standard smorgasbord of psychotherapies. One might call such tendencies "spirituality lite."[46]

Thus, there are clear dangers associated with the "spiritual but not religious" movement. At the same time, the tradition of Christian mysticism is all about people who enjoy deep connections with God. Quoting the late German theologian, Karl Rahner, Louis Dupré, a philosopher of religion, said that Christianity in the future will either be mystical or it will not be at all.[47] By "mystical" neither Dupré nor Rahner intended to include only extraordinary personal experiences of God's presence, visions and exceptional moments. Rather, they were referring

---

45. Wuthnow, "Spirituality and Spiritual Practice," a chapter in *After Heaven: Spirituality in American Since the 1950s* (Berkeley, CA: University of California Press, 1998), p. 319, as cited by Edwards, p. 34.

46. Lawrence Cunningham, *Notre Dame Magazine*, Autumn 2002, p. 2. Cunningham recommends a good test for the "spiritual but not religious" people: "Can you teach it to your children? Does it spill over into more loving relationships with others who are not part of your own nurturing community? An even better test: does a way of being spiritual help in moments of profound crisis, like coping with serious illness?" See also his most recent book, *An Introduction to Catholicism* (Cambridge University Press, 2009).

47. Louis Dupré, "Seeking Christian Interiority: An Interview with Louis Dupre," *The Christian Century* 114:21 (July 16, 1997), p. 655.

to religious experiences which are neither private nor extraordinary, but rather ones that lead people to a deeper personal understanding of scripture, the Sacraments and in prayer. The great mystical tradition never separated spirituality and religion. One fed and nourished the other. The experiential dimension of faith need not be opposed to the institutional dimension.

While the evaluations of this movement differ, the fact of its growth has been well documented. A poll conducted in May of 2009 by Trinity College reports that those Americans who do not associate with any religious tradition constitute the fastest growing segment of the national religious population. It now accounts for nearly one in six Americans. A Pew Forum on "Religion and Public Life" helps us to describe better just who these religiously unaffiliated Americans are. Instead of assuming that they are all atheists (still only 2 percent of the population), the Pew survey has discovered that few of these people have left religion because they thought that modern science had disproved religion's validity. Instead, many of these people seem to have been disenchanted with religious people and institutions. Almost half (four in ten) say that religion remains important in their lives, but that for now they have yet to find the right "fit" for themselves. And additional interesting finding is that 54 percent of Americans in families which were not attached to any religious tradition now belong to one.[48]

But reason for concern remains. Seeking personal religious experience directly can easily degenerate quickly into narcissism, especially in a consumerist and Internet culture that responds to an individual's immediate desires. An additional reason also gives cause for concern. Based on his own research, Robert Putnam reports that the 30 to 40 percent of "nones" (those who report no religious affiliation) has skyrocketed among younger Americans.[49] A large number of college students describe themselves on surveys as "nones." Even though very few high school youth describe themselves as "spiritual but not religious," it should be obvious why educators need to remain especially vigilant on their behalf.

However, the therapeutic character of religion today need not lead to narcissistic forms of religious belief and practice. Few things will help persons avoid narcissism more than being a part of a community which forms authentic individuals through personal discipline and the service of others. All the great religious traditions demand forms of asceticism, especially religious practices for people to enact together, to keep them on the difficult path toward transformation—never fully reached in this life. Religious writers remind us to seek not consolations of God, but the God of consolations. What the Australian Cistercian

48. See Dan Gilgoff, "Many Americans are Saying Goodbye to Religion, but not Faith," *US News and World Report*, June 2, 2009.

49. Dan Harris, "Young Americans Losing Their Religion," *ABC News*, May 6, 2009.

monk Michael Casey says of the monk can be applied just as well to every religious believer:

> Monastic life is not really about self-realization, in the immediate sense of these words: it is more about self-transcendence. These are noble words, but the reality they describe is a lifetime of feeling out of one's depth: confused, bewildered, and not a little affronted by the mysterious ways of God. This is why those who persevere and are buried in a monastic cemetery can rarely be described as perfectly integrated human beings.

Casey speaks of a "lifetime of feeling out of one's depth." His understanding of that search for personal religious experience is less likely to fall victim of narcissism. He describes self-transcendence as "a relentlessly grinding process. It makes each one of us the anti-hero in the drama of our own life: unknowing, incompetent, bumbling."[50] Casey's gritty realism about the spiritual journey is refreshing, balanced and hopeful: the more people realize their need for God's healing grace and the support of a community which performs their religious practices together, the more confident they become that the long journey to authenticity will be more God's work in them than their own.

The spiritual but not religious phenomenon can be interpreted positively. And indeed, there are some positive dimensions: a genuine search for the transcendent and a quest for personal authenticity. But given the consumerist and individualistic characteristics of the larger culture, religion too easily becomes a therapeutic instrument for personal fulfillment. Communal religious practices are dropped in favor of more immediately gratifying spiritual experiences. Young people especially need to be formed in religious practices that will make it less likely that their spirituality will be turn out to be an eclectic collection of personally preferred experiences, often delivered electronically, and sometimes chemically. The teaching of these religious practices in ways that deepen spirituality is one of the great challenges religious educators face today.

Conclusion

This chapter has described five characteristics of the culture in the United States. The last three of these characteristics—the dominance of media, the reduction of religion to the therapeutic and the growing disenchantment with traditional forms of religion—have had their greatest impact on youth. Other characteristics

---

50. Michael Casey, *Strangers to the City: Reflections on the Beliefs and Values of the Rule of Saint Benedict* (Orleans, MA: Paraclete Press, 2005), p. 4.

could have been described as well—such as consumerism, ethical relativism, a pervasive religious illiteracy coupled, ironically, with a greater sensitivity to the needs of people suffering in virtually any part of the world.[51] One of the key contentions of this book argues that for Catholic high schools to be effective, the teachers need to be especially aware of the influence of contemporary culture on them and especially their students.

Given the historical development of Catholic schools touched upon in Chapter 1 and some of the characteristics of contemporary culture sketched in this chapter, it is time now to devote a chapter to exploring the mission of the Catholic high school. In the introduction, I alluded to the biblical truth, "without vision the people perish," to emphasize the importance of a clear mission for an educational institution." Applying this biblical truth to an educational institution, we can say that "without a clear mission, a school fails its students." In what does the mission of a Catholic high school consist? How is it distinct from that of a public high school and from the growing number of charter schools? To these important questions I now turn. Subsequent chapters examine how, in the light of a Catholic high school's mission, administrators and teachers should understand their roles.

---

51. Taylor, *A Catholic Modernity?* pp. 30–32.

4

The Mission: Moral and Religious Formation

Introduction

Until the Enlightenment, most people assumed, give or take the occasional Machiavelli, that moral and religious formation went hand in hand. They understood that people should be fair and honest and kind, and they believed that religious practices and teachings reinforced these qualities. But the Enlightenment sought to separate the two by basing morality on reason alone and pushing "religion" (read, Christianity) into the private sphere, where parents on their own and within the family would hand on their faith to their children. For schools, further complications arose with the rise of religious pluralism: if people held different religious views, then their schools, in order not to become embattled, could only teach what people held in common: basic moral principles, not specific religious traditions.

This chapter explores three issues: first, how the leaders of public schools have largely abandoned the teaching of religion but have worked at moral formation, and the difficulties they've encountered in that effort; second, the critical importance of personal example in learning morality; and third, why the leaders of Catholic schools have an advantage over their public counterparts, since they, doing the work of moral formation, can draw explicitly upon a rich religious tradition that includes a doctrinal framework and religious and moral practices. I begin with a few notes from history that will provide some perspective on how, for a very long time, religious and moral education remained intimately linked. I then look at some of the difficulties public schools face when they try to provide character education and moral formation. Finally, I describe doctrinal dimensions and various practices of Catholicism and how they help Catholic schools provide rich moral and religious formation.

In our last chapter, I explained that contemporary culture does not do a good job of helping believers, especially Catholics, see the importance of communal religious practices and the doctrinal foundations of their faith. Moreover, the pervasive therapeutic shape of religious understanding today makes it more difficult for most people to grasp how a religious tradition legitimately makes claims that may not be seen as immediately satisfying. In this chapter, I argue that Catholic schools are uniquely situated to address and challenge the therapeutic, individualistic and a-intellectual character that marks the religious life of so many people today.

Moral Education: A Few Notes from History

At least as far back as the time of Greek civilization, people have debated education's purpose. The Greeks wondered whether virtue could even be taught. For Aristotle, persons are virtuous when they like and dislike what they ought. Aristotle speaks of the importance of "ordinate affections," or the appropriate personal response to situations and actions. He also told his followers that if people want to know what moral behavior is, they should examine closely the behavior of moral people.[1]

In much the same way, Augustine speaks of virtue as *ordo amoris*, the ordering of our loves, or the ability of persons to give every object the kind and degree of love it deserves. Throughout the centuries—from the lyceum of the Greeks to the catechetical school of Alexandria, and from the European medieval university to the nineteenth-century colleges in the United States and England—the moral education of students based on an explicitly religious foundation formed an essential part of education. From the founding of Harvard in 1636 until after the Civil War, college presidents, who typically were clergymen, taught a capstone course to those about to graduate. The course integrated moral philosophy, theology, and what we would now call psychology. It was all about moral formation.

Even in the 1890s almost all colleges and universities in the United States, most of which were originally founded almost exclusively by Protestant churches, continued to hold compulsory chapel services, and some required attendance at Sunday worship, even up to the time of World War II.[2] One should not assume, of course, that compulsory religious services were, by themselves, reliable indicators of effective moral education, nor that the only source of moral formation are religious services. The general assumption, however, was that common religious services contributed to the development of virtue.

As late as the 1950s, "it was not unusual for spokespersons of leading schools to refer to their schools as 'Christian' institutions."[3] When Duke University

1. Richard P. Geraghty, *The Object of Moral Philosophy According to St. Thomas Aquinas* (Washington, D.C: University Press of America, 1982). Geraghty explains that for St. Thomas, who followed Aristotle on this matter, moral philosophy was a practical science, one in which imitation and prudence played key roles.

2. Amherst College, however, retained compulsory chapel until 1967.

3. George M. Marsden, *The Soul of the American University: From Protestant Establishment to Established Nonbelief* (New York: Oxford University Press, 1994), p. 3.

adopted its founding bylaws in 1924, its mission statement read, "The aims of Duke University are to assert a faith in the eternal union of knowledge and religion set forth in the teachings and character of Jesus Christ, the Son of God." But by the early 1990s, Duke's newly installed president, Nan Keohane, admitted that only after she became the president did she discover that Duke's motto was *Eruditio et Religio*. That discovery, she admitted, made her uneasy since, in her view, the motto put an emphasis on religion that "seemed hard to square with the restless yearning for discovery, the staunch and fearless commitment to seek for truth wherever truth may be found that is the hallmark of a great university."[4] One can only wonder how she reacted when she also discovered the 1924 mission statement. In fact, today one looks long and hard to find clear affirmations of religious and moral purposes from leaders of public higher education. Required services, even on Catholic campuses, the last to give them up, are hard to find anywhere today except at a few evangelical colleges. Any explicit attention to religion in public primary and secondary schools began to disappear in the 1960s.

In summary, with the rise and then dominance of science, coupled with the pervasive influence of capitalism and professional education (divinity schools, along with schools of education, became poor sisters and exist now on the margins of their universities), the leadership of the clergy-presidents effectively ended on the college and university level. The growth of professional education nearly displaced classical education, in part because it was not considered practical, but also because classical education imparted moral formation. As a consequence of these developments, moral education no longer holds a central place in colleges and universities. Since the turn of the twentieth century, moral formation has gradually disappeared in public colleges and universities and since the mid-twentieth century from public schools as well. Where it has not disappeared, its appropriate format in a religiously pluralistic culture is hotly debated.

Moral Formation and Public Schools

In the light of this history, the question arises whether a similar shift from moral to technical education has taken place in primary and secondary education in the United States. As I have already explained, the common schools established by Horace Mann in the 1840s required the daily reading of the King James Bible and of the famous McGuffey readers. During the first one hundred or so years, these common schools set out quite openly to provide moral education through

4. Stanely Hauerwas, "Missing from the Curriculum," *Commonweal* (September 23, 1994), pp. 19–20. See also Michael J. Baxter and Frederick C. Bauerschmidt, "*Eruditio* without *religio?* The Dilemma of Catholics in the Academy," in *Communio* 22 (Summer, 1995), pp. 284–302.

discipline, the example of teachers, and the curriculum itself. Up through the 1950s, public schools kept both a religious and a moral focus by teaching morality and promoting religious practices that are best described as part of mainline Protestantism.

But the movements that pushed colleges and universities to marginalize moral education were also bound, some decades later, to affect primary and secondary schools. One blow suffered by the public schools, as explained in Chapter 1, was the 1963 Supreme Court decision to strike down the practice of reciting the Lord's Prayer and reading aloud sections of the Bible. According to one of the Justices, the reason for the Court's decision was religious pluralism: "Today the Nation is far more heterogeneous religiously... Practices which may have been objectionable to no one in the time of Jefferson and Madison may today be highly offensive to many persons, the deeply devout and the nonbelievers alike."[5]

Many supporters of traditional moral education believed that religious practices, such as reading the Bible, were very important for the purposes of moral education. In the absence of these religious practices, most public educators have since begun to avoid explicit moral education entirely. Since the late 1960s, most teachers in public schools steer clear from all discussions of the relationship between morality and religion, and as a consequence, moral formation has suffered. Nevertheless, most public educators realize that some basic moral formation needs to be imparted, but find that they face many challenges in efforts to do this.

By examining the challenges public educators face in addressing moral formation, especially in the light of the separation of moral from religious formation, Catholic educators can get a clearer sense of how the educational environment of Catholic schools, due to their distinctive approach to teaching and moral formation, enjoys an advantage over public schools when it comes to the moral formation of their students.

In recent years, some public educators have promoted what has come to be known as character education. While not explicitly referring to such education as moral formation, they promote the formation of certain virtues in their students—virtues such as honesty, fairness and responsibility. But they have encountered challenges even in these efforts. Some wonder whether they will actually end up promoting a religious orthodoxy of some sort if they teach their students specific virtues. Many teachers avoid in-class discussions about ethical issues, believing that students should discuss ethical issues only at home in their families and their churches. Some teachers believe that all that should be taught is what can be verified by science, or what is needed to be a good citizen: classes

5. Cited in Stephen L. Carter, "Let us Pray," *The New Yorker*, December 5, 1994, p. 62.

on science, government, reading and writing. Some teachers simply believe they are incompetent to teach ethics.[6]

In the face of such objections, people like Louis E. Raths, Merrill Harmin, and Sidney Simon recommended that teachers could at least help students simply clarify the values they already hold. These authors believed that neither students nor teachers should criticize any of the values that students expressed. Nor were teachers to affirm any values themselves. Thus, in the early 1970s, a number of schools began teaching "values clarification." In addition to this approach, some schools also taught Kohlberg's six developmental stages. According to Kevin Ryan, both approaches rarely succeeded informing students morally:

> Both approaches discredit the direct teaching of the core values upon which social life, particularly life in a democracy, depends and strongly suggest to teachers that the seeds of moral wisdom and ethical values lie within the child, and the teacher is to be a morally neutral facilitator. In other words, teachers, as representatives of the adult community, should have nothing to say about ethical issues nor can they provide any help to students' efforts to acquire the enduring habits of good character. Youth must discover these on their own.[7]

Moral formation requires more than the individual student thinking about his or her values; it is best achieved, as I shall argue later in this chapter, through participation in the practices of a religious tradition shared by and embodied in an exemplary community.[8]

Unlike most public school teachers who are reluctant to teach morality, most parents think teachers should. A poll in *The Wall Street Journal* showed that the great majority of the American public answered yes to the question, "Should our public schools teach standards of right and wrong?" However, only 33 percent of teachers agreed. Further, in the 25th Annual Phi Delta Kappa/Gallup poll,[9] over 90 percent of those polled believed that the public schools should teach the following values: respect for others, industry or hard work, persistence or the ability

6. See Roger Starratt for a summary of these objections, *Building an Ethical School: A Practical Response to the Moral Crisis in Schools* (Washington, D.C.; Falmer Press, 1994).

7. Kevin Ryan, "It's Back to Basics, But Teachers Haven't Gotten the Word," *Journal of Teacher Education* 45 (1994), p. 304.

8. E. C. Lageman, "Character and Community," *Teachers College Record* 96 (1994), p. 141–147.

9. Graham, Ellen. 1988, "Coping with Change: 'Values' Lessons Return to the Classroom—Educators Say Kids Today are 'Rudderless'", *Wall Street Journal, Eastern Edition*. September 26, 1988, p. 1.

to follow through, fairness in dealing with others, compassion for others, and civility or politeness. In a 1993 Gallup poll, 90 percent of those polled believed that public schools should teach honesty, racial tolerance, belief in democracy, and the Golden Rule. Two-thirds believed that the curriculum should teach sexual abstinence outside marriage.[10] Thus, unlike teachers, most parents and the general public believe basic values should be taught in public schools.

The stress seems to be on "basic values," that is, values on which there is a consensus. Thus, left out of such basic values is teaching a specific position on a divisive moral issue like abortion. Nor do parents and the public believe any specific religion should be taught. In other words, many parents seem to believe that it is possible to extract from religion certain common values that should be taught in public schools. Stephen Carter believes that "education for values should stick to the points where the society has reached consensus; otherwise, when religious (or nonreligious) parents complain that the schools are trying to wean their children from them, they will be right."[11] He also notes that education in morality has the support of both the cultural left, for example, by the People for the American Way, and the cultural right, as represented by William Bennett, whose book, *The Book of Virtues*, sold over two million copies. Bennett devotes a chapter to each of the following virtues: self-discipline, compassion, responsibility, friendship, work, courage, perseverance, honesty, loyalty, and faith.

Public universities face an even greater challenge in coming up with a consensus on basic values. The Carnegie Foundation tried to help public universities identify those "basic values" or "principles," as their report calls them. The report lists six of these principles for decision making and community building: (1) shared academic goals; (2) an openness marked by freedom of expression and civility; (3) justice through which very different persons are honored; (4) discipline practiced by individuals as students and by the community as a whole; (5) care for all members of the campus community; and (6) celebration of the heritage of the educational institution.[12]

Of course, it is not enough just to teach these values. Authors, like Alexander Astin the UCLA professor and educational researcher, distinguish between the explicit and implicit values of an institution. Explicit values are those found in the school's charter, its stated mission, and in the speeches of the principal to the

---

10. Elam, Stanley M., Lowell C. Rose, and Alec M. Gallup, 1993. "The 25th Annual Phi Delta Kappa/Gallup Poll of the Public's Attitudes toward the Public Schools," *The Phi Delta Kappan* 75:2, p. 145.

11. Carter, "Let us Pray," p. 73.

12. *Campus Life: In Search of Community*. A Special Report by the Carnegie Foundation for the Advancement of Teaching (Princeton University Press, 1990), pp. 7–8.

parents. The other values, the implicit values, are the ones which, in Astin's view, actually drive the school: the ones which determine the actual budget decisions, how faculty are chosen, what pedagogical techniques are used, and how students and faculty act and treat each other. When the two sets of values are in sync, a consistent message is sent and received; when the two are in conflict, the implicit message is the one that students absorb.

Astin also distinguishes between the explicit and the implicit curriculum and concludes that our most important moral message is often found in the latter rather than the former; that is, in "the teaching methods we use, how we grade and test our students, and how we treat each other as professional colleagues," but not in the actual subject matter we teach.[13] Twenty years after graduation, students seldom remember what they've been taught; however, they usually remember the character of the persons who taught them. Astin's research supports the aphorism that character is caught rather than taught. It is something like the common cold; you get it from those who have it, without knowing exactly how you picked it up.

A now familiar African proverb states it takes a whole village to raise a child. It is the whole extended family and neighbors interacting over the years that forms the character of a member of the group. Robert Coles, the child psychiatrist at Harvard, recalls his father telling his brother and himself as youngsters that "character is how you behave when no one is looking." But Coles thoughtfully asks, "Are we ever in a situation when no one is looking?" Coles states that morally mature people, wherever they may be, carry within them a company of witnesses. There is, therefore, no such thing as being alone. People are always, as it were, in public and always carry within them their village.[14]

Researchers and writers about moral formation like Astin, Carter, Bennett and others are clear that the entire school, faculty, curriculum, and co-curricular activities, should embody and communicate moral formation. One can only admire the effort on the part of public educators who wrestle with how they might undertake what traditionally has been called moral formation. They know that formation is important, but have difficulty coming to a consensus because of contemporary concerns about religion in public schools, about the intimate relationship between morality and religion, and about the challenges genuine religious pluralism poses in local schools. If one of the best ways to impart moral

---

13. Alexander Astin, "What Matters in College: Four Critical Years Revisited," *Chronicle of Higher Education* (November 11, 1992), p. B 4.

14. Robert Coles, *Call of Stories* (Boston: Houghton Mifflin, 1989), p. 198. See also his *The Moral Intelligence of Children: How to Raise a Moral Child* (Penguin Putnam Inc.: New York, 1986).

formation is through the personal example of teachers, then it has to be asked whether one can easily avoid serious consideration of religious dimensions.

Deeds, Habits and Religious Exemplars

Before considering the important role that religious teachings and doctrine play in moral formation, it is useful to consider first the important role that personal example plays in communicating moral formation to adolescents. C. S. Lewis once remarked that while he could understand the philosophy of idealism, he could not live it. When he referred in a conversation to philosophy as a subject, he was corrected by Bede Griffiths, who later became a Benedictine monk and a leader in the dialogue between Catholicism and Hinduism. Bede believed that philosophy was not a subject, but a way of life. In recent years, the central importance of traditions, that is, of sets of practices which existentially communicate meaning and create understanding, have been emphasized by thinkers such as Alasdair MacIntyre,[15] Heinrich Fries,[16] and Pierre Hadot.[17] In their view, philosophers have forgotten how important it is that they live what they teach. Real philosophy, these writers suggest, is less about conceptual fluency and verbal precision than it is about moral integrity, personal discipline, and practical wisdom. They stress the importance of linking preaching to one's practice. Therefore, greater attention needs to be given to personal example and practices.

Freud certainly stressed that the habits formed during childhood deeply affect the behavior of adults. William James, perhaps America's best known psychologist, underscores the importance of repeating good deeds from the earliest age:

> Could the young but realize how soon they will become mere walking bundles of habits, they could give more heed to their conduct while in the plastic state.... Every smallest stroke of virtue or vice leaves its never so little scar. The drunken Rip van Winkle, in Jefferson's play, excuses himself for every fresh dereliction by saying, "I won't count this time." Well! He may not count it, and a kind of heaven may not count it; but it is being

---

15. A. MacIntyre, *After Virtue: A Study in Moral Theory* (University of Notre Dame Press, 1981); and *Three Rival Versions of Moral Enquiry: Encyclopedia, Genealogy, and Tradition* (University of Notre Dame Press, 1990).

16. H. Fries, *Theology and Narrative: Selected Essays,* G. Hunsinger & W. Placher, eds (NY: Oxford University Press, 1993); and *Fundamental Theology* [*Fundamental Theologie*], R. J. Daly, S. J., trans., (Washington, D.C.: Catholic University of America Press, 1996). Original work published in 1985.

17. Pierre Hadot, *Philosophy as a Way of Life,* edited and with an introduction by Arnold I. Davidson (Blackwell Publishers Ltd., 1995).

> counted none the less. Down among his nerve-cells and fibers the molecules are counting it, registering and storing it up to be used against him when the second temptation comes.... As we become permanent drunkards by so many separate drinks, so we become saints in the moral... sphere by so many separate acts.[18]

One does not have to be a disciple of John Dewey to understand that what people do often deeply shapes how they think. It stands to reason then that not just the mind, but also the body needs to be involved in the educative process. This interplay requires more than the addition of a physical education class to courses that concentrate on learning concepts. What we do with our bodies and touch with our senses is more likely to remain in our minds. An ancient Chinese proverb puts it well: "When I hear, I forget; when I see, I remember; when I do, I understand." And among the physical and spiritual practices important for moral formation is the practice of silence. Few teachers challenge students to be still, to think quietly, and to listen attentively. Just getting students to sit still is no small educational achievement![19] When teachers help students learn how to be silent, to read silently, they may find those same students treating each other with more respect than before and performing acts of courtesy in the lunch room or even on the playing field.

How a person acts reaches deeper than the merely cognitive dimension, though of course both acting and thinking are important. If the heart is commonly reached, as John Henry Newman once put it, "not through reason, but through the imagination... by history..." and, above all, by persons,[20] then those

---

18. As cited by in R. Wilkens, *Remembering the Christian Past* (Grand Rapids, MI: W. B. Eerdmans Publishing Co., 1995), p. 135.

19. Thus Catholic philosopher Louis Dupré, writing against the "pragmatist heresy" in education, states: "What is needed is a conversion to an attitude in which existing is more than taking, acting more than making, meaning more than function—an attitude in which there is enough leisure for wonder and enough detachment for transcendence. Culture requires freedom, but freedom requires spiritual space to act, play, and dream in.... The space for freedom is created by transcendence" (*Transcendent Selfhood: The Loss and Rediscovery of the Inner Life* (NY: Seabury Press, 1976, p. 17), as cited in James L. Heft, S.M., ed., *Faith and the Intellectual Life: Marianist Award Lectures* (University of Notre Dame Press, 1996), p. 70.

20. The entire often-cited quotation from Newman's *An Essay in Aid of A Grammar of Assent* (1906, pp. 92–93): "...the heart is commonly reached, not through reason, but through the imagination, by means of direct impressions, by the testimony of facts and events, by history, by description. Persons influence us, voices melt us, looks subdue us, deeds inflame us. Many a man will live and die upon a dogma; no man will be a martyr for a conclusion." Obviously, Newman has a much richer notion of the meaning of the word "dogma," as we shall see shortly, than is typically found in our heavily Anglo-Saxon influenced culture. For him, dogmas are nothing more nor less than efforts to express in language the saving events and truths of the Gospel.

persons who have assumed central roles in the education of students—the teachers—can enter not just the minds of the students, but their hearts as well. And they do so, primarily, through their actions.

If people are moved by the example of others, if the deeds and behaviors of parents and teachers leave lasting impressions upon their children and students, then all schools, and especially Catholic schools, must attend not just to a teacher's academic competence, but also to that teacher's total impact upon students. How faculty teach, coach, supervise and walk the halls, may have a greater impact than their best class presentations. Therefore, besides attention to the "whole person" of the student, attention must also be given to the "whole person" of the teacher. Students experience teachers as whole persons, not just as a shoe salesperson whom they see rarely when they go shopping. As important as the impact of the whole person of the teacher is on students, it is very difficult to measure. Nevertheless, it is that elusive whole person that people instinctively apprehend. Assessing the moral impact of teachers involves much more than course outcomes and success on standardized exams; it requires reflection on the more subtle dimensions of moral education. As the philosopher and writer Iris Murdoch once put it:

> When we apprehend and assess other people we do not consider only their solutions to specifiable practical problems, we consider something more elusive which may be called their total vision of life, as shown in their mode of speech or silence, their choice of words, their assessments of others, their conception of their own lives, what they think attractive or praise-worthy, what they think funny: in short, the configurations of their thought which show continually in their reactions and conversation.[21]

In summary, the educative power of various practices, including the way we perceive and understand other people, should never be underestimated. Most all of these examples come from the general experience of humanity seeking to build better relationships with each other.

Some teachers, as noted earlier, hesitate to undertake character education because they claim that they are not experts in it. There may be a deeper reason for their hesitation. Stanley Hauerwas, a professor of theological ethics at Duke University, traces the lack of comfort many feel in being models to our democratic society: where everyone is supposed to be equal, where no one is to be placed

---

21. As cited in R. Wilkens, *Remembering the Christian Past*, p. 143.

above anyone else, and where no one should presume to be a model for students to emulate. Following Alasdair McIntyre, the Notre Dame philosopher, Hauerwas stresses the importance of the interaction between apprentice and master in the learning of a craft such as bricklaying. To learn to lay brick, it is not enough to have bricklaying explained. It is necessary to learn many skills, including mixing mortar, building scaffolds, handling a trowel, spreading and frogging the mortar (frogging means "creating a trench in the mortar so that when the brick is placed on the mortar, a vacuum is created that almost makes the brick lay itself"). When you learn bricklaying, you are actually entering into a history that has its own language, its own practices, and its own master craftsmen. Hauerwas concludes that "the accounts of morality sponsored by democracy want to deny the necessity of a master. It is assumed we each in and of ourselves have all we need to be moral." But masters are necessary if uninitiated people are to become moral, for being moral is a condition that requires initiation and training. Because of this widespread "democratic" but ultimately inadequate notion of moral formation, Hauerwas claims that the most effective moral education today comes through learning to play baseball, basketball, to quilt, cook, or lay bricks. He explains that "such sports and crafts remain morally antidemocratic insofar as they require acknowledgement of authority based on a history of accomplishment."[22]

Although Hauerwas may have stated his case too sharply in favor of experts—for even when people are the experts they continue to learn and need to improve, and too many experts discount the wisdom of ordinary people—his central insight is sound: character education is inescapably craftsman-like. It is a mistake, then, to separate intelligence from discipline, or discipline from virtue. This is why many who support character education strongly recommend various forms of service that takes students outside of themselves and makes them more aware of the needs of others.

A Catholic Vision of Life

By now, I hope it is clear that the example of teachers plays a pivotal role in the moral formation of their students. Teachers in Catholic schools are no exception in this regard. In Catholic schools, it is possible to join moral formation explicitly with a religious tradition. So at this point, it is appropriate to ask, what is the Catholic vision of the human person? Who are Catholics? Once I clarify what a Catholic vision of life is, I will then spell out some key Catholic doctrines, and then finally, at

---

22. Stanley Hauerwas, *After Christendom? How the Church is to Behave if Freedom, Justice, and a Christian Nation are Bad Ideas* (Nashville, TN: Abingdon, 1991), p. 101–102.

the end of this chapter, ask how this Catholic vision of life and Catholic doctrines should influence the moral formation offered in Catholic schools.

To start, it is important to state that Catholics are Christians. They affirm that God is One and is Three—one nature and three persons. They are people who believe in Jesus Christ who, risen from the dead, sends forth his Spirit. Catholics are also not just individuals, but a people, a community with a history and distinctive practices. Catholics remain Christians largely on account of those practices which nourish and challenge them through the Word and the Sacraments, and through a call to ministry and witness.

Not long after the first followers of Jesus were called Christians (at that time some pagans also called them "atheists" since they, the Christians, believed in only one God and not many gods as did the Romans) they acquired the name "Catholic," a word used either as a noun or an adjective, as in either being a Catholic, or being a Catholic Christian. Already in the third century, theologians and pastors were explaining that being Catholic meant, following the Greek language, something that is "throughout-the-whole." In other words, Catholicism extends itself, the Gospel, the good news of and about Jesus Christ, to everyone in every possible language. Thus Jesus tells us (Matthew 13:33) that "the reign of God is like yeast which a woman took and kneaded into three measures of flour. Eventually, the whole mass of dough began to rise." As the late Jesuit Walter Ong observed: "Yeast is a plant, a fungus, and it grows. It has no limits itself, but is limited only by the limits of whatever it grows in. The Church, understood as Catholic in this way, is a limitless growing reality."[23] Catholicism is comprehensive and broad. In this sense, Catholicism is inclusive of all that is good and true and beautiful.

Richard McBrien, in his widely used textbook entitled *Catholicism,* states that Catholicism "is characterized by a *radical openness to all truth and every value*. It is *comprehensive* and *all-embracing* toward the totality of Christian experience and tradition."[24] McBrien stresses that Catholicism typically affirms a *both/and* rather than an *either/or* approach to reality. Thus, Catholicism characteristically speaks not of "nature or grace, but graced nature; not reason or faith, but reason illumined by faith; not law or Gospel, but law inspired by the Gospel..." Therefore, being Catholic means preserving, affirming and living the fullness of the truth, rather than emphasizing one element of truth while ignoring another, or creating false dichotomies. The Church, for example, con-

23. Walter J. Ong, S.J., "Realizing Catholicism: Faith, Learning and the Future," in *Faith and the Intellectual Life*, ed., James L. Heft, S.M., (University of Notre Dame Press; Indiana, 1996), p. 32.

24. Richard McBrien, *Catholicism,* rev. ed., (CA: Harper San Francisco, 1994), p. 1190.

demned the teachings of Marcion (note that the Catholic Church condemns teachings, not persons), who thought the New Testament was wholly a Gospel of love, and therefore required Christians to exclude the emphasis on the law and to avoid acts of violence that he thought the books of the Old Testament condoned. The Church opposed Marcion's thinking and taught that both the Old and the New Testaments were valid (the New Testament fulfilled but did not replace the Old), that both contain the law and both issue the call to love, and that law and love are, therefore, not to be opposed.

To take another example, the Church has, since the middle of the fifth century, consistently taught that Jesus is both human and divine. In doing so, the Church opposed those who wanted to say that Jesus was divine but not human, or human but not divine, or both human and divine but schizophrenic (not one person). To this day, the temptation to stress humanity or divinity to the exclusion of the other remains, as is evidenced in Martin Scorsese's film, *The Last Temptation of Christ*, which stresses Jesus' humanity so much that one wonders how Scorsese's Jesus could have attracted and transformed disciples.

Does an emphasis on "both/and" mean that Catholics end up indiscriminately embracing everything and opposing nothing? Do Catholics end up legitimating too much, including, as some conservative Protestants fear, idol worship, and as some pacifists fear, war? This type of all-inclusiveness cannot be what "both/and" means. For Jesus himself condemned certain deeds—the desecration of his Father's house with crass practices of greed, the selfish ambition and blindness of his disciples, and the self-righteousness of certain religious leaders who lorded it over others. Rather, "both/and" must mean that all that is good is to be cherished, that false dichotomies are rejected (e.g., either law or love), and that tensions can be dynamic and creative, as in the case of the tension that exists between the prophetic and priestly roles in the Church.

McBrien describes three fundamental theological dimensions of Catholicism: sacramentality (the acceptance of tangible and finite realities as actual or potential carriers of divine presence); mediation (a corollary of sacramentality which means for the Catholic that grace comes through Christ, the church, and other signs and instruments); and communion (a still further corollary which means that all grace comes to us in and through community and communion with others and nature).[25]

Open to all truth, both/and, sacramentality, mediation and communion—these phrases and words can obscure as much as they clarify, unless we have concrete examples and practices that signify what they mean. Take the phrase,

---

25. McBrien, p. 1197.

"open to all truth." Are there not plenty of painful examples of Church leaders who have not been open to some theories of science (evolution), scholarship (which challenged the traditional understanding of the Mosaic authorship of the Pentateuch) and even some political theories (e.g., democracy, separation of church and state, religious freedom)? Indeed there have. How then are people to understand, then, what "open to all truth" might mean? One way to understand what "open to all truth" means is to examine the doctrine of creation—that everything that is has been created by God who continues to sustain it all in existence. If the doctrine of creation is true, then it follows that Catholics should learn everything they can about creation. Catholics should never fear the truth—for ultimately it all comes from and leads back to God.

Sacramentality simply means that God speaks to believers through his creation, through things. Since everything has been created in and through God, believers somehow experience God when they see the hand of the Transcendent One in earthly things. And though God can appear as an apparition in some personal form, the ordinary way in which God is present to believers is through ordinary contact with others. Christianity is not an "out of the body" experience; rather, it relies upon the human senses as the typical doorways to encountering God. Adding the dimension of communion emphasizes in a somewhat different but related way that the ordinary locus of revelation is interpersonal—that it is not the isolated believer who encounters God—the alone with the Alone—but rather believers gathered in faith with other believers—"where two or three are gathered in my name"—that they sense their oneness with God. Or, in more theological terms, mediation, according to Cardinal Avery Dulles, assumes that "God ordinarily comes to us through the structures that are given, especially those to which his gracious promises are attached, such as incarnation, scripture, sacrament, and apostolic ministry."[26] Similar descriptions of Catholicism can be found in the works of other writers.[27] Typically, such authors stress the importance of community, the dynamic interplay between faith and reason, the importance of both scripture and tradition, the centrality of both Word and Sacrament, and the unique way in which authority functions within the Catholic tradition, especially through the *Sensus fidelium* of all the baptized, and the ministries of the bishops and the pope.

---

26. Avery Dulles, *The Catholicity of the Church* (Oxford: Clarendon Press, 1985), p. 7.

27. Such as Henri de Lubac's *Catholicism*, Friedrich von Hugel's *The Mystical Element of Religion*; Yves Congar's *Tradition and Traditions*; Rosemary Haughton's *The Catholic Thing*; Walter Kasper's *An Introduction to the Christian Faith*; Dennis Doyle's *The Church Emerging from Vatican II*; and William Portier's *Tradition and Incarnation*.

It might also be helpful to think of Catholicism as a tradition, that is, a living reality that grows over time through the debates and practices of a community of believers. Unfortunately, for most people today, the word tradition suggests something that is old and frozen. In one of his classic writings on Catholicism, *Orthodoxy*, G. K. Chesterton famously distinguished between tradition and traditionalism. Tradition is the living faith of the dead, and traditionalism is the dead faith of the living. In this sense, tradition is a vital, developing, even at times contentious reality, the core themes of which are so profound that they are passed on from generation to generation. Traditionalism, by contrast, clings to forms that do not give life, and, as a consequence, are not worth passing on to the next generation of Christians.

Finally, one more description of Catholicism: it includes everybody. The Church is made up of all the baptized, those who are married and those who are single, those who are ordained and those who are vowed, those who are saints and those who are sinners, those who are rich and those who are poor. The Church as a whole continues on its pilgrim journey with constant interplay between the laity, the bishops and the theologians—an interplay that at times grows tense, but ultimately sheds light through the continuing guidance of the Holy Spirit. Some conservatives think "the Church" is only the bishops while some liberals think it is only the laity. The Church includes everyone, laity and bishops—both sinners. Neither the liberals who despair that the changes in the Church they think are needed will ever be made, nor conservatives that fear that Church is falling apart for lack of stricter exercise of Episcopal authority—neither has sufficient faith in the Holy Spirit.

In summary, Catholics are Christians. They are a community of faith which strengthens itself and celebrates Word and Sacrament. Under the guidance of the Holy Spirit and with the assistance of the bishops and theologians and the faith of all believers, Catholics preach the Gospel to everyone everywhere, a Gospel that affirms that Jesus is Lord. Catholics treasure all that is good and true and beautiful in the world, including music, dancing and wine. In these senses, we can think of Catholicism as universal, comprehensive and evangelical.

These teachings form the doctrinal basis of Catholicism, and, as such, the foundation and framework for the moral formation that takes place within it, whether the site of that moral formation is the family, the school or the parish. Critics of Catholicism often see so much doctrinal teaching as opposed to, or at least unacceptably limiting, a person's freedom to think for oneself. Before turning to one of the most misunderstood categories of Catholic teaching—the category of dogma—I want to address those critics who think that affirming dogmas makes thinking for oneself no longer possible.

Can Catholics Think for Themselves?

Is it possible to be a practicing and faithful Catholic and still think for oneself?[28] Aren't Catholics put upon by domineering members of the hierarchy? If they can't think for themselves, what kind of schools do they run? A recent study by Andrew Greeley and Michael Hout documents "significant anti-Catholic sentiment" among ordinary conservative Protestants who "believe that Catholics are not allowed to think for themselves, that Catholic statues and images are idols, and so on."[29] George Bernard Shaw once famously remarked that "a Catholic university" is an oxymoron, a contradiction in terms. In other words, the Church is threatened by creative thinking; therefore, to survive, it crushes independent thought.

While such critics are sometimes right about certain Catholics, they also confuse authoritative teaching with authoritarian teachers. Rather, Catholics, when they understand their tradition correctly, know that in the last analysis they alone must make up their minds; however, they also know that they should never make up their minds alone. Like people facing a serious medical crisis, Catholics don't hesitate to weigh options and get a second opinion before making a major decision. And in the tradition, there are also several—sometimes even multiple—opinions, some possessing greater authority than others. A genuine believer stays at the table, listening to many voices, stays engaged in honest and demanding conversation—remaining in a conversation which leads over time to deeper insight and understanding, indeed, to orthodoxy. For Catholics, of course, not all voices have the same degree of authority. In the last analysis, it is the voice of the bishops, particularly when they teach with infallible authority, that Catholics acknowledge and accept—but still, all the while, reflecting upon, and sometime only gradually appropriating, the meaning of those dogmatic teachings.

I believe that accepting revelation as true does not dull but rather sharpens the intellect, inviting believers to think more critically about more dimensions of life than if they were not to believe authentic revelation. For example, if Jesus is truly human and truly divine and not schizophrenic, then belief in Jesus calls us to explore our understanding of God in a new way—not as a distant disincarnate potentate, but as someone who as a vulnerable human being loves everyone so

---

28. See again John McGreevy's article, "Thinking on One's Own: Catholicism in the American Intellectual Imagination, 1928–1960," in *The Journal of American History* June, 1997, pp. 1–32.

29. Christian Smith, "Social Science, Ideology, and American Evangelicals," a review of *The Truth about Conservative Christians* (University of Chicago Press, 2006), in *Books and Culture*, November/December, 2006, p. 26.

deeply as to lay down his life for them; not as someone aloof, far away and untouchable, but as someone who could weep at the death of his friend; not as a cosmic force or a green halo of light, but as a person who can actually be encountered, because, in many ways, he is truly human, especially accessible in the Word and the Sacraments, in community, in all creation and in loving other persons. Jesus, as it has been remarked, is God with skin.

Such beliefs do not kill the inquiring intellect. A person who believes that Jesus is the human face of God, and that Jesus lives in the hearts of all those who truly seek Him—that same person desires to know and love others as fully as possible. The deepest human hungers are to know and to love, to be known and to be loved. If God has created heaven and earth, all that is visible and invisible (for example, angels), then Christians ought to learn all that they can about their world, learn to appreciate its beauty, and learn its laws and respect its integrity. And if Jesus is the Way, the Truth and Life (John 14:6), then Christians ought to seek to understand all that there is to understand and to live it as a tried and trustworthy way of life.

What all this has to do with education should be obvious. Consider just three consequences of the characteristics of Catholicism just described as they would relate to Catholic education. The first and most important dimension of education characteristic of Catholicism is the joining of intellectual with moral and religious education. Wisdom is not just the acquisition of a great deal of knowledge; it is also the ability to make sound judgments and how to practice that wisdom day-to-day. Bernard of Clairvaux, the eleventh-century Cistercian monk and doctor of the Church, put it this way:

> There are many who seek knowledge for the sake of knowledge: that is curiosity. There are others who desire to know in order that they may themselves be known: that is vanity. Others seek knowledge in order to sell it: that is dishonorable. But there are some who seek knowledge in order to edify others: that is love.[30]

To edify others does not mean to impress or dazzle them, but to build others up, to encourage them. What this statement meant in Bernard's day as well as today is that Catholicism is committed to moral formation in education, not just to the accumulation of facts and the development of marketable skills. There is a moral dimension that is inherent in knowing and understanding, as well as a moral dimension to be found in the art of teaching.

---

30. Cited in Mark Schwehn, *Exiles from Eden: Religion and the Academic Vocation in America* (NY: Oxford University Press, 1993), p. 60.

Second, from its earliest days, the Church has taken education seriously. Early on, Christians founded within the Roman Empire schools and libraries that soon became famous. In the Middle Ages it created the first universities in the West. In the United States, the Church has invested heavily in a wide array of educational institutions, from preschool to post-graduate education, from parish catechetical programs to adult education. Faith has nothing to fear from education and serious thinking. As Augustine once wrote, "No one believes anything unless one first thought it to be believable... Everything which is believed should be believed after thought has preceded... Not everyone who thinks believes, since many think in order not to believe, but everyone who believes thinks."[31] To believe rightly is to have thought before, during and after the act of faith.

A third and final dimension of education within Catholicism is the desire to know whatever is true. Early in the life of the Church, believers found much wisdom in the writings of the pagan authors. In rethinking all of Christianity in his own time, St. Thomas did not hesitate to draw heavily on the thought of the pagan Aristotle or the Jew Maimonides. And in this spirit, Catholic schools do not hesitate to teach all subjects. Catholics are more likely to establish liberal arts colleges than bible schools; that is, Catholic institutions teach not only the Bible, but also theology, philosophy and literature, mathematics, physics and chemistry—though Catholics still have something to learn from many Protestants about how to read and treasure the Bible. Catholics are interested in understanding the world, not escaping it; living in it thoughtfully, but not swallowed up by it. Salvation for Catholics is not from the world, but in and through it. Thus, once again, Catholicism is comprehensive, seeking not only a balance of revealed truths, but also a window into all that can be known. The qualities are not unique to Catholics, since other Christian groups share them; they are, however, characteristic of Catholics.

The desire to understand all that is, to question, to reach beyond what can be measured empirically, to take seriously both the moral and intellectual dimensions of education—all these habits should characterize Catholic education. Is it legitimate, then, to question dogmas?

Dogmatic Foundations of Catholic Education

At the beginning of this chapter we described how philosophy was first understood as a way of life before it became an academic subject. The first Christians referred to their religion as a "way." A "way" of living draws upon practices and

31. Cited in Robert Wilken, *Remembering the Christian Past*, p. 20.

rituals that form character. It is now time to reflect on some of the most central teachings of Catholic Christianity, dogmas. In developing a better understanding of the nature and limits of dogmas, it needs to be kept in mind that teaching—especially teaching dogmas—without supportive practices has little lasting effect and is quickly forgotten, just as practices without teaching are blind, since one does not understand what one is doing.

Through the living of "the way," Christians are enabled to articulate truths that they live, even if they live them always imperfectly. In fact, the truths of Christianity were first deeds and persons, and at its very foundation, the deeds and words of the Word, Jesus Christ. Knowing about his life, death and resurrection, and knowing through the scriptures what he taught during his life, Christians have from the earliest time found it useful and sometimes necessary to clarify and stress what needs to be affirmed about "the way," and what needs to be clarified about the teachings of Jesus, indeed, even about who Jesus is.

One of the least understood categories of belief in Catholicism is dogma. Dogmas clarify core teachings.[32] Through these official statements, the Church clarifies, defends and expresses fundamentally important—that is, saving—truths. The Church will never deny the truth of a dogma. However, the words used to express a truth of the faith may change. Such a change in language will be made in order to express more accurately the truth of the dogma. In 1999, the Catholics and the Lutherans agreed upon a newly formulated statement about justification, that is, about how Christians are saved through faith in Jesus Christ. To arrive at that agreement, Catholics and Lutherans needed to return to the controversies of the sixteenth century, and even more importantly to the revealed word of God, the scriptures, and see if after long and demanding conversations they could arrive at a more accurate understanding of the meaning of justification. While the 1999 Augsburg statement is not formally a dogma, it nonetheless illustrates well how the language used to express a truth of the faith might be improved upon.[33]

The most widely and regularly expressed dogmas of the Church are the creeds of antiquity, for example, the creeds of the councils of Nicea and Constantinople, which are recited each Sunday at the celebration of the Eucharist. These creeds

---

32. Flannery O'Connor, the Catholic novelist of the deep south, wrote: "There is no reason why fixed dogma should fix anything that the writer sees in the world. On the contrary, dogma is an instrument for penetrating reality. Christian dogma is about the only thing left in the world that surely guards and respects mystery," in *Mystery and Manners: Occasional Prose* (New York: Farrar, Straus and Giroux, 1969), p. 177.

33. Avery Cardinal Dulles, "Two Languages of Salvation: The Lutheran-Catholic Joint Declaration," in *First Things*, December 1999, pp. 25–30.

actually put into words—inadequate words to be sure—the saving events of history: that God the Father creates the world, that salvation may be found in the Son who dies and rises from the dead, and that the Holy Spirit continues to animate the Church with its ministries of preaching and the forgiveness of sins. Creeds are affirmed at baptism and constitute the core teachings of the Church.

Along with dogmas, Catholics also have difficulty understanding the dogma of infallibility. The Church distinguishes between infallible and non-infallible teachings. Infallibly defined truths are typically those important teachings over which, at one time or another, major disagreements arose, and the Church found it necessary to clarify what the teaching should be. One source of many disagreements has been apparent confusions about what the Bible teaches. For example, at one point in the Gospel of John, Jesus affirms that he and the Father are one; but at another point, he admits that not even he knows when the end of the world will happen, something that only the Father knows. Well, is or is not Jesus one with the Father? If he is one with the Father, why then doesn't he know when the world will end? And if he is not one with the Father, is he really divine? Or, to offer another example, at the Last Supper, Jesus says simply and directly of the bread and wine, "this is my body and this is my blood." But in the discourse on the bread of life in chapter six of the Gospel of John, he says that it is the spirit and not the flesh that is important. Such texts about the divinity and humanity of Jesus caused confusion among believers, as did those texts about the bread and wine and the best ways to understand Jesus' presence in the Eucharist. These are critically important matters of the faith of the Church. The Church then, in Council, after discerning the faith of the Church, interpreted the scriptures on these matters in an infallible way. Vatican II taught that the scriptures are utterly reliable in all things that are meant for salvation, implying that not all things in scripture are meant for salvation. Infallible teachings articulate those most central saving truths.

Another typical misunderstanding is the idea that Catholics are required to believe only infallible teachings. While it is true that infallible teachings are core teachings of the Church, they are not the only core teachings. Some infallibly true teachings of the Church are not infallibly defined: the need for repentance, for daily prayer, and the obligation to love God and neighbor. Teachings about love and repentance have never been infallibly defined because there has never been major disagreement over their interpretation and importance. Therefore, Catholics are obligated to accept more than infallibly defined truths. A Catholic does not, to paraphrase scripture, live on infallibly defined truths alone.

It is important that the Church distinguishes between infallible and non-infallible truths. If no distinction is made between such teachings, the ordinary

Catholic runs the risk of giving the same importance to a teaching on the real presence of Jesus in the Eucharist and a teaching about fasting during Lent. Most Catholics instinctively understand that the former teaching is more central to their faith than the latter. Sometimes Catholics argue about whether an official teaching is infallible or not. For example, some theologians believe that the official 1968 teaching of the encyclical *Humanae Vitae* that condemns artificial birth control is infallible, others do not. And even though canon 749 of *The Code of Canon Law* states that no teaching is infallible unless is it manifestly presented as infallible,[34] arguments over which level of authority stands behind certain official teachings are rather common in the history of the Church.

An important reason for the distinction between infallibly and non-infallibly defined teachings is that not all official teachings of the Church are necessarily true for all time. Up until the last century, the Church, based on a mistaken interpretation of certain texts of scripture and influenced by social conditions, officially taught that slavery was acceptable. The dignity and freedom of a human person is hardly an unimportant matter. The Church now, finally, condemns slavery; John Paul II stated that slavery is an intrinsic evil. That condemnation was enshrined in the teaching of Vatican II on religious freedom.[35] Suffice it to say that doctrines develop. It took nearly four hundred years for the Church to find appropriate language to express the central doctrine of the Trinity. Sometimes what was once taught is no longer taught. Some official teachings—not dogmatic teachings—of the past are now seen to have been false. The truth of dogmas, however, does not change and Catholics are required to affirm them. The Church is in a continual process of discerning the truth of the Gospel for our own times and continues to affirm some of those truths as forever true. They are dogmatic teachings.

Dogmas then form a normative conceptual framework for the Christian life. Part of a good Catholic education helps Catholics understand the importance of these central truths, these dogmas, for their own life and salvation. They also learn that though some teachings are not infallibly defined, they are nevertheless infallibly true. And finally, they also come to understand that the Church, like parents, is also human and can make mistakes in what it teaches. To understand these distinctions leads a person to a mature Catholic faith.

---

34. *The Code of Canon Law* (Collins Liturgical Publications, 1983), article 749, par. 3: "No doctrine is understood to be infallibly defined unless it is manifestly presented as infallible."

35. See John Noonan, *A Church that Can and Cannot Change* (IN: University of Notre Dame Press, 2005).

Catholic Schools: Dogmas, Moral Formation and Practices Together

Given the dogmatic foundation that Catholics have through their faith, how should moral formation be approached? What are some of the characteristic emphases and practices of Catholic schools that flow through that framework? How do these fundamental theological dimensions actually shape the practices and rituals of Catholic schools? Discussing the mission of a Catholic school by emphasizing practices and rituals that flow from Catholicism has the benefit of being more descriptive than an approach that would simply stress the Church's dogmatic teachings. Describing the way the faith shapes an educational culture allows us to see what the whole house, built on the foundation and supported by the framework, looks like.

To extend the metaphor, upon entering the house, that is, a Catholic school, what sorts of activities should be visible? In 1973, the bishops of the United States issued a pastoral letter on Catholic education entitled, *To Teach as Jesus Did.*[36] This valuable letter emphasized three dimensions of Catholic educational institutions that ought to distinguish them: teaching, community and service. Teaching all the subjects well, and especially teaching the Gospel of Jesus Christ; forming community through which the presence of God is experienced in the midst of a faith-filled people; and, after the example of Jesus, serving others—these three activities constitute the essential institutional qualities of Catholic schools.

If a Catholic school is clear about its religious and moral mission, it already enjoys a distinct advantage over public schools. Many studies (for example, one published in the US by the Rand Corporation, *High Schools with Character: Alternatives to Bureaucracy*[37]) have shown that an effective school requires both a vision of education held in common by students, faculty, and parents and the freedom to implement that vision. Catholic schools should strive for academic excellence within the context of a community of faith. But how many Catholic schools actually join the moral and religious dimensions of the education they offer? How many teachers understand how a Catholic theological vision enriches and deepens moral education?

Schools with a clear vision of their mission can afford to welcome all students. And for that matter, most Catholic schools are open to whoever applies. Though

36. *To Teach as Jesus Did: A Pastoral Message on Catholic Education,* National Conference of Catholic Bishops, November 1972 (Washington, D.C: United States Catholic Conference, 1973).

37. Paul T. Hill, Gail E. Foster, and Tamar Gendler, *High Schools with Character* (Santa Monica, CA: Rand, 1990).

open to all students, these schools should not, for fear of offending non-Catholic students, abandon their commitment to passing on the Catholic faith tradition. In some high schools, I have witnessed well-intentioned faculty who stress the school's Catholic identity, but have not learned how to do that in a way that is also ecumenically informed and sensitive. The United States is religiously pluralistic; most Catholic schools have students and teachers who are not Catholic. Teachers in these schools need to learn how to teach Catholicism in an ecumenically astute way.

Schools with a clear vision demand discipline so that order and civility support the common good. That all students are welcome doesn't mean that they can come and do whatever they want. Mediocrity in academics or irresponsibility on the part of students and faculty is not acceptable. Just as hard work is expected of students, competence and dedication are expected of the faculty. Such teachers deserve a living wage. At the same time, our schools must remain accessible to more than the rich. A continuing challenge facing most Catholic schools is balancing the demand for a living wage against an affordable tuition. More will be said in a later chapter about meeting this financial challenge.

Of course, every educational institution, especially primary and secondary schools, whether Catholic or not, should be a caring institution. The special reason for caring that should motivate teachers in Catholic schools is that every child is believed to be a child of God, created in God's image and likeness. To believe this, teachers may on certain days have to make a heroic act of faith. Nonetheless, every student is cared for when hurting and challenged when lazy. The Catholic school is a place of care and challenge because, ultimately, the members of the community, students as well as teachers, staff and parents, recognize themselves as part of the body of Christ. This theological foundation and framework should influence all the activities of the school. But if the theological framework is not understood, or worse, misunderstood as simply a matter of stricter discipline—a key advantage of Catholic education is lost.

Descriptions of the qualities of Catholic schools similar to those above can be found scattered throughout *To Teach as Jesus Did*. All the qualities mentioned in the bishops' document presuppose a confluence of several components that tend to be kept separate in public schools: for example, the moral and religious dimensions, moral formation and supportive religious practices, moral formation and the intellectual dimensions of religious beliefs.

To conclude this chapter on how Catholic high schools can integrate these dimensions, allow me to give examples of four characteristics that Catholic schools with a proper sense of their distinctive mission have. I am presuming that every Catholic school will continue to teach religion courses well and frequently, work to strengthen the ties between the school and the parishes from which many of the children come, and continue to cultivate in the students and faculty a deep sense of the richness of Catholic tradition. Of course, in reality, such all-encompassing expectations cannot always be met, in which case, the key advantage of Catholic high schools over their public counterparts may be weakened or even lost.

The first characteristic of Catholic schools—and here I am speaking mainly of Catholic high schools, which I know best—is that the teachers make an effort to put what they teach into a moral and theological context. That is to say, they strive to *integrate knowledge*. Critics of higher education note repeatedly that professors teaching various disciplines don't talk with each other. On the one hand, college students often select courses as if they were walking through a cafeteria line: they choose what they like more often than what they need. Professors teach their subject as if that subject were the only subject in the students' curriculum. Most of our primary and secondary school teachers, having attended such universities themselves, found their major area of study segregated from other areas of knowledge. As a consequence, the curricula of most of the high schools in which these college graduates now teach reflect a lack of integration similar to that which characterized their own college education.

An integrated education does not attempt to create strained amalgams such as "Catholic chemistry" or "moral mathematics." Nor does it refer to some more obvious points of collaboration that might be imagined, for example, between a religion teacher and biology teacher when offering sex education. Rather, it refers to science and humanities teachers thinking through the courses they teach so that they might together bring to light issues that are very important but rarely treated—issues that fall through the cracks that exist between these subject areas when they are not integrated. To offer but two examples, think of the learning that could be acquired by developing ecological themes from studying the history of industrialization while also reading novels by Charles Dickens and Upton Sinclair, or by linking the goodness of creation in a religion course with some themes from a physics or biology course. Anyone who has ever attempted the extensive collaboration that such efforts at integrating knowledge require knows the dedication and time it demands of teachers, who without the encouragement and support of principals, rarely are able by themselves to make this effort. Catholic schools should, therefore, not only build communities of faith, they should also support in their teachers efforts to integrate knowledge. We shall return to this question in our chapters on leadership and faculty.

Secondly, Catholic education communicates a sense of history. Until very recently, Americans have always moved west, have looked to the future rather than the past, and have placed their confidence in science and technology, which they hope can solve most, if not all, problems. However, just as on a personal level a sense of one's past makes possible a sense of one's own identity, so does an appreciation of history and tradition help strengthen a person's identity as a Catholic. John Henry Newman once wrote that to be deeply immersed in history is to cease to be a Protestant. Expressed with a bit more ecumenical insight, Newman's thought might be put this way: those who have developed a deep sense of history will appreciate different understandings of different peoples from different times, and in that process identify more readily the blind spots of their own time. Too many teachers know only their own subject, and even then only a recent version of that subject. Understanding the history of biology can be as enlightening as understanding current biology. Catholics without an historical sense may be able to identify with the Church's current institutional practices, but they often have little understanding of the meaning of those practices, and even less capacity to explain when and why these practices originated, and why they are important now for Catholics. Were more teachers educated in history, philosophy and theology, their efforts to integrate knowledge and understand history would be more successful than they currently are.

A third characteristic of a Catholic school should be its emphasis on art, speech and drama. Catholics grow spiritually within a tradition of liturgically celebrated Word and Sacrament. Besides the need to integrate knowledge and appreciate history, Catholics should develop more fully their sense of ritual and symbol—those ways of knowing and understanding that rely on intuition and aesthetics, on the power of narrative and on the beauty of music and dance. Otherwise, Catholics run the risk of reducing all knowing to ideas and technical skills.[38]

Hans Urs von Balthasar, a gifted and prolific Swiss theologian and priest, died in the late 1980s on the morning of the very day he was to be made a cardinal of the Catholic Church. Von Balthasar named his life work, a multivolume exploration of the nature of Catholic Christianity, *Herrlichkeit*, a German word which means "glory." He divided this multivolume work into three parts: Theo-aesthetic, Theo-dramatic, and Theo-logic. His conviction was that most people came to believe in God first through their awareness of beauty (aesthetic), followed by witnessing the actions of virtuous believers (dramatic), and only lastly through rational arguments (logic). In sequencing his volumes in this way, he suggests that ordinarily people need to experience beauty and be moved by the example of

38. All-male Catholic high schools especially run the risk of downplaying of the arts. Perhaps we should take a hint from the first Jesuit schools that did not even offer a religion class, but instead taught the great pagan authors, stressed the arts, and, in general designed their curricula to instill the virtue of *pietas* (see John W. O'Malley, "Jesuit History: A New Hot Topic?" in *America*, May 9, 2005, pp. 8–11.

others before logical explanations will make much sense to them. To ignore these steps would be like expecting a person who has never been in love to understand and personally identify with the lead characters of Shakespeare's *Romeo and Juliet*.

Perhaps inspired by von Balthasar's conviction, Cardinal Danneels of Belgium, at a gathering of Cardinals in Rome in 2001, asked whether the Church should make greater use of the notion of beauty as a "doorway leading to God." He acknowledged that God is truth and holiness and moral perfection. However, in each of these qualities, humans fall short. Truth attracts us, but people often do not act on it. Holiness and moral perfection are also attractive, but due to inescapable moral weakness, people are incapable of attaining such states. But beauty, he writes, "disarms; it is irresistible for our contemporaries. Young students spend hours discussing and holding forth about dogma (truth) and ethics (goodness). But when they listen to Bach's St. Mathew Passion, they are disarmed and surrender in silence."[39]

Beauty and an aesthetic sense are especially important in liturgy. In 1943, Pope Pius XII published an encyclical on the liturgy, *Mediator Dei*, in which he made the extraordinary statement that the Eucharist is the "source and summit" of the Christian life. To speak of the Eucharist as the "source" of the Christian life indicates that without the Eucharist, without both the power of the Word and the nourishment of the Sacrament, Christians would have little to draw upon for their spiritual life. To speak of the Eucharist as the "summit" suggests that being in love with God and with others creates more than a "peak experience." For the believer, such communion realizes the very purpose of life.

The Eucharist embodies and enacts a ritual that sustains and realizes the purpose of the Christian life. At its center is an action, a drama, an offering, a sacrifice, a transformation, a meal before which there is a proclamation of a saving word, and a preparation of gifts, which represent the work of the people, gifts which are transformed, and then returned to them, who also, through faithful participation, are to be transformed. During the celebration of the Eucharist people play different roles, such as those of presiders, readers, communion ministers, musicians and singers. And if the school is well-designed, the Eucharist will be celebrated in artistically shaped sacred space, with statues and colorful windows, flowers and incense, podium and pulpit, altar, crucifix and candles. Finally,

39. Cardinal Godfried Danneels, "Beauty and the Way to God," in *The Tablet* (December 21–28, 2002). We may ask just how many students we know would listen to Bach. Nevertheless, Danneels concludes: "Beauty can achieve a synthesis between truth and goodness. Truth, beauty and goodness: those are three of God's names and three paths that lead to him. But beauty has hardly been pressed into use by theology or religious teaching up until now. Isn't it time to do so?"

when all these elements come together, when these roles are enacted amidst song and silence, reverence and proclamation, then the participants experience the source and summit of the Christian life.

When people who lead Catholic schools enact the Eucharist as it ought to be enacted, a profound dimension of Catholic education is realized: how to speak, to listen, to read in public, to sing, to move, and how to be silent. How to understand symbols and enact ancient rituals of washing and genuflecting and blessing and bowing, standing, sitting and kneeling—all these actions educate, that is, draw out of people what is deepest in them—the desire for God and for communion with others. Is every Eucharist experienced as a "source and a summit"? Of course not—not any more than every meal at home is experienced as a family encounter. Moreover, the celebration of the Eucharist with high school students presents its own challenges. Yet, when the Eucharist is thoughtfully prepared, respectfully approached and fully embraced, transformations abound, profound connections are made, and understanding deepens.

Using the liturgy as an example of ritual underlines the importance of more than the cognitive and conceptual in education. If before the Second Vatican Council too many devotions unconnected with scripture and the Sacraments distracted Catholics from the heart of the Gospel, now after Vatican II Catholics are only beginning to develop and rediscover devotions, that is, rituals and communal practices, which help them individually and as communities to strengthen the living of the Christian life. A greater sense of awe and reverence needs to be recovered in liturgies. Rituals embody understandings in palpable and communal forms. As already has been mentioned, Catholic schools, and especially Catholic high schools, should be recognized for devoting as much time and emphasis to the arts, to drama, music, and the humanities, as they do to science, social science and mathematics.[40] Nietzsche once remarked that "the trick today is not to arrange a festival, but to find people capable of enjoying one."[41] Catholic schools should be populated with people who have learned how to love festivals; know how to host and enact them; and how to teach others how to appreciate music, the proclaimed Word, and the artistic environment that lifts the spirit—all qualities that a community that knows how to celebrate liturgy values.

Having attended and presided at a number of Eucharistic liturgies at Catholic high schools, I have the impression that in at least some instances a golden opportunity is being missed. Frequently, the songs that are chosen and the quality of

---

40. The most elaborate rituals in our schools should not be sporting events, the athletic marching band, the prom and various rituals associated with homecoming weekend.

41. Quoted by Josef Pieper, *In Tune with the World: A Theory of Festivity*, translated from the German by Richard and Clara Winston (NY: Harcourt, Brace & World, Inc., 1965), p. 10.

singing do not reflect an informed and rich grasp of Catholic liturgical tradition. How to overcome this problem requires more than a priest who can preach effectively to high school students (already a high expectation), but also faculty who will take the time to prepare the students for a liturgical celebration.

The fourth and final characteristic of a Catholic school is its service orientation. One manifestation of this characteristic is the awareness that "cooperation is a more basic comprehensive category of human relationship than competition."[42] Service is a step beyond cooperation, for service places the needs of others first. Ultimately, after the example of Christ, service is the emptying of oneself, laying down one's life for others. Students should see this level of dedication in their teachers, whom we have spoken of earlier as their "models," both inside and outside the classroom. Indispensable are teachers who lead and mentor their students in service. Any way that parents can be drawn into this gospel-inspired activity will create a greater congruence between their influence on their children and the mission of the Catholic school.

It can be quite a challenge for Catholic educators who promote service to form an integral link between the Gospel mandate to serve others and helping out in a soup kitchen. The tendency to associate religion only with "vertical" activities, like silent personal prayer, and associate "horizontal" activities like helping others with simply doing good deeds is pervasive. Similarly, Catholics often miss the ethical ramifications of celebrating the Eucharist just as they do the theological basis for Christian service. A Catholic school, with a mission framed by deep dogmatic teachings should and can do a better job of integrating the vertical and the horizontal than a public school where explicit references to religion and God's role in all of life are absent.

Conclusion

In recent years, despite the secularization of public school curricula, public educators have struggled to find ways to communicate basic moral values to their students. But their efforts have met much opposition, especially from fellow educators who worry about crossing over from moral formation to religious indoctrination. Catholic educators have an advantage in these matters. In their efforts at moral education, they can openly draw upon a sense of the Gospel, a love of history and religious tradition, an integrated curriculum, an aesthetically moving celebration of the Eucharist, and a commitment to service motivated by the example of Jesus. But Catholic schools continue to close. Would schools that

---

42. Monika Hellwig, "Reciprocity with Vision, Values and Community," in *The Catholic Church and American Culture,* ed., Cassian Yuhaus (NY: Paulist Press, 1990), p. 92.

embody a full vision of Catholic education as described in this chapter still be closing? Would parents not take up two jobs to make it possible for their sons and daughters to have such an education, such a clear alternative to what public schools can offer? What prevents more of our schools from developing a fuller embodiment of a Catholic vision of their mission? We turn now to a discussion of the key roles that educational leaders must assume if Catholic schools are to be clear and attractive alternatives to public schools.

5

Leadership: Theological Sources

Introduction: Distinct but not Separate

In most Catholic high schools, principals have greater authority to make decisions locally than do their counterparts in public high schools. In his important 1983 study, *High School,* Ernest L. Boyer quotes a public high school principal from a Midwestern suburb:

> I go almost every year to conventions for principals, and there's always a speech telling us we need to be educational leaders, not managers. It's a great idea. And yet the system doesn't allow you to be an educational leader...There's so little we have to control or change. The power, the authority is somewhere else, though not necessarily the responsibility.[1]

One of the distinguishing characteristics of Catholic schools, both primary and secondary, is the high degree of local authority that principals enjoy. But at how many of our Catholic high schools do the leaders make the best use of that extensive authority? And even more importantly, on what foundation should their authority be based?

In the previous chapter, I stressed the critical advantage that Catholic schools have over public schools: they can draw upon both rich theological doctrines and an extensive moral tradition. I gave several examples of how the theological vision should shape a Catholic understanding of the moral dimensions of education. A vibrant vision for Catholic education joins intimately the theological and the moral dimensions. This chapter focuses on the theological foundations of leadership in Catholic schools and the next chapter on the moral dimensions. Catholics may distinguish but should never separate these two rich sources that together create a distinctive educational mission.

I am devoting two chapters to the issue of leadership precisely because in Catholic high schools principals can and do enjoy much greater discretion in making policy and setting priorities than do their public school counterparts. Second, I am convinced, as I stated in Chapter 1, that competent and compelling

---

1. Ernest L. Boyer, *High School: A Report on Secondary Education in America* (New York: Harper & Row, 1983), p. 219.

leadership is critical for the survival and flourishing of Catholic high schools. In recent years, a certain egalitarian spirit ("we are all leaders") has tended to minimize the crucial importance of strong local leadership for an educational community. Third, I have devoted one chapter to primarily theological themes about leadership and a second to moral themes. I think the emphasis in each chapter is different but related, and this rich interplay between the theological and moral is simply one more treasure that the Catholic tradition offers to those engaged in institutional leadership. And fourth, I explained in the last chapter that the leaders of public schools have a difficult time dealing explicitly with moral education, partly because of the controversy such efforts frequently generate among parents and faculty, and partly because they are not allowed to root that education in any religious tradition. Again, the leaders of Catholic schools enjoy a distinct advantage in being able to unite both moral and theological dimensions and enjoy serving a constituency that supports their mission.

Some Preliminary Personal Reflections

After completing fourteen fascinating years of academic administration, I moved into a university professor position that allowed maximum freedom for teaching and scholarship and working more closely with other faculty in faculty seminars.[2]

When I think about academic leadership, I find myself recalling vividly the feelings I had after completing my first year as chair of a large and rambunctious department. I then told a friend: "I no longer have the luxury of belonging to a clique; I can't pass on gossip about certain members of the department; I have to find ways to be helpful to individuals whom I don't particularly like; and I have to keep a certain distance from all the members of the department, even my close friends, so as to remain equally accessible and at least appear fair to everyone." I paused and then added, with a smile, "I hate this job; it is forcing me to be virtuous!" Indeed, positions of administrative leadership demand personal asceticism, as do the roles of teacher and parent. Administrative leadership in an educational institution demands a capacity to work with many different types of

2. For several years, I conducted a seminar for about a dozen faculty that lasted a full semester and included financial support for individual summer research, all focused on their disciplines as they related to Catholic intellectual traditions. For a description of the first seminar, see "Ethics and Religion in Professional Education: An Interdisciplinary Seminar," in *Current Issues in Catholic Higher Education*, Association of Catholic Colleges and Universities, Vol. 18, No. 2 (Spring 1998), pp. 21–50; also published in *Enhancing Religious Identity: Best Practices from Catholic Campuses*, eds. Irene King and John Wilcox (Washington, D.C: Georgetown University Press, 2000), pp. 175–199. I have also published articles on three other of these faculty seminars.

persons; in fact, administration itself constitutes a liberal education—it challenges a person to help very different persons to commit themselves to a common vision and task.

During the years that I held such positions—all in a Catholic university—I found some of those challenges of leadership particularly demanding. For example, I asked myself how I should articulate the Catholic tradition without causing some members of the faculty to dredge up memories of bad experiences they have had with that tradition. How do I sharpen the Catholic identity of an institution when members of its faculty have many different religious backgrounds? How could I emphasize the value of the Catholic tradition without appearing to promote ideas from the distant past that now seem irrelevant, or even detrimental, to current needs? But if then I don't draw on that tradition, how would I keep strategic planning from ending up with goals which are virtually the same as those of a secular university? For example, should the emphasis on "diversity" among faculty and students be the same at a Catholic university as it is at a secular university? These questions are important also for faculty, principals and presidents of Catholic high schools, though the ways in which they can be addressed at a high school often differ from how they are handled at a university.

I also faced the challenge of persuading individuals that the changes I thought needed to be made were important. For example, since the late 1970s, the university had been involved in developing a more integrated general education program. Our first efforts at this had left much to be desired; in particular, the content of the courses approved for general education lacked integration. A smaller, more highly integrated, core curriculum program already thriving within the university became a good example, a prototype if you will, for greater integration in the larger curriculum. Few things support a needed change more than successful visible examples of the proposed change. Even if the example is a small pilot project, I found that actually showed that an improvement could be made. These examples created an atmosphere more open to change, especially if they are led by persons whom the rest of the faculty respects. Credible examples persuade more effectively than fervent exhortations.

Fourteen years in administration also convinced me that leadership takes many different forms, that a particular style of leadership moves some people but not others, and that no form of leadership inspires everyone. To compensate for inevitable blind spots that even the best of leaders have, I found that mentors, on and off campus, can play a key role. Leaders tend to live a lonely existence; all the more reason for leaders to have a few confidants with whom they can share their hopes and doubts, to whom they can vent their frustrations, and from whom they can seek guidance.

Choosing between what might work well at particular time and what is right in principle but not timely constitutes one of the more difficult decisions in leadership. For example, to launch a major program in theology when faculty positions are being cut might be in principle what the institution needs, but the timing is poor. Or, take the example of money given to a university by a corporation whose products are immoral—that might be very attractive, but in principle unacceptable. What should be done? Or the practice of awarding financial aid only to prospective students who can pay more of the cost of tuition than to qualified students from poorer families in need of financial aid may improve the school's bottom line, but not meet its moral obligations. Pressure from alumni to muzzle a certain teacher or demands by rich donors to cancel a course they find offensive test an administrator's convictions about the freedom of the school to conduct its own business in the way the faculty and its Catholic tradition determine is best.

Finally, I came to realize that people are more fragile than I had thought, and that words of encouragement and appreciation contribute more to morale than merely articulating high standards. I still have to work at acknowledging the achievements of others. On the other hand, I have found that some people harbor grievances that they have allowed to fester for years, usually against previous administrators, only to reiterate their grievance to the new person in the administration. Personal hurts seem to linger a very long time. I also learned that publicly criticizing people, even those without grievances against the administration, rarely "sets the record straight." I often found that patient endurance, accompanied by a restatement of the mission, the wiser way to go. Personal criticism should be given privately, but even then it takes considerable skill to make such conversations feel constructive to the person criticized.

Personal experiences in university administration have not been my only source for trying to understand leadership. My experience has been informed by two other sources. First, and most important, I have drawn on the Christian tradition, which in its own way has continued to shed light on the meaning of community, the role and responsibility of leaders within communities, and the nature of the human person. In this chapter, I will explore five theological themes in the Christian tradition that have been valuable to me and strike me as particularly important today for educational leaders. Since secular literature on leadership rarely draws explicitly from biblical sources and the Christian tradition, a straightforward exposition of ideas rooted in the Christian theological tradition and relevant to leadership should prove helpful to people with responsibility for Catholic education.

Second, over the years, I have read a number of books on leadership, some of which I have found to be helpful. I will refer frequently to one book in particular. Along with the five theological themes, I will introduce complementary insights that can be found in some current leadership literature. But before taking up the theological insights, it is useful to clear away some debris—I am thinking of Christian books about leadership that distort the Christian tradition.

Christian Tradition: Avoiding Distortions

Students of history are more aware than most people how easily different periods of history can refashion the Gospel in their own image and likeness. Even though Jesus speaks to every age, people of every age have not always been willing to listen to his teachings, or when they do listen to them, they hear in them only what they want to hear. Some people listen selectively for to listen carefully is too threatening. They block out everything disagreeable; they don't allow themselves to be challenged and don't learn. It is very easy to listen selectively. And the irony is that if you tell such people that they listen selectively, they listen selectively to your statement that they listen selectively. Unfortunately, a number of Christian authors writing about leadership fall into this trap. They give selective descriptions of Jesus and picture him as an entrepreneur, a capitalist, an urban reformer, a hippie or the world's most successful ad man.

For some reason, during the mid 1990s, a number of such books about Jesus appeared, for example, Laurie Beth Jones' *Jesus CEO* (Hyperion, 1996), and Mike Murdock's *The Leadership Secrets of Jesus* (Honor Books, 1996) and *God's Little Devotional Book for Leaders* (Honor Books, 1997). Murdock's 1997 book, one in a series of such books written also for couples, men, moms, students and so on, begins each chapter (two pages in length) with a biblical passage followed by an inspirational commentary that can be read in a minute. The message remains the same: Jesus was a great leader who knew how to influence people and attract followers.

The temptation to reshape the image of Jesus to fit our own immediate needs, to shape his image to fit our own biases and even prejudices seems to affect everyone. An example from an earlier part of the twentieth century will illustrate the problem. In 1925, Bruce Barton published *The Man Nobody Knows*, which sold over a half-million hardcover copies and has recently been returned to print. Barton saw himself as rediscovering the real Jesus of scripture, instead of a Jesus who had been emasculated by liberal Protestantism. Emphasizing Jesus' vigor and gregariousness was Barton's way of convincing people that Jesus could speak to "modern man." In the process, Barton emphasizes Jesus' humanity at the expense of his divinity, presenting him as an advertising genius whose every word and gesture give sales managers today all they need to know to be successful. The tone for the book was set by the opening quotation, "Wist ye not that I must be about my father's *business*?"[3]

In a *Christianity Today* article Andres Tapia, "who at 34 lives in postboomer-prebuster limbo," claims that an attractive portrait of Jesus for Gen Xers can be seen clearly in the Gospels. According to Tapia,

> Jesus was in his early thirties when he began his public work; he had no career path and no place he could call home. His greatest battles were against the dogmas of his day, and he showed little faith in institutions and rules and regulations. Rather his message was of a Father full of grace, and the context of his work was his personal relationships. He built community, first with his small group of 12, and then across class, gender, racial and lifestyle lines. He liked a good party, even turning water into wine to keep one from ending prematurely. He spoke against injustice and did not have the stomach for inauthentic people. He thought globally but acted locally.[4]

Needless to say, there are elements of truth in the portraits of Jesus drawn by Barton and Tapia. However, their description of Jesus misleads business people and panders to Gen Xers in ways that make it less likely that they will encounter the real Jesus.

Ultimately, such distortions root themselves in their inability to transcend themselves, to open themselves to an understanding that is other than what they already think. To avoid this danger of distortion, people should form their picture of Jesus through a careful study of scripture, and in conversation with other Christians who are different from themselves and who have lived in earlier ages and faced different challenges. Such conversations help people develop understandings of Jesus which are not simply their own projections.

In other words, those who work within the whole span of Christian tradition, which includes a rich two-thousand-year-old conversation, have a better chance

---

3. See Patrick Allitt's "The American Christ," in *American Heritage* (November 1988), pp. 128–141, at p. 139. Not only entrepreneurs distort the image of Jesus, but also academics. C. S. Lewis' fictional character, Screwtape, a retired devil, acts as a consultant for his nephew Wormword, just beginning his career as a professional tempter, and suggests to him that devils need to wean their subjects from sincere devotion and participation in the sacramental life. Gradually then, God becomes remote and shadowy: "Instead of the Creator adored by its creature, you soon have merely a leader acclaimed by a partisan, and finally a distinguished character approved by a judicious historian," in *Screwtape Letters* (Macmillan Paperback Edition, 1970), p. 107.

4. Andres Tapia, "Reaching the 1st Post-Christian Generation X," in *Christianity Today*, Vo. 38, No. 10, (September 12, 1994), p. 17.

of avoiding distorted portraits of Jesus. Catholic tradition carries within itself the thought of literally millions of people across the centuries. The more fully believers make the multifaceted Catholic tradition their own, the more they transcend being merely contemporary. Indeed, a person immersed deeply in a religious tradition can bring the wisdom of that tradition to bear on the present.[5] Apart from the discipline, indeed the asceticism, of studying carefully such a tradition, people end up mainly with projections. According to the Bible, people who worshiped what they fashioned with their own hands committed idolatry.

Five Christian Themes Relevant for Leaders

I turn now to that Christian tradition to see what theological insights there might be there to help enrich our understanding of leadership. If these insights are drawn from the New Testament and the core experiences of committed Christians, they are likely to last more than a generation. There have already been enough waves of secular leadership literature in just the last fifty years to make a reader aware that popular portraits have quickly come and just as quickly gone. The author of an article that appeared in the *Administrative Science Quarterly* wonders about this rapidly changing parade of ideas about leadership:

> As we survey the path leadership theory has taken, we spot the wreckage of "trait theory," the "great man" theory, the "situationist" critique, leadership styles, functional leadership, and finally, leaderless leadership, to say nothing of bureaucratic leadership, charismatic leadership, group-centered leadership, reality-centered leadership, leadership by objective, and so on. The dialectic and reversals of emphases in this area very nearly rival the tortuous twists and turns of child-rearing practices, and one can paraphrase Gertrude Stein by saying, 'a leader is a follower is a leader.'[6]

In view of such rapidly changing theories, it may be asked whether my own reflections on "Christian leadership" will not simply add another theory to the wreckage pile. I do not think they do. The five themes I am about to describe are deeply embedded in a two-thousand-year-old tradition of faith, which in turn draws

5. See T. S. Eliot's "Tradition and the Individual Talent," in *The Sacred Wood* (University Paperbacks, 1969), pp. 47–59. For Eliot, the poet learns what is to be done only when "he lives in what is not merely present, but the present moment of the past...," and when "he is conscious, not of what is dead, but of what is already living" (p. 59). See also Aidan Nichols, "T. S. Eliot and Yves Congar on the Nature of Tradition," in *Angelicum* 61 (1984), pp. 473–485.

6. Warren Bennis, *On Becoming a Leader* (Reading, MA: Addison-Wesley Publishing Company, 1989), p. 39.

upon thousands of years of Jewish tradition. These five themes have demonstrated real sticking power. What then are some of the themes that can be drawn from that tradition? And more practically, how might they be of assistance to those who lead educational institutions?

Let me begin this part of the chapter by naming the five theological themes that I wish to emphasize: the Church as a community, the way in which holiness requires the transformation of the whole person, the diversity of the gifts of the Holy Spirit, the prophetic imperative, and the fragility of people. That Christians worship a trinity of persons helps them see that the importance of community is located in the very nature of God. That holiness requires a transformation of the whole person—soul, strength, body, and *mind*—suggests that holiness involves not just how one acts, but also how one thinks. The ability to recognize a diversity of gifts prepares the Christian community for leadership that assumes many forms. The doctrine of original sin reminds us that everyone is fragile and wounded, that no system is perfect, and that care and forgiveness can be every bit as important as giving direction and setting high standards.

At different points in the description of these five theological themes, I will refer to a book by Ronald Heifetz, *Leadership Without Easy Answers*.[7] Among the leadership authors I have read, Heifetz's thought strikes me as especially profound. His key ideas, it seems to me, reflect a wisdom about leadership that complements and underscores the wisdom of the Christian tradition. Like many leaders, Heifetz deals with real, complex situations for which there are no simple answers. He focuses, as we shall see, on working with groups and leading institutions, and recognizes that leadership necessarily takes many forms given different situations. He does not romanticize what leaders do, nor ignore their difficulties. He understands that institutional change takes time, that people need to be carefully brought along, and that ultimately effective change is not imposed. Therefore, I will refer to some of Heifetz's ideas to help illustrate the wisdom that the Christian tradition embodies.

1. A Community of Persons

The first theme emphasizes that Christians should be especially aware that they are part of a community with a long and rich history. Rather than be led into thinking that persons create themselves, Christians recognize that they are a part of a larger family, larger indeed than an individual's biological family. In the

7. The Belknap Press of Harvard University Press, 1994. Heifetz surveys the theories of leadership, reducing them ultimately to four (pp. 16–23): (1) the "great men"; (2) the "situationist"; (3) the "contingent"; and (4) the "transactionist."

chapter on American culture, I spent some time describing the tendency of Americans to be highly individualistic. In an address on leadership given in 1990 to the Catholic bishops, sociologist Robert Bellah contrasted the thinking of John Locke, so influential in shaping the early political and economic thought in the United States, with the covenantal tradition of the Bible. Locke's vision of the human condition starts with adult individuals who through their own work acquire property which they protect by choosing freely to enter social contracts that set up a limited government.[8] Bellah asks where these individuals came from, and whether they had parents who taught them a language with which they could make contracts about such matters. But Locke, Bellah notes, wrote nothing about these matters. By contrast, a covenant is not a "limited relation based on self-interest, but an unlimited commitment based on loyalty and trust." Self-interests are transcended for the sake of the community. In covenantal thinking, an individual is rooted in community rather than the community being at the service of the individual.[9]

For Christians and Jews, God initiates the covenant. That covenant forms people who through the generations continue to shape their members. Communities, especially large ones that trace their history back two and even four millennia, repeat stories and perform rituals. They cultivate memory; without memory, they have no identity. Participation in the Christian community requires people not only to hear the stories that have made them who they are, but then to tell their stories to others, and join with others in reenacting rituals that in turn tell them who they are. In other words, membership in the Christian community requires persons to recognize that they are formed from birth (and even earlier—the biblical call of the prophets assures them that in preparation for their calling they were already being formed in their mother's womb—see Jeremiah 1:5). A community is shaped by the stories they repeat, and formed by the rituals they celebrate. Every individual is part of a community.[10]

---

8. Terry Eagleton, a sharp critic of liberal democratic consumerism, writes that "liberalism fosters an atomistic notion of the self, a bloodlessly contractual view of human relations, a meagerly utilitarian version of ethics, a crudely instrumental idea of reason, a doctrinal suspicion of doctrine, an impoverished sense of human communality, a self-satisfied faith in progress and civility, a purblindness to the more malign aspects of human nature, and a witheringly negative view of power, the state, freedom and tradition" (*Reason, Faith and Revolution* [Yale University Press, 2009], p. 94).

9. Robert Bellah, "Leadership Viewed from the Vantage Point of American Culture," in *Origins*, Vol. 20, No. 14, (September 13, 1990), p. 219.

10. John T. McGreevy's book, *Catholicism and American Freedom* (W. W. Norton and Company, 2003) explains that Catholics in the United States, the single largest religious group in the country by the mid-nineteenth century, interacted with the then-dominant Protestant notion of freedom, which typically stressed the individual over the community. With numerous historical examples, he shows how Catholics insisted that moral formation was essential for the responsible exercise of freedom.

Some contemporary writers on leadership, by contrast, oppose looking to ancient traditions for models of leadership. They seem in some ways to be similar to those who separate spirituality from religion. They think that the formative influence of a biblical covenantal community would have to be out of date, even stifling, and therefore a straightjacket from which persons need to be liberated. In their view, communities with ancient traditions automatically are not sufficiently flexible to allow for creative leadership. As a result, these writers present "spirituality" as a liberating force and "tradition" as a restrictive imposition. They seem to think that to be creative, people need to leave behind traditions that depend on the repetition of communal practices and rituals. For them, vital spirituality is freed from dogmas, communal practices, clerical overseers, indeed, from all obligations to a community rooted in history. Once freed from these restrictions, individuals are able to tailor spiritualities to fit their particular needs. One of the most striking recent examples of the "spirituality without religion" approaches to leadership may be found in Peter Vaill's book, *Managing as a Performing Art*. He writes:

> The real premise here is that our tendency to equate discussions of spirit with discussions of religion is a significant part of our problem as a society and as a profession of managers.... Religion has rendered the question of spirituality almost undiscussible [*sic*] except within a framework of doctrine and language that sound stilted and artificial to many in the world of work.[11]

It is not necessarily a bad thing that writers on leadership and management take spirituality seriously; problems arise, however, when they oppose spirituality to tradition and "religion." Leaders of Christian institutions are better served if they recognize that the Christian tradition, with its various practices and rituals, fosters a rich and multifaceted spirituality, one that is, at the same time, both personal and communal. Leadership thrives from and within a community.

Once, while being pressed to answer a reporter's question about her "style as a leader," Dorothy Day, the founder of the Catholic Worker Movement, finally

---

11. (San Francisco: Jossey-Bass Publishers, 1989), pp. 212–213. For Vaill, spirituality starts within the self, focuses one's own spiritual development, and characterizes all true leadership (p. 223). See, however, Eamon Duffy, Reader in Church History in the University of Cambridge, who wrote: "What worries me about the whole 'spirituality' industry...is the support it gives to the notion that growth in faith, hope and love is a matter of cultivating what you might call our holy bits—which rarely include the brain." And again, "I distrust the implication that the spiritual is something which starts when you close your eyes and retreat inwards, that it is about your *soul*, which in our culture is a notion almost invariably associated with subjective feeling." *Priests and People*, November 1997, p. 452.

responded: "Leadership isn't only something in you, in a person—your personality. Leadership depends on where you are as much as who you are, and it depends on the company you're keeping." Every time the reporter returned to the question of her personal authority and style, she "came back at him with a plea that he realize how much of our actions depend on the people we're here to learn from: we take our cues from them."[12] Day underscores the importance Christian tradition gives to community, and does so when she points out the critical importance of community for leadership.

The leaders of Catholic high schools, however, don't just find themselves in the midst of a given community. They should actively shape their community, especially their leadership team and the faculty. Years of university administration have convinced me that one of the biggest mistakes deans and department chairs make is to retain, often out of fear of hurting people or appearing to be authoritarian, mediocre staff that they've inherited from their predecessors. A mediocre staff triples the time leaders then have to spend on details, time that they should be giving to strengthening the mission of their schools.

Just as important as recruiting an excellent staff is recruiting good teachers. I noted in an earlier chapter that pastors with grade schools put little importance on the recruitment and formation of their teachers.[13] I would argue that the recruitment and formation of staff and faculty are the most important responsibilities of those who lead Catholic high schools. The capacity of faculty to work together as a team, or better as a community, is crucial to the school's success. Max De Pree, the chairman emeritus of the Herman Miller Company, once observed that "major college coaches recruit carefully and diligently because they know their success as coaches depends on their recruits' potential."[14] In Catholic schools, principals have much greater latitude in recruiting faculty than their public school counterparts, who are often limited by tenure and seniority systems. It is difficult for me to imagine anything more important for principals than constantly being on the lookout for good staff and excellent teachers who as a community are enthused about the mission of the school.

---

12. Robert Coles, "On Moral Leadership: Dorothy Day and Peter Maurin in Tandem," in *America*, June 6, 1998, p. 10. According to the Memorial Library Newsletter (Marquette University), May 1994, p. 1, "The Dorothy Day Catholic Worker Collection," Day was "widely regarded as the most influential lay person in the history of American Catholicism for her steadfast living of the Gospel message."

13. I don't want to be unfair to these pastors. Perhaps they feel as though they already have very dedicated staff who need little additional attention. The survey questions, however, do not allow for a response from the pastors that would make this clear.

14. Max De Pree, *Leading Without Power: Finding Hope in Serving Community* (San Francisco: Jossey-Bass, 1997), p. 87.

Part of the continuing formation of staff and faculty requires deeper immersion in the great Christian story. Identifying oneself as a part of the Christian community that lives from its founding stories and traditions need not lead to stilted rituals and deadening indoctrination. People who live consciously within a tradition realize, as noted in the previous chapter, that traditionalism—not tradition—is the straightjacket.[15] This distinction between tradition and traditionalism means that people participate in a community that transcends a single time and only one place. Apparently, Vaill has never been shaped by or exposed to such a vital religious community. When leaders understand that spirituality ought to be embedded in a tradition, they will more easily recognize that people flourish not just as individuals but rather as members of communities that engage in practices that form whole persons.

2. Moral and Intellectual Formation Together

Because Christians realize that they understand themselves best when they remember they are members of communities that are enriched by tradition, they join moral and intellectual forms of learning, which is the second theme that I want to emphasize. It is important for Catholic educators to understand the theological basis for the intimate relationship between moral teaching and intellectual development. Jesus told his followers that they must love the Lord their God not only with their hearts, but also with their minds, and to do so with all their strength. Intellectual development should never be separated from moral development. An intellectual who has no moral compass is dangerous; a moral person without intellectual formation may give good example, but has a hard time saying why—and in the worst case such a person may not be moral, since knowing is an important dimension of doing. Educated Christians understand that they need to develop both their minds and their morals.

As we saw in the last chapter, some public schools have promoted "character education" to ensure a greater degree of civility, decency and respect among students. In the setting of a public school, advocates of character education have found it difficult to teach about any one religion out of respect for the religious diversity of their faculty and students. What is more, they have decided that it would be wise not to speak about religion at all. Leaders of Catholic schools are free, as I argued in the previous chapter, to draw on the resources of their own

15. See also Jaraslov Pelikan's *Vindication of Tradition: The 1983 Jefferson Lecture in the Humanities* (New Haven: Yale University Press, 1984). At the beginning of this series of lectures, Pelikan quotes Goethe's *Faust*: "What you have as a heritage, take now as task; for thus you will make it your own."

religious and educational tradition. They can teach the deep religious roots of morality.[16]

The link between knowing and doing is not automatic. From the time of the Greek philosophers on, it has been recognized that knowledge, the intellectual dimension of learning, does not always translate into virtuous behavior, the moral dimension. Thus, to know is not necessarily to do. The brightest are not always the best. Writing about the contribution of the Catholic philosopher Josef Pieper, Lutheran Gilbert Meilaender spells out the close relationship between learning and virtue, suggesting that the more persons mature morally, the more likely it is that they will be able to learn what is true. He quotes Pieper who once wrote that we have "lost the awareness of the close bond that links the knowing of truth to the condition of purity." Drawing on Pieper's insight, Meilaender believes that in order to know the truth people must become persons of a certain sort.[17] Kierkegaard once described a believer as someone who was in love, and Pascal thought people needed to love things before they could really know them.[18]

In other words, in the Christian vision of life, to see deeply into reality, one must be religiously transformed—or more accurately, embrace the life-long process of religious transformation. Just as the practices of the community's traditions supply the context for that religious transformation—our first theme—so the intimate relationship between intellectual and moral education—our second theme—elucidates two principal goals of Catholic education: formation in the faith and intellectual growth.

3. A Variety of Gifts

A third theme from the Christian tradition recognizes that leadership takes many forms. St. Paul develops this theme better than any other New Testament writer. In his first letter to the Corinthians (12: 4–11) he states that "there are different gifts but the same Spirit." Among the gifts he mentions are those who manifest "wisdom in discourse" and others who have the "power to express knowledge." Some have the power to heal and others the power to be prophetic. Some enjoy the gift of tongues and others the ability to discern spirits. Later (verses 27ff) he

16. "Ethics" is a term that has its roots in the Protestant tradition and has been taken over by professional communities who produce ethical codes for their professions; for example, they develop ethical codes for engineers and medical doctors, but do not root those codes in any specific religious tradition. Catholicism prefers to speak of "morality," by which it understands a set of behaviors that flow from certain religious beliefs. In the Catholic tradition, "moral theology" is a faith-based reflection on how the disciples of Jesus should live.

17. Gilbert Meilaender, "A Philosopher of Virtue," in *First Things*, Number 82, April 1998, p. 17.

18. See Terry Eagleton, *Faith, Reason and Revolution*, p. 120.

tells Christians that they are the body of Christ, in which different organs play different roles, all of which are important. At this point, Paul explicitly mentions teachers and administrators. This rich variety of gifts is to be used for the good of the community: "To each person the manifestation of the Spirit is given for the common good" (v. 7). Not only is there a variety of gifts, but leadership itself comes in a variety of forms.

Persons who appreciate a wide variety of things are said to have "catholic tastes"; they are said to be cosmopolitan. As mentioned earlier, the Catholic tradition characteristically emphasizes the wisdom of a both/and rather than the either/or approach. In that capacious spirit, Catholic theologian Hans Urs von Balthasar describes four models of discipleship, singling out the New Testament figures of Mary, Peter, Paul and John.[19] Or to give another example, the canonized saints of the Catholic Church are hardly clones: Thomas Aquinas and Thérèse of Lisieux (the Little Flower), Francis of Assisi and Augustine, Elizabeth Ann Seton and Edith Stein. Leaders of very diverse religious congregations, whose members include all sorts of personalities and may be living all over the world, have for centuries faced leadership challenges at least as great at the modern corporation or school.

Often these very different embodiments of holiness praised lesser-known persons whom they testified made it possible for them to become the persons they had become. In our own time, Dorothy Day, a striking embodiment of the virtue of justice and love for the poor, claimed that were it not for the less well-known Peter Maurin, an eccentric and chronically disorganized individual, she would have accomplished little. According to her, he was the "needler," the one who kept pointing out what God "wanted doing." She disdained any attribution of leadership to herself, although people today readily identify her as the person who has inspired several generations of people to live simply and act justly.[20] Despite her many disclaimers, Dorothy Day had a certain charismatic impact.

A very different form of leadership was exercised by John Henry Newman, recently beatified. He was by nature shy and temperamental, hardly what today we might call outgoing or dynamic. In his one attempt to be an academic leader, he failed. Invited by the Irish hierarchy in 1853 to found a university in Ireland, he ultimately returned to England, disillusioned, after several wearisome years of

---

19. See for example his *The Office of Peter and the Structure of the Church*, trans. by Andree Emery (San Francisco: Ignatius Press, 1986), pp. 204–287; also *Church and World*, trans. by A. V. Littledale (New York: Herder and Herder, 1967), pp. 44–111; and "Theologies of Religious Life and Priesthood," by David N. Power, O.M.I., in *A Concert of Charisms: Ordained Ministry in Religious Life*, edited by Paul Hennessy (New York: Paulist Press, 1997), pp. 82–83, where Power notes that von Balthasar respects the various "callings" in the Church, allows none to be placed above the other, and emphasizes their interdependence.

20. Coles, "On Moral Leadership." Maurin also warned Day that "if you're going to teach people, you'd better be clear about what you want to come of it, because a teacher is a leader and if a teacher doesn't know that, there's trouble to pay" (p. 9).

fruitless effort. But during that time, he gave several lectures about the nature of university education that became a book entitled *The Idea of a University*. This book has continued to influence generations of educational leaders. Was Newman not a leader in a very real sense? Are there not many ways to exercise significant leadership? As we shall see, he would never have been included on the list of effective leaders in most contemporary books on the topic.

Charismatic leadership can be just what a particular institution needs at a certain point in its history. However, at another time a given school might most need a leader with strong management skills. Another school might need a change-agent, and still another someone who can heal hurts and rebuild trust. Charismatic leadership tends to be overemphasized in current leadership literature. As Heifetz points out, charismatic leaders have no problem getting followers, but seldom succeed in getting people who follow them to face their problems, or the problems of the institutions they lead.[21]

Warren Bennis, for example, writes in *On Becoming a Leader* that those leaders who "forge the future" will have certain things in common: a broad education, boundless curiosity and enthusiasm, belief in people and teamwork, a willingness to take risks, devotion to long-term growth rather than short-term profit, commitment to excellence, readiness, virtue and vision.[22] Wow! That's quite a list. Bennis distinguishes "leaders and managers as the differences between those who master the context and those who surrender to it.... Managers wear square hats and learn through training; leaders wear sombreros and opt for education."[23] The authors of books like these attribute to leaders characteristics that approximate divinity.[24] Over

---

21. Heifetz, pp. 13–14. Later, he writes: "When the stress is severe, we seem especially willing to grant extraordinary power and give away our freedom. In a historical study of thirty-five dictatorships, all of them emerged during times of social distress. Unhinged from their habits, people look with greater intensity to authority figures for remedies" (p. 65).

22. Bennis, pp. 201–202. If this list were not daunting enough, Bennis adds: "And as they (these leaders of the twenty-first century) express themselves, they will make new movies, new industries, and perhaps a new world. If that sounds like an impossible dream to you, consider this: it's much easier to express yourself than to deny yourself. And much more rewarding, too." In the last analysis, leadership is reduced to creative and aggressive self-expression, which Bennis describes as "the most basic human drive" (p. 123); "'letting the self emerge' is the essential task for leaders" (p. 113).

23. Bennis, pp. 44–45. He apparently means that managers are linear and unimaginative in their thinking, while leaders are creative and multifaceted in their thinking.

24. The tendency to inflate the desirable qualities of a leader is hardly new. In the nineteenth century, a member of the Board of Trustees at Yale described the characteristics of the person they were seeking to fill the position of president as follows: "He had to be a good leader, a magnificent speaker, a great writer, a good public relations man, a man of iron health and stamina, married to a paragon of virtue. His wife, in fact, had to be a mixture of Queen Victoria, Florence Nightingale and the best dressed woman of the year. We saw our choice as having to be a man of the world, but an individual with great spiritual qualities; an experienced

the years, I've read hundreds of resumés, some of which were sent to me by people who seemed to believe that they could meet just about any expectation. Basic Christian insights into leadership temper the messianic expectations of leaders.

I have stressed the importance of the community and tradition, the intimate connection between intellectual and moral education, and the multiple forms in which leadership can be exercised. Two more themes from the Christian tradition shed further light on the meaning of leadership.

4. The Prophetic Dimension

Our fourth leadership theme is the prophetic dimension. Prophets are dangerous, and scripture warns that true prophets are called, not self-appointed, to their difficult role. Some people who do appoint themselves prophets relish confrontation and exude self-righteousness. True prophets are able to raise uncomfortable truths that actually guide and bind the Christian community together. Fr. Thomas Reese, S. J., once described as one of the most important roles of leadership is "to identify the dominant contradiction at each point in history."[25] Since the prophetic dimension can be so provocative, I need to explain carefully how it might function in the leadership of Catholic schools.

Christians inherit a tradition, reaching back all the way back to Hosea, Isaiah and Jeremiah, that teaches that everyone, especially the poor and the marginalized, are God's children, that people should not be defrauded of their earnings, that kings and princes and appointed officials are accountable for their actions, and that justice is the necessary condition for lasting peace. Throughout the nineteenth and the first half of the twentieth century, Catholic schools helped many generations of poor immigrants acquire an education that made it possible for them both to learn about their faith and to participate fully in the larger society, which in many ways wanted to exclude them from benefits to which they were entitled. These schools were vehicles of social justice.

In our own day, the challenge remains much the same, but with a slightly different twist. Rather than Catholic immigrants arriving mainly from Europe,

---

administrator, but able to delegate; a Yale man, and a great scholar; a social philosopher, who though he had the solutions to the world's problems, had still not lost the common touch. After lengthy deliberation, we concluded that there was only one such person. But then a dark thought crossed our minds. We had to ask—**is God a Yale man?**" Cited by Frank Rhodes, "The Art of the Presidency," *The Presidency* (Vol. 1, No. 1) (Spring 1998), p. 17. Ironically, Rhodes goes on in the article to spell out his view of a president's responsibilities that, while a little less idealistic than those listed for the Yale presidency, nonetheless would, in my view, still remain very difficult, even for a gifted mortal, to fulfill.

25. Cited by John Coleman, S.J., "Dimensions of Leadership," in *Origins,* September 13, 1990, Vol. 20, No. 14, p. 225.

African Americans, Hispanics, Haitians, and Asians are the latest arrivals to the United States. Many of them live in the inner city. But like European immigrants, many of them are also poor and continue to suffer discrimination. In suburban America, however, most Catholics now comprise the "haves" rather than the "have nots." For some of these Catholics, the Church's social teachings sound like socialism, or as one wealthy friend of mine remarked, like "the Democratic Party at prayer."

At their June 1998 meeting, the American bishops issued a statement in which they acknowledged that "our social doctrine is not shared or taught in a consistent and comprehensive way in too many of our schools, seminaries, religious education programs, colleges and universities."[26] Among the themes highlighted in the letter from the bishops are the civic duties of families and communities; human rights and responsibilities; the option for the poor and the vulnerable; universal health care coverage; the dignity and rights of workers; and care for God's creation. The bishops ask that the leaders of Catholic schools help their faculty learn more about the social teachings of the Church and integrate them into their curricula. Both the new inner-city immigrants and the suburban Catholics, however, have similar spiritual and religious needs; both need religious and moral formation and can therefore benefit immensely from Catholic education.

Two obvious consequences flow directly from a serious personal appropriation by Catholic educators of the social teachings of the Church. First, Catholic schools should never be havens for the well-to-do who want their children to get a bigger piece of the financial pie. The leaders of some Catholic high schools publicly tout each spring the number and dollar value of the academic scholarships their seniors win, featuring them prominently in local newspapers. Of course, graduates of Catholic schools should succeed; the definition of success, however, should include not just financial awards, but also, and even more importantly, discipleship.[27] Ultimately, Catholic educators should hope that their graduates transform society, not "fit seamlessly" into the highest rungs of its social hierarchy.

The second consequence of implementing Catholic social teaching is the hard work that competent implementation requires. Such implementation requires the difficult and complex work of social analysis. Dom Helder Camara, the bishop of Recife, one of the poorest dioceses in Brazil, famously remarked,

---

26. "Sharing Catholic Social Teaching: Challenges and Directions," in *Origins*, July 2, 1998, Vol. 28, No. 7, pp. 102–106.

27. See the writings of John Coleman, S.J., especially "Discipleship and Citizenship," in Mary Boys, ed., *Education for Discipleship and Citizenship* (New York: Pilgrim Press, 1988); "Discipleship and Citizenship: From Consensus to Culture Wars," in *Louvain Studies* Vol. 17, No. 4 (Winter 1992); and "Under the Cross and the Flag," *America*, May 11, 1996.

"When I give food to the poor, they think I am a saint; when I ask why the poor do not have bread, they think I am a communist." Social analysis and social change go beyond doing service within the system and being kind to everyone. They require individuals to study the causes of poverty, to work for more equitable and just treatment of people—especially the poor—and to risk their own status and standing for the sake of those who are less fortunate.

Jesus was crucified, among other reasons, because he spoke truth to power. The work of justice is just that—work, hard work. It can also be dangerous work. But it is not enough just to denounce injustices. Institutions need reform, and that requires the formation of leaders, and long-term attention to policies and their careful implementation. Real reform requires dedicated leadership willing to serve for not just a year or two, but for life. Few teachers engage in social analysis, and those who do often do not do it competently; too many become partisan advocates who have done little of the careful analysis of the systemic complex causes of injustices.

Having emphasized the prophetic theme, it is important to remember that the primary purpose of education is for students to learn, not to become social activists. If upon graduation the alums of Catholic schools dedicate themselves to the poor, they should be celebrated. At the high school level, however, it is probably best to sow seeds, to equip students with the skills that will help to assure that if they do decide to do something, they do more good than harm. Again, the teachers' witness imparts the most lasting lessons. In several Catholic high schools, teachers mentor students doing service projects that link them directly with people in need. Memories of these service experiences, especially when teachers have done their best to help students recognize that such service is an integral part of their identity as Christians, will likely bear continual fruit during the rest of the students' lives.

The prophetic dimension often comes into conflict with the pragmatic dimension. Prophets call people back to the covenant, to what they ought to do. Prophets specialize in stating what is right and wrong. They call wayward people to live moral lives. Much of contemporary management and leadership literature avoids discussion of what is right and wrong, and stresses instead "effectiveness." Effectiveness can be understood as turning around a failing company, or, on a more personal level, knowing how to realize one's own potential. Though a Catholic school must surely demonstrate achievement, both academic and moral, leaders of Catholic schools must ask deeper questions than those of effectiveness.

Because Catholic schools draw on both a religious and moral tradition, they can ask what the most worthy goals are. Suppose, for example, that students in a social studies class are introduced to the case of a company that discovers that one of its products—say even its most lucrative product line—causes serious ecological damage. If the company closes down that line, it will have to lay off half their workers. Also assume that the company doesn't have the money to do the research necessary to produce a less destructive product. What is the most moral course of action? The issues are complex—but such moral issues need to be addressed. The leaders of the company should not ignore the ecological problem and aim only to make as much money as possible. Social analysis requires that profits always be weighed against benefits, especially the common good, the impact on the poor, and the effect on the environment.

Consider another example of "effectiveness," one that assumes that getting something done it more important than asking whether it should be done. In the March/April 1998 issue of the *Harvard Business Review*, Joseph Badaracco Jr. wrote an article about "character building." He illustrated his thesis with three examples of individuals who forged their character at "defining moments when a manager must choose between right and right." The article employed throughout the language of "values" and "principles." His third example, the most useful for our purposes, tells the story of Eduoard Sakiz, the CEO of Roussel Uclaf, a French pharmaceutical company, who wanted to introduce into the international market the abortifacient pill RU-486. In the conclusion of the article, Badaracco praises Sakiz who "not only stayed closely connected to his personal values and those of his organization but also predicted what his opponents and allies outside the company would do. The result was the introduction of a drug that shook the world."[28] Though Badaracco wrote an article about morality and principles, his discussion of Sakiz's character-building "defining moment" skipped over the moral dimensions of Sakiz's actions. He addressed none of the moral issues that the RU-486 pill itself raises. Sakiz, Badaracco concluded, was masterfully "effective," and, in that very effectiveness, had made it possible, at least from a Catholic perspective, for millions of people to commit a moral evil with greater ease and more privacy than ever before.

In contrast to Badaracco, Heifetz goes beyond the typical "value-free" approach of the social scientists who dominate this field of literature. Heifetz notes that if leadership is reduced to effectiveness or the moving of masses of people to act, then both Hitler and Gandhi were effective leaders. He asks fundamental questions such as "leadership for what?" and "to whose benefit?" Such questions help us correct the flawed approach that concentrates on effective

---

28. Joseph L. Badaracco, Jr., "The Discipline of Building Character," in *Harvard Business Review* (March–April, 1998), p. 124. The idea of character being shaped by "defining moments" as the time when people must decide between two alternatives, both of which seem right, has merit. My argument, however, is that the author focuses on the defining moment, and not on the moral dimensions of the issues that need to be weighed before making a decision. Obviously, if a person holds the traditional Jewish view, for example, that a fetus becomes a human being only after 40 days, then the moral analysis of bringing to market RU-486 becomes quite different.

procedures alone. Badaracco presented the business leader as someone whose character had been deepened by this "defining moment." From Heifetz's approach to leadership, Badaracco's definition of leadership lacked moral analysis. There has to be more to leadership than effectiveness and successful tactics.

Facing the moral questions that go beyond mere effectiveness requires not only careful thought, but also consistency and courage. For leaders of Christian educational institutions, an emphasis on the prophetic dimension of the Christian life will require that ends and not just means be examined. Students need to learn how to analyze the structures of society and understand that they have an obligation to act with justice. Leaders of Christian educational institutions form graduates who believe they have an obligation to do what they can to make the world more just.

Prophets rarely occupy positions of official authority. God called them to a difficult ministry that required them to confront and correct kings and priests. No wonder people in authority find prophets annoying, even threatening. Moral leaders recognize the truth of what prophets say. In schools, prophets may well be members of the staff and faculty. A healthy school community fosters the honest expression of opinion. Strong leaders do not dismiss their critics, but give them a fair hearing, and even protect them from those in the organization who, because of an exaggerated sense of loyalty to them as leaders, might try to marginalize and even silence such critics.

Official authority does not exhaust the forms of authority. If it did, many prophetic people would not be able to exercise moral leadership—think of Martin Luther King Jr., Lech Walesa, Vaclav Havel and Mother Teresa. Indeed, reliance on official authority alone runs the risk of extinguishing the prophetic tradition. The Catholic tradition, building on the experience of the Jewish prophets, recognizes that official authority needs to heed prophetic authority. Among other things, this means that in a Catholic school, leadership is never dull, since the prophetic dimension is honored.

5. Fragility of Persons

Finally, the Christian tradition recognizes that people are fragile. People are broken and in need of healing. Our fifth theme, it can be said, affirms the Christian doctrine of original sin. The Christian vision of life assumes that people sin and fail, and are need of redemption.[29] The doctrine of original sin invites leaders to

---

29. Typical of much of the New Age spirituality is a vision of happiness and fulfillment that escapes tragic choices or loss. In an otherwise fine CD by Barbra Streisand, *Higher Ground*, one of the songs, "Lessons to be Learned," assures us that there are "no mistakes, only lessons to be learned." Surely in such an imaginary universe, there is no hell but only various forms of heaven in which everyone is blessed, regardless of behavior.

be more compassionate. They do not presume that everyone, if only they tried harder, could be perfect. Institutions are created by imperfect people. Overly zealous efforts to "perfect" institutions make them even less human. Leaders need patience. They realize that people need not only to be led, but also need to be allowed time to adjust to and then embrace change.

The situations that leaders face vary greatly. Heifetz recognizes this complexity and distinguishes three types of situations, those in which (1) the problem and the solution are clear; or (2) the problem is clear but the solution requires learning; or finally (3) neither the problem nor the solution is clear. A leak in the cafeteria ceiling provides a clear definition of the problem with an obvious solution. Rapid turnover of faculty poses a clear problem, but the solution requires learning to determine the actual causes and an appropriate response. But suppose the problem is a hard-to-answer question. Suppose it is asked how the sciences and the social sciences should be understood and taught at a Catholic school precisely because it is Catholic. How many teachers and principals would have a clear sense of the problem, much less an understanding of how to solve it? While it may be clear to many in a Catholic school that it ought to be truly and distinctively a Catholic school, the same degree of consensus rarely exists on what that would mean concretely in terms of curriculum other than, perhaps, the teaching of religion. And suppose further that the problem to be solved was not limited to the curriculum, but also included the moral formation of not just the students but also the teachers. In such a case, both principals and faculty must work hard to think these issues through together, initiating and evaluating changes designed to impart a distinctive educational experience, in terms both of curriculum and of moral formation.[30]

Heifetz is particularly aware of the time that people need in order to embrace change and of the skills that leaders need to acquire in order to help individuals and communities to undertake the difficult process of change.[31] He understands the fragility of human beings. And, as we have also seen, he does not limit effective leadership only to the impact of charismatic personalities. Rather, he emphasizes those forms of leadership that guide processes which direct peoples' attention to real problems, sift information for reliability, frame issues, make room for conflict and the unexpected, and clarify ways to make decisions.[32] Such leaders do not need to appear to have all the answers; rather, they need to know how to help a group arrive at solutions together. Heifetz describes those who avoid the hard

30. Heifetz, see pages 69–76.

31. Heifetz, pp. 76 ff. See especially his description of how a physician (Heifetz is a medical doctor) might handle a patient who must deal with the reality of terminal cancer.

32. Heifetz, pp. 113 ff.

work of change as engaging in "work avoidance" behavior. The reasons for such behavior are many, including fear of change, refusal to assume any responsibility for the problem, unrealistic expectations of what the leader should be able to do, natural human insecurity, and simply refusing to admit that there is a problem.[33]

When problems loom large, people put great pressure on their leader to solve the problems as soon as possible. But in difficult situations, it is the good leader who chooses to keep a certain but not overwhelming pressure on others. The leader does this to make it more likely that an appropriate urgency will be sustained until together, as a community, a resolution can be found. But sustaining pressure is not enough. Leaders also assist the community by framing the issues, and perhaps even orchestrating some conflict while working carefully at the same time to contain disorder.[34] Biblical prophets usually utter either promises or denunciations. Leaders involve others to help bring about needed change. Rather than denunciation, thoughtful criticism and encouragement for co-workers keeps most people engaged in working together for a solution.

Leaders need to recognize their own weaknesses too. Not long ago, I came across an article in a religious magazine entitled, "Who Feeds the Shepherds?" Indeed, how many teachers and administrators recognize and provide for their own nourishment? How many carve out time for refreshment and renewal? In his book, *The Seven Habits of Highly Effective People*, Steven Covey tells the story of someone who comes upon an individual in the woods trying to saw down a tree. The individual looks exhausted and when asked how long he had been at the task, responds, "for hours." When the visitor suggests that he take a moment to sharpen the saw, the individual tells him he doesn't have time to do that since he is so busy sawing.[35]

Frank Rhodes, the very successful president of Cornell University, pinpointed several reasons why leaders of educational institutions fail to do their task well. The first is exhaustion: "Lack of sleep, no time for exercise, short-

---

33. Heifetz illustrates "work avoidance" on the level of national leadership by discussing the SDI (Strategic Defense Initiative) that President Reagan attempted to effect. Instead of learning how to deal with the new world reality—the necessity of international interdependence and cooperation—Reagan avoided that hard task and proposed instead a "technical fix" which in the opinion of many respected scientists was technically impossible in the first place. See pages 40–48.

34. Heifetz puts it this way: "...the cook regulates the pressure of the holding environment [a term that Heifetz uses to describe when one person can hold the attention of another in order to help that person change] by turning the heat up or down, while the relief valve lets off steam to keep the pressure within a safe limit. If the pressure goes beyond the carrying capacity of the vessel, the pressure cooker can blow up. On the other hand, with no heat nothing cooks" (p. 106).

35. Stephen R. Covey, *The 7 Habits of Highly Effective People* (New York: Simon & Schuster, 1989) p. 287.

ened vacations, and repeated involvement in crises are the warning signs on the road to personal exhaustion."[36] Ernest Boyer described principals of high schools as being in a state of "perpetual motion," always "on the run with a wide variety of people in brief, episodic fashion."[37] Leaders need to sustain themselves not only with time for reading, but with responsible work habits that will allow them not only to read, but to keep clear their priorities, keep close to their families and loved ones, and, as I have emphasized, draw upon the insights of the Christian tradition. Ordinary people often expect leaders to be extraordinary; they forget that everyone, including even the best leader, is only human.

Workshops on leadership rarely feature what this fifth theme clarifies: that people are fragile and insecure. Hard-nosed leaders urged to understand the fragility of people will hear in such advice something they don't want to do: coddle people and accommodate incompetence. But most people are unable to be what idealistic leaders expect them to be. Despite the old Disney theme song that told people that who they are is not important, but only that they wish upon a star. Well, who people are does matter. Even though Jesus told his disciples that they would receive whatever they asked for in his name, in the garden of Gethsemane, that advice didn't work, even for him. There, in the garden, Jesus sweated and then shortly after shed his blood. If the son of God experienced genuine limits in his sinless humanity, so will fragile humans who know their sinfulness.

A focus on positive thinking, on being able to be whatever one wants to be, certainly has its limits. But if popular leadership gurus avoid dealing with this aspect of the human condition, a few major writers and even some popular singers still address it clearly. Walker Percy, the Catholic novelist, once asked: "Is it too much to say that the novelist... is one of the few remaining witnesses to the doctrine of original sin, the imminence of catastrophe in paradise?"[38] The songwriter and singer Bruce Springsteen explains, in a remarkable interview, the power that Flannery O'Connor's stories have had on his craft:

> The really important reading that I did began in my late twenties, with authors like Flannery O'Connor. There was something in those stories of hers that I felt captured a certain part of the American character that I was interested in writing about. They were a big, big revelation.... There was

36. Frank Rhodes, "The Art of the Presidency," p. 17.

37. Boyer, *High School*, p. 222.

38. Cited by Robert Ellsberg, *All Saints* (Crossroads, 1997), p. 235.

> some dark thing—a component of spirituality—that I sensed in her stories, and that set me off exploring characters of my own. She knew original sin—knew how to give it the flesh of a story.[39]

If indeed people are fragile, if they are burdened with a "dark thing" that can be spoken of only with the deeper language of religion, then leaders need to realize that people will need time, understanding, and support to change. Leaders will realize that defense mechanisms must be dealt with carefully to avoid needlessly threatening people who may already feel threatened. Leaders will rather gradually help others to open themselves to the work that is at hand.

Conclusion

The Christian tradition offers valuable wisdom for leaders of Christian educational institutions. It reminds them that besides being their own persons, they are even before that members of a community blessed with different skills and gifts, committed to both intellectual and moral learning, aware and appreciative of the many forms that leadership takes, challenged by the social responsibilities that flow from the Gospel and, finally, sensitive to the fragility of everyone, especially themselves and those with whom they work and teach. Drawing explicitly upon these theologically grounded themes in the building of the school community of teachers and staff is something that leaders of Catholic schools can do that public school leaders are unable to do. Moreover, Catholic school leaders not only have access to such rich theological sources,

39. "Rock and Read: Will Percy Interviews Bruce Springsteen," from *Double Take*, published by the Duke University Center for Documentary Studies, Issue 12, Spring 1998, p. 2. Springsteen described his work as "food for thought," addressing "how we live . . . and how we ought to live in the world" (p. 4), an effort to "establish a commonality by revealing our inner common humanity, by telling good stories about a lot of different kinds of people" (p. 5), and sustained by "companionship which means breaking bread with your brothers and sisters, your fellow human beings" (p. 9). Springsteen reflects the Catholic imagination. Writing to a Cecil Dawkins on December 9th, 1958, Flannery O'Connor pinpoints "an incomplete understanding of sin" as the cause of Dawkins' dissatisfaction with the Church: "This will perhaps surprise you because you are very conscious of the sins of Catholics; however, what you actually seem to demand is that the Church put the kingdom of heaven on earth here right now, that the Holy Ghost be translated at once into all flesh. . . . Christ never said that the Church would be operated in a sinless or intelligent way, that it would not teach mortal error. . . . The Church is founded on Peter who denied Christ three times and couldn't walk on water by himself. . . . Human nature is so faulty that it can resist any amount of grace and most of the time it does. The Church does well to hold her own; you are asking that she show a profit" (*O'Connor: Collected Works*, The Library of America (NY, NY, 1988), pp. 1083–1084.

they also have much greater freedom than their public counterparts to build a distinctive vision of education by drawing explicitly upon these sources. These five theological themes, however, are not the only sources. Catholic educators can also draw upon a rich moral tradition that offers even further insight into the Catholic vision of educational leadership. These moral virtues are the subject of the next chapter.

6

Leadership: Moral Sources

Introduction

In recent years, a veritable explosion of literature on moral life based on the idea of virtue has shifted the focus away from one's individual choices and acts to one's formation in a community and the development of one's virtues. In his book introducing moral theology to college students, William Mattison writes at the beginning of his chapter on virtue that the moral life is more than any given action.[1] When people say of someone who they know well, "That's just not like her," they are distinguishing between that person's character and one of her deeds.

C. S. Lewis, whose many books are filled with illuminating examples and apt metaphors, gave the example of two persons playing tennis, one an excellent tennis player and the other not. On occasion, the excellent player, he explained, might miss a shot, just as the unskilled player might once in a while get lucky and make a great shot. No one expects the unskilled player to make good shots regularly or the excellent player to make bad shots regularly.[2] Lewis explains, "What you mean by a good player is the man [or woman] whose eye and muscles and nerves have been so trained by making innumerable good shots that they can now be relied on." Repeated efforts to develop a skill are what is called a habit. Excellent players possess this "habit of tennis" even when they are not playing. It is that capacity, as distinguished from particular acts, that is called a virtue.

The classical moral tradition describes four such virtues: prudence, justice, fortitude and temperance. These virtues are especially important for leaders,

---

1. William C. Mattison III, *Introducing Moral Theology: True Happiness and the Virtues* (Brazos Press, 2008), p. 57. The renewal of scholarly interest in the virtues may well have been triggered by the excellent study of Stanley Hauerwas, an evangelical Protestant, who published the groundbreaking study, *Character and the Christian Life: A Study in Theological Ethics* (Trinity University Press, 1975). A short book on the virtues for leadership, but filled with many rich examples, is Alexandre Harvard's *Virtuous Leadership: An Agenda for Personal Excellence* (Scepter, 2007). The classic sources, of course, remain Aristotle and Aquinas, and in recent times, Josef Pieper.

2. Mattison also cites Lewis' example (p. 62). I vividly remember this very example when, in 1969, in order to find some relief from the rigors of graduate studies, I read for the first time Lewis' classic, *Mere Christianity*. In my now tattered 1969 MacMillan edition, Lewis' example of the tennis player may be found on p. 77.

because they provide inner capacities leaders will need to draw upon to make decisions that require careful analysis and may admit of many solutions. Some moral theologians criticize the emphasis on virtues because having a virtue does not insure that the right decision, or the right tennis shot, will be made. An emphasis on virtues also seems too abstract. But this is precisely the value of the virtue emphasis: it stresses the importance of developing good *habits*, including the ability to make wise practical applications of principles to the many complex situations people face in everyday life.[3] Hence, it is important to know about the moral virtues; they should be part of any discussion about leadership. Leaders can benefit greatly from developing these virtues in their work and their lives; but in addition to developing moral virtues, Catholic educators are also able to draw explicitly upon the theological sources discussed in the previous chapter.

This chapter unfolds in two steps. First, I offer a description of the four moral virtues and how important it is for people to acquire all four, especially if they are to be good leaders. Having a good grasp of the theological dimensions outlined in the previous chapter is important but not enough; dozens of often complex decisions need to be made daily by leaders in Catholic high schools. Being able to draw on both a theological vision and moral habits, leaders can then develop a deep sense of the unique mission of a Catholic school and possess the skills needed to effect that vision. Second, I will look at five more specific challenges, not unrelated to those that face the Church, that confront leaders of Catholic high schools. To meet these challenges adequately, leaders in Catholic schools need to develop the four moral virtues.

The Four Moral Virtues

The four moral virtues are called cardinal virtues, from the Latin word *cardo*, meaning "hinge," since all other virtues depend on a person developing these four. The order in which the four cardinal virtues are traditionally listed is instructive: first is prudence, followed by justice, fortitude and then, finally, temperance. Prudence is the virtue that helps a person know what ought to be done. For Thomas Aquinas, prudence is a quality of judgment that permits a person to discern the good that should be done and then to do it. Prudence is more than perceiving the good thing that should be done, it also is doing it. In typical brevity, Aquinas writes that prudence is "right reason in action," that is, prudence enables a person to assess accurately a situation so that the course of action will be appro-

3. Of course, there are some absolutes, rules that bind in all circumstances: for example, genocide, the killing of innocent people, and slavery are always wrong.

priate. In this sense, prudence is both intellectual and practical: it has to do with perception and action. Prudence includes both *insight* and *foresight* (*pro-videns* in Latin). Leaders do their best to understand a complex situation, act appropriately, and then evaluate the consequences of their decision.

Sometimes what should be done is obvious; it may be the simple application of a rule. For example, pay your taxes. At other times, situations can be complex. For example, how to increase teacher morale? There may be several appropriate ways, some better than others, one that would be best to start with, and some that are effective only once a good start is made. Prudence helps a person evaluate the possibilities in the light of the actual situation at the school, and then act in a way that indeed increases teacher morale. The prudent person understands how and where to start a process, and how to continue on it. But possessing the virtue of prudence is no protection against sometimes making an imprudent decision.[4]

In the last chapter, I emphasized as one of the theological themes that Christians are deeply interdependent, that is, always part of a larger community. This communal dimension means that prudence has a social dimension since wise leaders, when possible, consult carefully before making major decisions. As I wrote earlier in this book, people should make up their own minds, but they should never make them up alone. Consultation can be done in a variety of ways. A school leader can consult with someone outside the school, for example, another principal. Or, a school leader may consult her staff, or key members of the faculty, or hold a meeting of the entire staff and faculty to understand better what might be the best course of action in a given situation. Being well-educated doesn't ensure that a person will size up a situation accurately. Intelligent people do not necessarily have an advantage in making prudent judgments. Those who are raised in the Christian tradition with its practices of love and prayer, even though they may lack formal education, may well exercise more prudence than the well-educated. As Lewis noted, "…an uneducated believer like Bunyan was able to write a book that has astonished the whole world." Ordinary people can have "street smarts," just as Ph.Ds can be clueless.

Another of the theological themes I described in the last chapter is the prophetic task of working for justice. Again, according to Thomas, it is the "function of justice to carry out the order of reason (that is, what prudence discerns to be

4. Peter Drucker writes, "Nobody learns except by making mistakes. The better a man is the more mistakes he will make—for the more new things he will try. I would never promote a man into a top-level job who has not made mistakes, and big ones at that. Otherwise, he is sure to be mediocre. Worse still, not having made mistakes he will not have learned how to spot them early and how to correct them" (cited by Alexandre Harvard, *Virtuous Leadership,* p. 66).

good) into actual existence."[5] The "order of reason" might be understood best today as "fairness": "it includes honesty, give and take, truthfulness, keeping promises, and all that side of life."[6] We usually associate justice with laws. Colleges teach courses in criminal justice. The virtue of justice does not ignore laws, but affirms that there is something deeper than law, which law is meant to protect, namely, virtue. As one moral philosopher put it, the person "who rejects evil not because it is forbidden, but because it is evil, is truly free."[7] Some laws can be unjust.

Justice gives others what is due to them. It means observing the Golden Rule, as we find it stated in the Gospel of Matthew: "Do unto others as you would have done unto you" (7:12). There is of course much debate over what is owed to others. Is universal health care a right or a privilege? Can war be just or are the pacifists right? Is capital punishment moral or should it be abolished? Justice is oriented to the "common good," which a Vatican II document described as "the sum total of social conditions which allow people, either as groups or as individuals, to reach their fulfillment more fully and more easily."[8] The common good of a school embraces everyone—students, teachers, staff, administrators, parents and the larger community. When a school is run justly, everyone benefits. The interactions within a school that is justly run are hardly fixed or frozen; rather, those interactions are dynamic, sometimes strained, sometimes smooth, and most often a cause for celebration. In general, it can be said that leaders of schools act justly when they enable people to work well together so that students may truly learn and mature. Leaders acting justly commit themselves day in and day out to making multifaceted decisions that further the mission by supporting just interactions among all the members of the school community.

If prudence helps leaders size up a situation accurately and pursue a good course of action, and justice gives them a dynamic vision of the common good, fortitude supplies them with the courage to do what needs to be done. Fortitude is manifested in two kinds of courage: the kind that faces great danger (for example, the possibility of martyrdom) and the kind that is able to stick with difficult tasks (e.g., the grind of administration or correcting a stack of essays). Thomas distinguishes between endurance and attack; for him, anyone who

---

5. Josef Pieper, *The Four Cardinal Virtues* (University of Notre Dame Press, 1966), p. 125.

6. Lewis, p. 76.

7. Robert Spaemann, *Main Concepts of Morals* (Munich, 1986), cited by Alexandre Harvard, *Virtuous Leadership,* p. 138.

8. *Gaudium et Spes*, article 26, par. 1, in *Vatican Council II*, ed., Austin Flannery, O.P., Costello Publishing Company (1996), p. 191.

remains committed to all that justice requires over a long period of time shows the essence of fortitude more than the person who responds courageously at the moment of attack. Enduring over the long haul, of course, may sound passive. But it need not be, especially when one remembers that to endure is to avoid discouragement and to persist even when one's efforts to bring about justice seem not to succeed. Educational leaders especially should remember the distinction Thomas makes between endurance and attack, since it is easy to be worn down by the multiple daily demands of one's responsibilities—demands that can be likened, in the words of one veteran administrator, to being trampled to death by rabbits. Leadership of institutions is more like a marathon than a sprint. A person who endures will "preserve cheerfulness and serenity" in the midst of a neverending quest for justice.[9] To die as a martyr for one's faith requires a moment of great clarity and courage. To live one's faith each day demands endurance and patience. St. Teresa of Avila states that living one's faith daily is the prerequisite for growth in holiness.[10]

At the beginning of the last chapter, I recounted how, after my first year as the chair of a large academic department, I complained to a friend somewhat facetiously that I hated the job because it forced me to be virtuous. Part of what I had been experiencing was that compared to being a faculty member, I had less control over my time than as department chair. To carry out those multiple administrative demands, as well as continue to teach, required endurance and courage.

It is difficult to get people to take leadership positions—since they often realize that the demands are endless. Some fear making mistakes. The word "courage" has a rich etymology: the English word comes from the Latin *cor* and from the French *coeur*, both meaning heart. Leadership demands "a lot of heart." When we describe people as "having heart," we are not just speaking about strength that comes from their intelligence. It is helpful to think of the heart as located at the center of the person, midway between the head, or intelligence, and the gut, or passion. Courage then is not just an intellectual quality, nor simply the expression of passion, nor something characteristic of people who are only physically strong. Rather, courage is something much more encompassing, something that describes the entire person.

The English Dominican theologian Herbert McCabe wrote a marvelous short and eloquent catechism entitled *The Teaching of the Catholic Church* (Michael Glazier, 1986). His catechism shows that it is possible to put into a

---

9. Pieper, p. 129.

10. Pieper, p. 137. He quotes St. Teresa of Avila who wrote: "I assert that an imperfect human being needs more courage to pursue the way of perfection than suddenly to become a martyr."

question-and-answer form an intelligent and sophisticated exposition of the faith. For example, in answer to the question, "What is courage?" he writes:

> Courage is a disposition of our feelings of aggression which inclines us, characteristically, to face up to and deal with difficulties and dangers for the sake of doing what is good: a courageous person is neither over-aggressive or timid; is angry about the right things at the right time and is prepared to suffer patiently when it is necessary, and even to die for the sake of justice or in witness to the gospel.[11]

In the light of this succinct but rich description of the virtue of courage, it becomes apparent that feelings of aggression can be positive, but require a balanced or moderate expression; that anger can be legitimate, but at times should not be expressed; and that finally, witnessing to the Gospel requires courage, even the courage needed to face martyrdom.

If prudence is often caricatured today as prudery, temperance, the last of the four moral virtues, is often confused with the denial of all pleasures. Perhaps the word temperance is too readily associated with those who wanted to ban all drinking. For Thomas, all virtue is found in the mean, not in the extreme; or, as my father used to remark, after drinking one beer, it's the abuse, not the use, of alcohol that is the problem. Moreover, temperance refers to all pleasures, not just to drinking. It helps us to desire what is reasonable, and if our desires are unreasonable, not to act on them. Let me give two examples of how educational leaders might apply this virtue. The first has to do with anger.

When I was provost (the university equivalent of a principal's role), I was blessed with a gifted assistant. When I got an angry letter from a faculty member, my instinct was to write back immediately with equal passion. My assistant, who proofread all my letters, set up, with my consent, what we called a "three-day file." There she placed all letters she thought expressed too much anger on my part. After three days, she brought the letter back to me and asked if I still thought I should send it. Almost always, I decided not to and drafted a more temperate letter. The second example is a problem that most leaders have: they are workaholics. Temperance recommends that everyone have their proper quotient of pleasure. Too few leaders know how to relax or take time away from the job. Families too often take second place to the job. How to overcome this very real problem takes discipline. It helps when a person you report to asks if you are

---

11. Herbert McCabe, *The Teaching of the Catholic Church* (Wilmington, DE: Michael Glazier, 1986), Question No. 234, p. 68.

getting enough vacation time, whether you are taking enough time off, and whether you'd like to go to a play or see a movie. I recall a wise rabbi who said that said each of us will be held accountable to every legitimate pleasure that we have allowed to pass by us in this life. I fear that few leaders report to people as wise as the rabbi who said this.

Before I begin to look at some of the major challenges that face today's leaders of Catholic high schools, three additional insights into the moral virtues need to be mentioned. First, how do these four virtues interact? It takes only a little reflection to realize that they all depend on each other. No one of the four can be exercised in a virtuous way and be acted on in isolation from the other three. Josef Pieper writes: "Fortitude...points to something prior...Prudence and justice precede fortitude...only he who is just and prudent can also be brave."[12]

Take, for example, the virtue of courage. Is it possible for a person to possess any of the other three virtues if he or she does not also possess the virtue of courage? If a person thinks she is prudent, but lacks courage, isn't she then likely to do only what is safe? If a person thinks he is just, but acts justly only when it is approved by others, does that person really possess the virtue of justice? If a person prides himself on his temperance, but lacks courage, will he ever put himself at risk for good reason? I could raise the same question about prudence, suggesting, for example, that courage without prudence ends in fanaticism. And so on.

Second, the value of understanding and exercising the moral virtues is that they are practical. "Practical reasoning" is an important subject in moral philosophy. We rely on such reasoning every day when faced with problems that have no single correct solution. Life is messy. Leaders often have to deal with complex decisions that involve interpersonal relations, how to motivate staff and teachers, or how best to lead a process of institutional change.

Third, the virtues are developed primarily through practice. When asked what good behavior is, Aristotle replied that good behavior is what a good person does. Developing leadership skills is often done on the job. By doing apprenticeships, asking the advice of mentors, and watching how good leaders do their work—these are among the best ways to acquire the moral virtues.

All this emphasis on the practical may obscure that it is crucial for practices to be moral—the purpose of activity must be moral. At the risk of oversimplifying, the theological dimensions of leadership lay out the truths—the foundations and goals of the Christian life—whereas the moral virtues equip Christians with the skills to live those truths and realize those goals. But to explore further in this chapter how educational leaders might exercise the moral virtues requires

12. Pieper, *Fortitude and Temperance* (New York: Pantheon Books, 1954), pp. 18–19.

that I discuss some of the challenges leaders of Catholic high schools face today. The second half of this chapter describes five such challenges. As I showed in the previous chapter, people have different ideas about what constitutes leadership. The five challenges I now discuss are sufficiently complex that they admit of no simple solution—hence the importance of practical reasoning and the moral virtues.

1. The Shift to Lay Leadership

The first challenge facing the Catholic Church today is the massive shift from religious to lay leadership. The rapid decline in the number of religious sisters and brothers, who up until 1965 ran and staffed the vast majority of Catholic primary and secondary schools, has fueled this shift.[13] It is not uncommon currently to have only a few older religious serving in a school where they once constituted the majority of the faculty. In many of these situations of diminished membership, the religious orders have chosen to create a "sponsorship" relationship with the lay leadership. According to research by De La Salle Christian Brother Frederick C. Mueller, sponsorship relationships take many forms.[14] However, all of these forms involve at least two things: first, the intent to preserve the charism and influence of the religious congregation; and second, the desire "to share responsibility with lay colleagues to accomplish the mission."[15]

What is meant by the "charism" of a religious order? The word comes from the Greek and means "gift." It refers to God-given gifts to persons or groups for the sake of the common good. The Apostle Paul affirms that "to each is given the manifestation of the Spirit for the common good.... All these gifts (charisms) are activated by one and the same Spirit, who allots to each one individually just as the Spirit chooses" (1 Cor. 12:7, 11). A special charism is bestowed on the founder or foundress of a religious community, and attracts and shapes those who feel called to become part of their communities. Thus the charism of a religious community refers to the distinctive spirituality and mission of the order. Thus, to

---

13. For example, in the mid 1960s there were over 16,000 Christian Brothers (founded by St. John Baptist de La Salle); by 1986 there were 8, 858, and since then the numbers have continued to tumble to about 5,000 (see *Letter From Rome*, by Robert Mickens in *The Tablet*, February 6, 2010, p. 33), with those remaining brothers advancing in age (see Kevin M. Todd, O.S.B., "The Evolution of 'Association' as a Model for Lay/Religious Collaboration in Catholic Education," in *Catholic Education* [Vol. 12, No. 3, March 2009], p. 330).

14. Frederick C. Mueller, "Sponsorship of Catholic Schools: Preserving the Tradition," in *The Catholic Character of Catholic Schools*, eds., Youniss, Convey and McLellan (Notre Dame Press, 2000), pp. 38–61. See also the Todd article mentioned in the previous footnote.

15. Mueller, p. 52.

mention the better known religious orders, the Franciscans can be said to have a charism for the practice of poverty and simplicity. Dominicans are known for preaching and education. The Jesuits are known for intellectual leadership and their work in universities. When religious orders are able to attract new members, their charism is obviously vital. Most orders, however, experience periods of decline and need reform. Even in the best of times, all the members do not embody their order's charism with equal power and visibility.

Mueller lists the tough challenges that religious communities who sponsor schools inevitably face:

> How do they deal with specific works which historically were a part and parcel of the very identity of the religious congregation, a part of its nature, purpose, spirit, and character? Are the members of the religious congregation willing to share responsibility with laity or do they insist on employer-employee relations? Are lay teachers and administrators willing to accept apostolic co-responsibility for the integral formation of students or do they wish to remain academic professionals? Is the Catholic population at large willing to prize religious-lay collaboration or do they continue to judge Catholicity by the number of religious?[16]

As the main source of an order's distinctive character, the charism can be shared with laity and co-workers, for example, in educational institutions. Many orders are now quite consciously doing that with the ever growing number of lay co-workers. Religious orders naturally resist changing or giving up their charism, especially when it is quite distinctive and valued by its members. As a consequence, special challenges arise when two or even three congregations join together to sponsor the same school: How should they decide to promote their respective charisms? Is it possible to promote at the same time two or three charisms in one institution? What if one congregation has a more defined and attractive charism than the other? What if five members of one congregation are on staff but only one member of the other congregation? In an effort not to offend members of other religious communities with which they work, should lay leaders who collaborate with these communities minimize their distinctive differences?

Or even more painful to think about is this challenging question: if an order has in recent years been unable to produce any educational leaders from its own

---

16. Ibid., p. 43. Mueller reports two other important findings. First, too often these relationships are unwritten and remain only informal. Second, very little communication takes place between religious communities, though through such conversation much could obviously be learned.

membership and unable to attract new members, should it presume that its charism should still shape the policies and ethos of their now lay-led school? Some orders have written well about their charism, spirituality and philosophy of education. Yet, how influential can a religious community's spirituality and philosophy be if they are not visibly embodied by the religious community's members in the very institutions they founded? Cardinal Newman was distressed by two eminent leaders of the Church of England who claimed that Christianity could be best promoted by reading literature and studying science. In disagreement, Newman claimed, as mentioned in an earlier chapter, that people are moved and transformed not first by the written word or the use of reason, but by meeting people face to face. The further removed religious actually are from interacting with students and faculty, the less likely it is that their charism, their very persons, will influence their students or their lay colleagues. Instead of taking positions on boards of trustees and in the principal's or the president's office, some religious communities are now speaking of the "preferential option for the young." They assign their few remaining members to teaching positions so that they might interact directly and daily with students and other faculty; they leave the administration and governance of their institutions to their lay colleagues.

In the light of the declining demographics of religious orders, and the hybrid sponsorship arrangements a number of them have made in individual schools, special challenges face the people who lead those schools, especially if they are lay persons. It takes both courage and wisdom for a lay leader to find the best ways to handle the sensitivities of alums and the few remaining religious, especially when the schools are sponsored by more than one religious order. It takes both courage and wisdom for a lay leader to persuade some religious that the school's Catholic identity is more fundamental and important than their order's charism, though a particular charism can provide an attractive way to embody Catholicism. It takes both courage and wisdom for a lay leader to tell a religious that he or she should retire from the classroom, or to remove from the faculty a religious who refuses to adjust to the new realities of lay leadership in the school.

In a growing number of Catholic schools, it has become necessary to develop a clear sense of Catholic identity without the assistance of any professed religious. It is sobering to note that three-quarters of all religious orders founded before the year 1600 no longer exist.[17] And while the Holy Spirit seems to raise up new forms of religious life at times of great change in the history of the Church, only the Church, and not any single religious order, is promised to exist until the end

17. Raymond Hostie, *Vie et Mort des Ordres Religieux* (Desclée de Brouwer, 1972).

of time. Even then, it is not known if at the end of time the Church itself will include a great number of people from all the nations, or only a faithful remnant huddled together in an alien land.

Despite such a gloomy possibility of an embattled remnant of believers clinging to the faith at the end of time, there is good reason, even in these difficult times, to remain confident. Given the decrease in the number of religious, the focus now needs to be on forming the next generation of lay Catholic educational leaders. It is time to invest more fully in the formation of lay leadership in the way that religious orders in the past invested in the formation of their own members. Most important for the lay leadership and faculty is a religious formation and an intellectual understanding of the great Catholic tradition of education, a point we will return to shortly. Since for centuries religious and priests have taken care of Catholic education, the development of a strong lay spirituality rooted in Catholicism has yet to take place. The need has existed for decades, but few dioceses or orders have addressed that need until very recently. It will take preparation, prudence and persistence (fortitude) for lay leadership to take over these formation programs and provide a vision of Catholic education that effectively communicates the faith to the next generation.

Leaders in Catholic schools often feel overwhelmed by multiple demands. Recent research on administrators in Catholic high schools shows that even in those schools that have both presidents and principals, principals still complain that they don't spend enough time as educational leaders.[18] One of the most important forms of educational leadership today is setting the moral and religious climate of the school, and educating the faculty in Catholicism and supporting their spiritual growth.

The president/principal model, which about half of Catholic high schools have now adopted, makes successful fundraising more possible. It also supports better business and financial planning, and an improved public image. But this administrative model runs the risk of being mainly market driven. When the majority of the faculty and administrative staff were members of vowed religious communities, paying the bills was not as difficult, and a thriving array of Catholic grade schools (feeder schools) made marketing for Catholic high schools almost unnecessary. Today, however, when most of the staff and faculty are lay persons, the addition of a president allows for a clearer focus on development, marketing and financial management.

18. Bro. William Dygert, C.S.C., "The President/Principal Model in Catholic Schools," *Catholic Education: A Journal of Inquiry and Practice,* Vol. 4. No. 1 (September 2000), pp. 16–41.

2. Formation of Lay Boards

In the past, the majority of the presidents came from the ranks of Catholic school principals. While this is still the case,[19] presidents in the future may be recruited from a variety of backgrounds, including the business world. When a school adopts a model that is market driven and hires leaders who come from business backgrounds one may end up with the sort of situation that now exists at a number of Catholic colleges and universities, that is, a board of trustees with considerable business acumen, but without an equal grasp of the religious and intellectual mission of the institute. If lay boards choose presidents with backgrounds similar to their own, then the religious leadership of the school may be seriously attenuated.

The formation of lay trustees and advisors to help sustain and develop Catholic schools constitutes a second challenge. Leaders of Catholic schools have little experience historically in forming and working with lay boards of trustees and advisors. When in the late eighteenth and early nineteenth centuries lay people in South Carolina, Philadelphia and elsewhere sought greater responsibility for the financial affairs of their parish church—including setting the salaries of the clergy and assuming the power to appoint them as their pastors—the bishops, with few exceptions, rose up in opposition. The central issue was, in the words of Patrick Carey, "how American or how republican and democratic could the ancient Catholic hierarchical institutions become and still retain their continuity with the Catholic tradition."[20] Many bishops wanted and obtained the legal status of a "corporation sole," which gave them full ownership of all diocesan property and the authority to appoint priests pastors. The degree of Episcopal control has remained so strong that any lay involvement has typically been reduced to offering advice, which bishops and priests are free to ignore. The question of how and in what ways lay persons should participate in the governance of Catholic schools has returned today with considerable force since so many lay persons are well-educated professionals who often have more management and economic expertise than many religious and bishops. Such lay persons expect, and sometimes have publicly demanded, greater transparency and accountability from bishops, especially in financial matters.

Before the 1960s, most Catholic colleges and universities did not have lay boards of trustees with real fiduciary responsibilities; nearly all such boards that then existed offered only advice to the religious who owned and ran the

---

19. See *Dollars & $ense,*, published by the Secondary Schools Department of the National Catholic Education Association (Wahsington DC, 2007), p. 9.

20. Patrick Carey, *Catholics in America: A History* (Praeger: Westport CT, 2004), p. 27

universities. The superior of the religious community who staffed the university was also its president, and his or her staff, members of the same religious community, made all the major decisions. Canon law still stipulates that lay persons have no authority over vowed religious or priests.

In more recent years, some high schools, typically those owned and run by religious orders, have also appointed lay boards with various degrees of authority and responsibility.[21] The relatively short time these new governance structures have been in place make it difficult to judge their overall effectiveness. However, there are some obvious advantages and problems. Ideally, a good board of trustees means that at the top there is not just the principal or the president, but a number of talented and committed people who take responsibility for setting major policies, clarifying and supporting the school's mission, maintaining the physical plant, and, of course, raising money. More pointedly, if lay boards of Catholic schools founded by religious communities follow the example of the development of effective lay boards at colleges and universities also founded by religious, then those school boards should ensure a greater degree of independence from the direct control of the local bishop. Such boards also protect their schools from the occasional unwanted intervention by some highly opinionated parents and wealthy alums in the local community.

The way in which the constitution of the board is drawn up can enhance that independence. The independence I am advocating here is not freedom from the influence of the local bishop, nor even less freedom from the obligation of the leadership of the school to strengthen the school's Catholic identity. Rather, this independence ensures the school's freedom, supported by the guidance and influence of the bishop, to shape its sense of Catholicity, one that will enhance the school's religious and moral distinctiveness. On the other hand, there have been problems, not the least of which has been, as mentioned previously, boards of trustees whose financial competence sometimes exceeds their understanding of the school's religious mission. Too often the few religious who serve on these boards become intimidated by highly accomplished lay persons with their professional secular competencies and forget their own special competencies related to the moral and religious mission of the school. As the saying goes, it is true that if there is no margin there is no mission. It is

---

21. The 2007 NCEA report *Dollar & $ense*, reports that "while school boards are ubiquitous, they vary in governing authority. Overall, 46 percent are policy making; 54 percent are consultative/advisory. 36 percent of schools with a board report having a two-tiered board structure, but only 16 percent of diocesan schools and 13 percent of parochial schools report having a two-tiered board structure, in contrast to 63 percent of the private, religious community-sponsored schools and 32 percent of the private, independent schools, which report two-tiered boards" (p. 9).

also true that to focus on margin apart from the mission spells the end of any distinctive identity for the school.

How should the president or principal of the school address the tendency of some board members who focus only on finances? They should spend more time forming and working with these board members. When I have asked various presidents and principals how much time they spend educating and forming their board members, they tell me that compared to fund raising and public relations, they spend very little time educating their boards. Many presidents of Catholic colleges and universities have discovered that to advance the mission of their institution, the most important thing that they can do is to recruit and build a strong, educated, dedicated and generous boards of trustees. Like any other important effort, such an ongoing effort takes time, certainly more than only a little of a president's time. Board formation is critically important, and will become even more important in the future. Unless the board is attended to, involved and engaged, they will not develop an appropriate level of responsibility for the school. And unless they understand their role well, the most dedicated of them may be tempted to enter into the operational level of the school, an area which properly belongs to the administration and the faculty. As another old saying goes, board members should keep their nose in and their hands off the daily workings in a school.

The prudent leader of a Catholic school carefully evaluates candidates before inviting them to become members of the board or the advisory group. The only criterion for board candidacy should not be their wealth. Second, boards should always include several people who understand well not only the religious mission of the institution, but who also are quite familiar with the managerial and business needs of the school. It is always helpful to have the president or principal of another Catholic high school serve on the board. Third, part of the agenda of each board meeting should include ongoing board education about the mission of the school. It requires intelligence, understanding and courage to find the appropriate relationship between the needed secular and religious competencies, and to guide the conversation that explores the best ways for laity, clergy and religious to collaborate and exercise authority.

Such formation obviously requires setting aside more time. It also requires money. Where will that money come from? It should come from wealthy Catholics and others concerned about the future of Catholic education, from the religious orders and from diocesan funds. Most Catholic universities began serious fund-raising only in the last thirty years; leaders of high schools and grade schools need to organize such efforts for themselves, even though most dioceses, strapped as they are for funds, seem wary of lay boards with real authority. Lay boards of trustees with real responsibility and authority constitute one of the key elements of future success for Catholic high schools.

Most religious communities in the United States are now property rich and personnel poor, and most face huge medical costs for their retirees. But the number of retirees will soon decrease as will the funds needed to cover their health care. As a consequence, some orders, with a considerably reduced membership, will still have property and endowments. I would suggest that these orders consider setting up another endowment for the sole purpose of the formation of lay leaders in Catholic schools, be they teachers, administrators or board members. The interest from the endowment could be used for several purposes. For example, several years ago the national Association of Catholic Colleges and Universities (ACCU) trained a group of people who went around the country conducting two-day workshops to help trustees understand better the Catholic educational mission, and how to support it more effectively as board members. These workshops were demanding (I personally conducted several of them), well organized, and very well received. It would take a few small adjustments to the workshop design to adapt it for Catholic high school boards.

3. Lay Spirituality

Besides the challenges involved in dealing with sponsorship arrangements made by religious orders in schools led by lay persons and the effective functioning of boards for Catholic high schools, there is a third challenge—that of developing philosophies of education and forms of spirituality appropriate for laity in leadership and staff positions. Some religious orders have been effective in sharing their educational charism in ways that have led their lay colleagues to embrace that charism wholeheartedly. But lay leaders, who in increasing numbers are leading diocesan schools, face a somewhat different challenge than that faced by lay leaders in schools founded and led by religious orders. How do they develop a spirituality and philosophy of education that is authentically rooted not necessarily in the charism of a religious order but in the larger Catholic tradition?

The development of Catholic lay spirituality and philosophies of education is not as easy as some may assume. It took hundreds of years from the founding of Christianity for religious orders to form and develop their own proper spiritualities; the forming of truly lay spiritualities will not be done in a year or even a decade. To say that lay spiritualities need to be developed is not to suggest that for centuries laity have not found ways to grow in holiness. It is more a question of spiritualities that are not the creation of religious for the laity, but spiritualities created by and for lay people.

Long before the Second Vatican Council, thoughtful voices, especially that of St. Frances de Sales (1567–1622), called for the development of spiritualities appropriate for lay persons. And though the Second Vatican Council (1962–1965) declared that all the baptized—and not just religious and priests—are called to holiness, the Church still has a long way to go to develop genuine lay spiritualities. Lay spirituality now includes not only being open to having and educating children, but deepening love for each other through sexual relations. It was only in the 1970s that retreats such as Marriage Encounter were designed by married people for married couples; before then, celibates, some of whom were excellent preachers and spiritual directors, gave retreats to the laity, the men attending one retreat and the women another. Members of religious orders often advised lay people who wanted to develop a deeper spiritual life to take up several practices of their orders, such as daily mass or saying the sacred office. These practices, of course, are good in themselves, but not always practical for lay persons, especially those who are raising families. This situation is now changing, but not rapidly enough.

Parallel to the challenge of developing lay spiritualities is that of developing "lay philosophies" of Catholic education. Lay leaders can, of course, learn much from the distinctive philosophies and pedagogies developed by religious communities. But lay leaders, especially those in diocesan schools, need to develop their own distinctive and localized visions for Catholic education. It is unlikely that a "generic" vision of Catholic education for a diocesan school will engage people anymore than a generic religious charism will engage those working in schools founded by a religious congregation. More and more lay people, especially those in leadership positions in diocesan high schools, need to develop distinctive visions of Catholic education.[22]

It takes both prudence and courage to develop a spirituality that as yet does not exist in sufficiently clear forms for Catholic laity. It takes discipline to search the past for all possible insights that would help educators live a deeper spiritual life today. It takes wisdom to read the new signs of the times, and create some new emphases and practices that help lay people live the spiritual life as the lay people that they are, not as "lay religious." Some things can be learned in this regard from the experience of Protestants. But they forced themselves to develop lay forms of spirituality because, with few exceptions, they simply got rid of all forms of religious life. The challenge for lay Catholics is to create lay spiritualities that draw from but not imitate spiritualities more appropriate for priests and religious. Catholics are only beginning to develop lay spiritualities for educational institutions—a truly daunting challenge, one that will require courage and wisdom to meet it.

---

22. See my "Toward a Theology of Ecclesial Lay Ministry," in *Together in God's Service*, published by the NCCB, Subcommittee on Lay Ministry and Committee on the Laity, 1998. The essay was written with a view to what the bishops call "ecclesial lay ministry." However, its application to a lay theology of education should be evident.

Two things occur to me that may speed up the development of these spiritualities. I suggested in the previous discussion the creation of endowments, not just by religious orders but also by dioceses. Another way to use the endowment is to support the education of leaders and teachers in Catholic high schools. Those who are preparing for leadership roles should have the opportunity for graduate education in theology. But a typical Master of Arts degree in theology will not be as helpful as a degree that would combine with theology courses those that also cover institutional management and leadership. Unfortunately, few such degrees exist. That is why a second and parallel use of the endowment should be devoted to supporting apprenticeships in which the future leaders of Catholic schools can study, under the guidance of an excellent principal, what it means to lead a Catholic high school. Without such financial assistance, the demands of time on people whose lives are already filled with demands of teaching and family make such educational opportunities rare.[23]

4. Hiring and Forming Faculty and Staff

The fourth challenge is the hiring and forming of the faculty and staff. One of the general norms (art. 4, par. 4) of *Ex Corde ecclesiae,* the 1990 letter from John Paul II on Catholic higher education, states that to protect the Catholic identity of the institution, Catholic teachers should constitute the majority of all teachers in every Catholic educational institution. The actual text uses the word "should," not "must." In some parts of the world, for example, Japan or India, it would be very difficult to find enough Catholic teachers to constitute even a significant minority. On the other hand, it makes sense to me that, all things being equal, Catholics should be hired for leadership and faculty positions in Catholic schools. When the hiring circle needs to be widened, Christians should be preferred over non-Christians, and humanists who respect the religious mission of schools over nonreligious people simply looking for a job. People with administrative experience know that some disaffected Catholics contribute less to the realization of the mission of the school than do some well-disposed Jews and Muslims. In an age that criticizes "ghetto Catholics" and "sectarian" institutions, it takes courage

23. A recent study of principals in Catholic schools in Australia showed that most lay principals felt unprepared for their role as the religious leaders of their schools, and often felt they were simply "thrown into" administration with little formation, and have consistently found that they simply do not have the time to read or study. This is a sad commentary that any enlightened board would remedy immediately and forthrightly, finding ways to support the preparation and continuing formation of their major academic officers (see Angelo Belmonte and Neil Cranston, "The Religious Dimension of Lay Leadership in Catholic Schools," in *Catholic Education*, Vol. 12, No. 3 [March 2009] pp. 294–319.)

to seek competent Catholics first as teachers and staff, and prudence to know how to hire people who are not Catholic but who support and contribute to the mission of a Catholic school.

A group of faculty with special responsibility for the mission of the school, the religion teachers, should be Catholics—but not just any Catholics. They need not only to teach the faith, but also, and even more importantly, to witness to it. Today, religion teachers need to know not only the Catholic tradition, but also know something about other Christian traditions as well. Many religion teachers know little about the ecumenism and the conversations among Christian churches since the Second Vatican Council. The same could be said about the general state of ignorance among religion teachers concerning the current state of important interreligious dialogues. This ecumenical and interfaith knowledge is important for two reasons: first, one of the best ways to come to a deeper understanding of what it means to be Catholic is to interact on a theological and personal level with others who are not Catholic; and second, a growing number of our students and even faculty are not Catholic.

In many of today's Catholic high schools, the members of the faculty are more diverse in religion and opinion than in the past. Since most members of the faculty turn to popular media for the news, they will find there a regular stream of scandal stories, some of which involve Church leaders and prominent Catholics in some current controversy, such as, the sexual abuse of minors, whether women should be ordained, should priests be required to be celibate and cohabitation before marriage.[24] Given this diversity among faculty and the focus of the media, leaders of Catholic high schools need to organize, on a monthly basis, opportunities for the faculty to learn more about the Catholic tradition in general and the mission of the school in particular.

Students in many Catholic schools come from increasingly diverse religious traditions. A not insignificant number of students come from marriages in which the parents are not of the same faith; many of them ask questions about other denominations. Teachers prepared to deal thoughtfully with this new diversity will likely teach a capacious, and therefore more authentic, form of Catholicism. Are the religion teachers prepared to respond thoughtfully to the questions and concerns of these students? Serious ecumenical awareness means having the courage to see oneself through the eyes of persons who sometimes do not agree with one's own religious tradition and commitment. It requires courage to recognize the strengths of other religious traditions and not just point out their

24. The US media knows that sex and gender arguments sell. I've rarely seen informed media coverage of a doctrinal issue as a doctrinal issue; doctrinal issues are presented primarily as issues of authority and persons in conflict.

deficiencies, and alternately, to accept the deficiencies of one's own tradition and not just trumpet one's own strengths—and to engage in this sort of thinking without losing one's fundamental commitment to one's own religious tradition. Increasingly today people believe that it makes no difference whether one is a Catholic or a Protestant, or even a nonreligious humanist so long as one is a good person. It is less easy today than in years past to assume that one has all the truth and that others of a different faith are lost (though, in the second grade, I was told just that by a teacher who assigned my Protestant father to hell). Catholic leaders and teachers must avoid both indifference and absolutism: the only acceptable approach requires both courage and wisdom.

An emphasis on diversity and appreciating differences can lead to indifference. In recent years, educators, especially on the university level, have committed themselves to promoting a certain type of diversity. They believe that diversity among students and faculty creates a better educational environment. In primary and second schools, diversity has been emphasized, but with a slightly different emphasis, as "multiculturalism." This cultural and educational movement emphasizes the importance of respecting and celebrating differences, especially the differences of racial and ethnic minorities. In its best forms, multiculturalism opposes racism and all forms of prejudice that refuse to affirm the genuine dignity of each human being, a foundational component of Catholic social teaching. It opposes the presumption that European culture is the best of all cultures. In recent years, the Church itself has become more aware that it is no longer just a Latin European Western community of faith. How to enter sympathetically into quite diverse cultures, retain unity (not uniformity) in one's own culture and promote a strong sense of Catholic identity constitutes one of the great challenges of the future.

In my judgment, these movements, with certain qualifications, are both significant and needed. A creative and courageous way to respond to these movements is to follow the lead of the Spirit at Pentecost; there, the apostles, gathered in prayer with Mary the mother of Jesus, spoke the same saving message in multiple languages. People from many different cultures, the Acts of the Apostles tells us, could understand the good news and embrace it. On that great day, many new believers were added to their number (Acts 2:47). But we also know there were problems. Language groups formed cliques. Certain people were ignored. The wealthy set extravagant tables for themselves and ignored the poor members of their own Eucharistic community. The early Church had to learn how to address these problems, how to form a genuine but diverse community.

There are lessons here for Catholic high schools. Many of them, especially those in the suburbs, cost more and more to attend. Thus, there is a great danger that they have become enclaves for the affluent. Some parents send their children to Catholic schools because there are few of those "others" there—few people of color, few of the poor. The leaders of these schools need to work hard to educate their students and their families about the importance of opening the school to "others," especially the poor, who desire a Catholic education.

That being said, however, there are nonetheless certain approaches to diversity and multiculturalism that are based on a false idea of tolerance. Stressing tolerance above every other value is not the attitude that best meets the challenges of diversity. Jesuit social ethicist David Hollenbach writes that:

> There are many indications in the United States today that tolerance of diversity occupies the place held by the common good in the thought of Aristotle, St. Thomas Aquinas and Ignatius of Loyola. Tolerance, not the common good, has become the highest social aspiration in American culture.[25]

To support his claim, Hollenbach cites, among other studies, the work of sociologist Alan Wolfe's 1998 study, *One Nation After All*, which explores what the American middle class thinks about public morality. Wolfe's study gives us both good news and bad news. The good news is that instead of a war between cultures, something close to a consensus exists on what is most highly valued by the middle class: the highest good now is tolerance. The bad news is that the highest good is tolerance. Wolfe suggests that an 11th commandment should be added to the biblical Decalogue: "Thou shalt not judge."[26]

Though a blessed alternative to violence, tolerance is not the highest good, because people who oppose making judgments contradict themselves. To say that no one should judge is, obviously, to make a judgment that no one should judge. Thus, if someone criticizes another person for judging, they are judging that the other person is judging. Even when a person prudently determines that an issue is not yet ripe for a judgment, their decision to suspend judgment is a judgment to suspend judgment. Thomas Aquinas taught that judgment is the highest act of the intellect, for to judge rightly is to be in contact with reality as it really is. And anyone who regularly judges rightly, St. Thomas continues, is a person who is wise. Therefore, a person's only choice is not to avoid judging, but to judge in a certain way, that is—to use a word we examined at the beginning of this chapter—to judge carefully, an act which requires, of course, one of those very important moral virtues, prudence.

---

25. David Hollenbach, S. J., *The Common Good and Christian Ethics* (Cambridge, 2002), p. 24.

26. See Hollenbach, pp. 24–30.

Being inclusive and affirming the truth is difficult and complex. First of all, tolerance actually requires that there be differences, or there is nothing to tolerate. Allowing those of different religious and political beliefs full participation in society is good and should be protected. A distorted notion of tolerance requires either that we ignore differences (an insult) or obliterate them (an assault). Neither approach recognizes the human dignity of people who are different from each other.

For Catholics to believe, as they should, that their religious tradition embodies the fullest means for salvation will, in a culture that champions a form of tolerance that refuses to make qualitative judgments, sound arrogant. However, I think that Catholics would be wise to recognize that despite the gifts of their faith and religious tradition, they can learn something from Mennonite Churches about witness to social justice; from the Evangelical Churches about their love for scripture; and from the Lutheran Churches, to cite just one more example, about their emphasis on that salvation is a gift, and also their from their great choral tradition (remember, Augustine said whoever sings prays twice). It should be added that when Catholics say that their tradition offers the fullest means of salvation (which includes, for example, the Sacraments and the hierarchy), that affirmation does not for one minute guarantee that Catholics are holier than Protestants; indeed, God may judge Catholics the more severely given the privileged means they enjoy.

Leaders in Catholic schools need to focus on the issue of truth, not just on finding the least common denominator to help everyone "just get along." It is simply not true to say that all the great religions teach the same thing, any more than it is true to say that as long as persons are sincere, it doesn't matter what they believe. It helps when Catholic leaders can admit faults and deficiencies in their practice of the faith, and point out what they can learn from other churches and religious traditions—even as they affirm the central truths of their own faith. It also helps to admit that, at times, we are just not sure what to think about a complex social and moral issue. There is no small need of prudence and courage in all such matters.

Finally, if the leaders of Catholic schools have good reason to give preference to hiring, when possible, Catholic teachers and staff, they also need to give attention to the percentage of the students who are Catholics. For those schools who have many more applicants than seats, a preference should be given to Catholic students. Why run a Catholic school if not first to help Catholics become educated in their own tradition? Even when a majority of the student body is not Catholic, Catholicism should still be the core of the religion program and shape the educational philosophy of the school. Non-Catholic families who send their children to Catholic schools should know from the beginning that the school is committed to a clear Catholic mission; at the same time, they should be reassured that there will be no coercion in matters of religious belief and practice. Again, such a carefully balanced position is not easy to maintain. It is neither arrogance nor an indiscriminating form of tolerance.

5. The Teaching of Religion

Fifth and finally, next to the ongoing formation within the Catholic tradition for the entire faculty, the leaders of Catholic schools need to be especially attentive to the quality of their religion teachers. It was not that many years ago that religion courses were almost exclusively taught by priests and religious. Some of these teachers were great; some were not. I have the impression today that in too many Catholic high schools, many of the faculty and even some administrators do not give religion teachers the respect that is due them. Students who come from Catholic grade schools sometimes think that they've heard it all before. Other teachers in the school may feel that such courses really have little use, at least in comparison to learning how to read and write and do math and science. Or, worse yet, at some Catholic high schools for boys, sports may dominate everything, and the coaches, not even the principal, sometimes seem to run the school.

For these reasons, it is important that the atmosphere of the school clearly support the explicitly religious dimensions of the curriculum and the school day. It is also important that the faculty who teach religion be competent and recognized as such, not only by their students, but also by the rest of the faculty. Needless to say, religion courses need to be demanding and rich in content. School leaders need to create opportunities, with at least some financial assistance, for continuing education for religion teachers. In some parts of the country, diocesan certification programs for teachers are useful, especially if the school itself does not have the resources to provide in-service formation for their teachers. Research, however, shows that religion teachers learn the most from theology courses taken for credit at Catholic universities.[27] This suggests an important role that Catholic colleges and universities, in cooperation with dioceses, could (and some certainly do) perform when they offer such courses for people preparing to teach religion. Some of the school's own religion teachers can be invited to give talks to the rest of the faculty in monthly settings such as I described earlier.

One further concern: some people at the high school level fear that the recent Vatican document on Catholic colleges and universities, *Ex Corde*

27. Paul Galetto, O.S.A., "Religious Knowledge and Belief of Lay Religion Teacher in Catholic Elementary Schools," in *The Catholic Character of Catholic Schools* (Notre Dame Press, 2000), p. 134.

ecclesiae, will require orthodoxy not only in what teachers teach, but also in their own personal opinions on a wide range of teachings, including non-infallible teachings. In a discussion on this point pertaining to those who teach theology at the university level, Archbishop Daniel Pilarczyk, now emeritus, of the Cincinnati archdiocese (who happened also to chair the Episcopal committee charged with drafting guidelines for granting and withdrawing the *mandatum*) stated his opinion that the *mandatum* pertains to what is taught, not to what an individual teacher might personally think about a particular teaching. He also explained that the *mandatum* does not govern the teacher's personal life, unless it can be construed as a form of teaching. Needless to say, this is a very complicated issue, which involves fidelity to the magisterium, freedom of conscience, the importance of the witness of a teacher's life, the degree of authority attached to a particular official teaching, and what one should and should not say in the classroom to students who are at different levels of maturity—to name only a few of the complications.

Again, such complexity escapes the coverage media gives to stories about Church controversies—which again is one of the many reasons why continuing education for faculty is so important. I doubt that any guidelines could be written that could anticipate all the possible conflicts that could arise on these matters in any school. In a recent article, Mary Angela Shaughnessy, S.C.N., describes some of the most recent legal complexities the leaders of Catholic high schools face today, including teachers in invalid marriages, faculty who are publicly pro-choice on abortion, an unmarried female teacher who becomes pregnant, and multiple examples of "boundary issues" between not only faculty and students, but between faculty.[28] She explains why it is that faculty and students in Catholic schools do not have the same rights as they would were they in public schools. More by way of witness and belief is expected of faculty in Catholic schools than in public schools. Catholic school leaders need to understand these legal matters to avoid suits. At the same time, and even more importantly, leaders of Catholic schools also need to appreciate the great freedom, as paradoxical as this may sound to public school teachers, they have that enables them to offer a religiously grounded education.

Knowledge of the law will help avoid some major problems. But many of the conflicts that will inevitably arise will be resolved best only through prudent judgments made by wise and fair administrators sensitive both to the traditions

28. Shaughnessy, "Civil Law and Catholic Education: Past, Present and Future," in *Catholic Education,* Vo. 12, No. 4 (June 2009), pp. 519–535. See also Charles J. Russo, "Canon Law, American Law, and Governance of Catholic Schools: A Healthy Partnership," in *Catholic Education,* Vol. 13, No. 2 (December 2009), pp. 185–204.

of the Church and the particulars of the local situation. Best of all, of course, are teachers and administrators who both believe and do their best to live the Catholic faith. In conflicts over these matters, nothing will be more important than to have school leaders supported by capable and dedicated board members able to approach these complicated matters with common sense and a commitment to the religious, moral and educational mission of the school.

Attending to the Poor: The Bigger Picture

Before concluding this chapter, we need to examine one of the major challenges we face in a liberal, democratic society. Otherwise, the discussion of the virtues of leadership may seem very abstract and philosophical. It is easy to talk about being a virtuous individual, but what can that possibly mean when we think about the large and challenging ways in which contemporary society itself seems to make the practice of virtue so difficult? Moreover, unless leaders in Catholic schools keep in mind the Church's fundamental commitment to the poor, they may become so absorbed in the immediate questions that face their school that they loose perspective. In the United States, to say nothing of other parts of the world, widespread poverty exists in the midst of extraordinary affluence. A scandalous gap of resources and personnel separates many inner-city from suburban schools. Unlike the poor, urban Catholic immigrants Catholic schools served one hundred years ago, many of those now living in the inner city are black, Haitian, Asian, and Hispanic.[29] Many of them are not Catholic; almost all of them are poor and suffer various forms of discrimination.

By contrast, the challenge in the suburbs, where most Catholics (except in the Southwest) are middle class if not affluent, is to teach the social justice message clearly and compellingly. In the inner-city schools, where often many of the students are not Catholic, the challenge is to be clearly Catholic and ecumenically oriented at the same time. The problems posed by economic inequality are complex, much more complex than the kind of simple solutions proposed by people with little experience of the long and hard process of working for social change or balancing a budget. And as different as the social and economic realities are for these two groups of people, they often share many of the same problems: broken families, drug and sexual addictions, violence, consumerism,

29. The "Notre Dame Task Force on the Participation of Latino Children and Families in Catholic Schools" reports that "while 75 percent percent of Latinos in the U.S. are Catholic, only 3 percent of Latino children currently attend Catholic schools," and that they thrive better in Catholic than public schools (see "Latino Families, Catholic Schools and Educational Opportunity," in *Origins*, Vol. 39, No. 31, [January 14, 2010], p. 506).

spiritual impoverishment, and the endless distraction of a hyperactive media and the Internet. Whether the families who send their children to Catholic schools populate the inner cities or the suburbs, they all need attention and formation that is both moral and religious.

I do not have the competence to present systemic solutions to deeply entrenched economic disparities. For understandable reasons, Catholic social teaching about capitalism remains ambivalent, especially since the recent economic crisis. However, certain observations, even by this nonspecialist, seem warranted. For example, an economy that favors the rich, assuming that they in turn will help the poor, has underestimated the greed that motivates many people, both rich and poor. On the other hand, for the government to attempt to take care of everyone—which is hardly the current situation—can lead to the weakening of individual initiative and creativity. The continuing challenge for people in the United States is how to generate wealth in ways that also meets the demands of social justice. That is a difficult question that admits of no single answer. Many leaders in the national community need a vision of the common good and all the skills of the moral virtues to achieve it.

Educators should not be naïve about the challenges and tensions that will arise, especially in suburban settings, when the social teachings of the Church are taught. The parents of wealthy students may feel criticized when Catholic social teaching is emphasized. The fact that many Catholic schools depend upon philanthropy to survive makes all this additionally complicated. Unless wealthy persons give generously to Catholic educational institutions, especially those in the inner city, many poor people will not be able to attend them, and those schools will continue to close. It is often difficult to promote the social justice teachings of the Church, and at the same time win a strong degree of philanthropic support from people of means. On the other hand, the Catholic community continues to have some real success along these lines. It is possible to advocate for the poor without condemning the rich. After all, there are wealthy people whose consciences are well-formed, and who focus on the common good and especially on the needs of the poor.

In understanding such complicated challenges, three groups of people unfortunately offer little help. First, many politicians actually distort the root causes of poverty. To be elected, they typically over-simplify complex issues; once in office, however, they move to a pragmatic center and continue business as usual. Both Democrats and Republicans frame issues in ways that make it difficult for thoughtful Catholics to be a member of either party without serious disagreements. There is a great need for more pro-life Democrats and social justice Republicans. My emphasis is on the need for *more*, since there are some pro-life Democrats and some social justice Republicans. We need more Catholics who wed their opposition to abortion to a commitment to the needs of the poor.

Besides politicians, there is second group of people, overly-zealous social justice advocates, who offer little help to those who wish to teach Catholic social teachings and create thoughtful ways to implement them. These zealots equate social justice only with direct action—picketing, lobbying, boycotting. To be clear, I am in favor of all these activities for just causes, even if sometimes these confrontations provoke strong reactions. If I opposed such tactics, I would have to oppose the nonviolent witness of Gandhi and Martin Luther King. However, I admire both of them. So, what is the problem? The problem is that some zealous advocates of social justice skip over the difficult work of social analysis and downplay the need for education rooted in a religious and moral tradition. They prefer instead to confront and denounce.

But there is a third group that constitutes perhaps the biggest problem. I am thinking of the many Catholics who think that any religious or theological comment on the economy is inappropriate, especially by religious leaders. These people have been influenced by a false understanding of the separation of church and state. They think that religion should be kept out of politics, and bishops should remain in the sanctuary. They make the same mistake many people in the public school system make: they sharply separate religion and public morality. While it is true that the Gospel should never be reduced to partisan politics, if that same Gospel does not have a political impact, it is anemic.

I am confident that access to a good education is one of the best ways over time to help the poor overcome their poverty. Fr. William Byron, S.J., has it right when he stated that running good Catholic schools is a great act of social justice:

> Catholics, the bearers of this tradition of Catholic social thought, clearly believe in the importance of education—not simply religious education for the protection and cultivation of faith, but education of every person's full human potential for enjoyment of a full and productive life. You will search in vain for a person who is well educated and also involuntarily poor. Hence, an important strategic step in the reduction of poverty (a social justice issue) is the provision of sound education.[30]

For Catholic education to be an act of social justice depends at least in part on what the students learn, not just that they are "highly educated," and enter prestigious universities. Therefore, leaders of Catholic high schools need to shape their

---

30. William Byron, S. J., "Ten Principles of Catholic Social Thought," in *Origins*, Vol. 33, No. 17 (October 2, 2003) p. 284.

mission so that their schools become centers for formation in the moral virtues—centers where students are taught the skills to make decisions about their calling and how they are to live out that calling as disciples of Jesus. Most injustices cannot simply or quickly be fixed. Idealists project utopias, visions of "the best" that become the enemy of even "the better." There is no perfect system; if there were, T. S. Eliot wrote, then no one would have to be good.[31] Worst than even the idealists are the indifferent: namely, those Christians who radically separate from the public sphere an important role for their religious and theological tradition.

To do social analysis well will require, first from teachers, the prudence to identify carefully the real issues (no small accomplishment); to understand what might be done and how; and then to have the courage to confront such issues in ways appropriate for them and their students, taking into consideration their level of maturity. None of this emphasis on social justice can afford to replace the foundational skills of reading, writing, speaking, thinking and praying; without these skills, the witness of students as Christians committed to social justice will be misinformed and inarticulate.

Conclusion

People who can be described as being on the "far right" and the "far left" in the Church often lack sufficient confidence in the guidance of the Holy Spirit. A few hearty people deal well with situations that are not black-and-white; they enjoy meeting challenges. If they do this well, they will be making good use of the moral virtues. On the other hand, people unable to handle ambiguity are prone to make black-and-white decisions and in the process can do serious harm to the faith.[32] In this time of transition and confusion, a constant return to the foundations, to the core of the educational vision, requires drawing upon both theological and moral sources.

The previous chapter outlined five theological themes important for clarifying and directing the Catholic mission of education. This chapter added a description of the moral virtues, and then discussed five challenges that, to be

31. T. S. Eliot, *The Rock*, cited by Harvard, p. 50.

32. According to the Dominican Simon Tugwell, "The Church has known many different moods in the course of her history. Sometimes she appears to be very confident of herself and of the value of her message, sometimes she seems rather to be a bit confused and unsure of herself; sometimes she boldly tells everyone exactly what they ought to be doing, sometimes she gives the impression of groping the darkness. And it is not necessarily in her 'best' moments, when she is most confident and clear, that she is most true to herself" (cited in *Commonweal*, October 9, 1998), p. 2.

addressed adequately, require prudence (good sense); justice (a commitment to the common good, with special attention to the poor); fortitude (courage in the face of difficulties); and temperance (a sense of balance and moderation). Taken together, the theological and moral sources for Catholic education form a rich template for leadership in the schools that offer students a truly distinctive education. It is now time to turn to those students, and ask questions about who they are and how they think. Without such knowledge, teachers miss an important opportunity shape the next generation of Christians.

7

Students Today: Descriptions

Introduction

Over the past four decades, most leaders in Catholic primary and secondary education have preoccupied themselves with three main issues: demonstrating the academic quality of their schools; balancing the budget (especially difficult given the cost of lay salaries and the overall disappearance of religious brothers and sisters from Catholic education); and rethinking what it means to have visibly Catholic school without religious and priests. Another issue of great importance is the impact of the larger culture which deeply shapes the personalities and attitudes of students. A better understanding of today's adolescents in Catholic high schools will help educators learn how to teach them, what to emphasize, and how to structure key activities in the school. Understanding adolescents requires that the deep cultural trends described in chapter two be explicitly recognized and evaluated in the light of the Catholic tradition.

Judith Viorst, a psychiatrist and author of *Necessary Losses,* offers one portrait of the typical adolescent:

> A normal adolescent is so restless and twitchy and awkward that he can manage to injure his knee—not playing soccer, not playing football—but by falling off his chair in the middle of French class.
>
> A normal adolescent has sex on the brain—and very frequently in hand.
>
> A normal adolescent describes as two major goals in life (1) putting an end to the threat of nuclear holocaust and (2) owning five knit shirts with a Ralph Lauren label.
>
> A normal adolescent plunges from agony to ecstasy—and back again—in under thirty seconds.
>
> A normal adolescent shifts from viewing her parents as merely fallible to regarding them as wrong about virtually everything.[1]

1. Judith Viorst, *Necessary Losses: The Loves, Illusions, Dependencies and Impossible Expectations That All of Us Have to Give Up as We Grow Older*, (Simon & Schuster, 1998), p. 152.

Viorst's clever set of generalizations about adolescents offers a starting point in understanding high school students. More recently, however, extensive studies on adolescents designed specifically to shed light on their religious thinking give the leaders of Catholic high schools detailed and more relevant information about their students. Christian Smith, a leading sociologist of religion, led an extensive study of the religious and spiritual lives of American teenagers. In his book, *Soul Searching,* he devotes a chapter to Catholic teenagers, in which he concludes: "Getting from where the majority of US Catholic teens currently are with regard to their religious faith and lives to achieving the huge religious potential that appears to exist for Catholic teens would seem to require that the Church invest a great deal more attention, creativity, and institutional resources into its young members—and therefore into its own life." "Undeniably," he adds, "the future shape of the US Catholic Church depends on it."[2] Unfortunately, it seems that not enough people in the Catholic community really believe this.

I've already argued that too many laity and clergy have doubts about the value of Catholic schools. To make clearer my case for the value of Catholic schools, this chapter returns first to the question of the shape of the culture of the United States. More specifically, it examines the results of several national studies on adolescents and their religious beliefs. I also describe how some leaders in the neurosciences think that adolescents are at a special developmental point in their lives—right where religious beliefs can take deeper root. One of the most important conclusions of these studies is that the experiences youth have during their formative years roughly between ages eleven and twenty-one will have especially profound consequences on the way they think and act for years to come. Certainly, youth will adapt and change over the course of their adult lives, but these adaptations and changes will occur within rather stable parameters influenced by the experiences they had during their teenage and young adult years. Therefore, the years that youth spend in high school can have an important impact on the rest of their lives. In the light of these studies, I conclude the chapter with several recommendations for working with adolescents in Catholic high schools.

Major Changes in the Culture

In turning our attention to the primary purpose of Catholic education as it relates to students today, I will necessarily explore, among other things, key cultural changes that have affected not only them, but their teachers and parents as well. In chapter two, I singled out five characteristics of contemporary culture, the last

2. Christian Smith with Melinda Lundquist Denton, *Soul Searching: The Religious and Spiritual Lives of American Teenagers* (Oxford University Press, 2005), p. 217.

three of which—the media, the therapeutic trend, and the "spiritual but not religious" movement—especially affect young people today. I wish to mention here two additional cultural developments which have made it difficult to connect with adolescents on a religious level.

First, unlike today, the Catholic subculture of the 1950s included big families, neighborhood communities tied to a parish (50 percent of which had thriving Catholic grade schools), a Catholic Church with apparent stability and strength, and by 1960, euphoria and a sense of pride over the election of John F. Kennedy, the first Catholic ever elected president of the United States. But this coherent and vibrant Catholic subculture dissolved in a relatively short time due to the post–World War II economic boom, the GI Bill which made college accessible to many men and some women who otherwise would have been unable to go to college, and the subsequent move of many Catholics to the suburbs. Affluence increased access to media and entertainment and fostered the individualism which has taken deep root among Americans. When these suburbs were shredded in the '70s and '80s by unprecedented numbers of divorces and the widespread use of drugs, the impact on children reverberated in the schools.[3] Today, many of our young people are emotionally insecure and lack confidence in their ability to love.

Second, besides the dissolution of the Catholic subculture, there has been a change that has directly affected our Catholic schools. I am thinking here again of the virtual disappearance of the religious orders that in the not-too-distant past virtually dominated Catholic grade schools and by their sheer numbers and visible presence profoundly influenced Catholic high schools. If the larger culture had not become so aggressively secular and sexually preoccupied as it has, and if Catholic communities and families had remained strong and together, the loss of the religious as educators would not have had as dramatic an impact that I believe it has.

Simultaneous with these two cultural changes, there has been a nearly pervasive coarsening of popular culture. A wide range of low-level and vulgar entertainment is now available to adolescents, often in the privacy of their own bedrooms. Experts estimate that 40 percent of Internet traffic carries pornography and, if one listens carefully to the lyrics of most popular songs (my students tell me that to concentrate on the lyrics of songs is to miss their point), what one

3. One manifestation of the divorce culture affects the Protestant community in its own distinctive way. An article published in the *Wall Street Journal* (June 26, 2009), describes a steady drop in attendance at Sunday school classes in Protestant churches, due in part to the number of children whose parents are divorced: "On any given Sunday, many children of divorced parents are out of town, visiting 'the other' parent" (Charlotte Hays, "Why Sunday Schools are Closing").

hears is a constant stream of words about "love" that in reality promotes sex and self-absorbed sensuality. The erstwhile forbidden "f—" word is now everywhere in the lyrics of song, on the screen, and especially on TV comedy stations that feature stand-up comedians. Many young people seem not to notice the vulgarity and crudity, as they tap and sway and bob to the rhythm of these songs, watch TV, and laugh at vulgar jokes and expressions. In short, the popular culture, in which most of our adolescents are immersed, does not support or promote their formation as Catholics, as Christians, or indeed, as citizens. These trends deeply influence adolescents in ways that lead them to accept as normal what only a few generations before would have been shocking.

I do not want to give the impression that there are no positive dimensions of modern culture—such as its emphasis on human rights; the value of personal freedom and individuality; and its capability, especially in the US, for philanthropy and generosity mentioned earlier in this book. Nor do I want to suggest that there were no real problems in the Catholic subculture of the 1950s, such as racism and sexism (both continue to plague our culture and Catholicism), and a uniformity in the Church that made creativity and legitimate diversity more the exception than the rule.[4] Nor do I want to suggest lay people are not capable of being excellent teachers and religious educators. What, then, am I saying?

What I am saying is that, to paraphrase Bob Dylan, the times have changed and changed profoundly. Not only have the times changed, but also the people and the culture that they both create and are shaped by have changed, and many of these changes have made carrying out the mission of the Catholic high school more difficult than ever before. Assuming that I have been basically accurate (and surely there is room for disagreement here) in my descriptions of these three major changes—that is, changes in our larger culture, in our Catholic subculture, and in the staff of our schools—then there is much to do if youth are to be educated and formed in the faith in Catholic high schools. The most typical way to measure change is by comparing similar things in different periods of history.

The Contemporary Shape of Religious Sensibility

Individualism is part of the genetic code of Americans. It affects today's adolescents, but in enhanced ways, especially in their attitudes toward religion. The

4. See John T. McGreevy's *Parish Boundaries: The Catholic Encounter with Race in the Twentieth-Century Urban North* (University of Chicago Press, 1996).

philosopher Charles Taylor illuminates the challenges educators face today. Fellow philosopher but nonbelieving Richard Rorty once described Taylor as one of the ten most important philosophers writing in the world today. Sociologist of religion Robert Bellah tells us that two important facts need to be kept in mind about Taylor. First, among widely read philosophers today, Taylor is one of only two (the other is Alisdair MacIntyre) who is a practicing Catholic. And second, he is "unusually knowledgeable about the social sciences... and is primarily concerned with the intellectual, ethical and religious meaning of modernity."[5] We can turn to Taylor, therefore, for additional evidence for the importance of understanding individualism and its consequences.

Taylor delivered the prestigious Gifford Lectures in 1999, which were published in 2007 in a much expanded version (over 850 pages) with the title, *A Secular Age*. One of the key themes of that major work was already nicely developed in a small 2002 volume, *The Varieties of Religion Today*.[6] Taylor shows why the Harvard religious psychologist and pragmatist philosopher, William James, whose own classic *Varieties of Religious Experience*, presented as the Gifford Lectures in 1899 exactly one hundred years before Taylor's, remains so contemporary. James had little use for churches and organized religion; instead, he focused on the religious experience of individuals, "the feelings, acts and experiences of individual men in their solitude." Those who seek God through churches experience God, James believed, at "second hand," as a "dull habit." Thus, the real locus of religion is the individual, not the community and its communal practices. Rather, for James, real religion is to be found in first-hand experience, not in reciting formulas and performing traditional rituals. He wrote:

> The word "religion," as ordinarily used, is equivocal. A survey of history shows us that, as a rule, religious geniuses attract disciples, and produce groups of sympathizers. When these groups get strong enough to "organize" themselves, they become ecclesiastical institutions with corporate ambitions of their own. The spirit of politics and the lust of dogmatic rule are then apt to enter and to contaminate the originally innocent thing; so that when we hear the word "religion" nowadays, we think inevitably of some "church" or other; and to some persons the word "church" suggests so much hypocrisy and tyranny and meanness and tenacity of superstition

---

5. Robert Bellah, "New Time Religion" (review of Taylor's *Varieties of Religion Today*) in *Christian Century* (May 22–29, 2002), pp. 20–24.

6. Harvard University Press, 2002.

> that in a wholesale undiscerning way they glory in saying that they are "down" on religion altogether.[7]

James had trouble appreciating Catholicism and community prayer. For Catholics, the community is central, and their religious practices, such as the Sacraments, cannot be celebrated by lone individuals. Dogmas, as explained in Chapter 3, are important, and if rightly understood, liberating. Tradition is valued since it literally shapes the Catholic community. But as Taylor explains, "What James can't seem to accommodate is the phenomenon of collective religious life, which is not just the result of (individual) religious connections, but which in some way constitutes or *is* that connection."[8] At the heart of that connection, Taylor continues, is the fact that the Church is a sacramental communion. When Catholics say that they don't "get anything out of Mass," they have connected with neither the community nor the Sacrament.

This deeply ingrained American strain of individualism and the primary authority of personal experience have, as already mentioned, long been a part of the US cultural landscape. On the other side of the ocean, Newman singled it out in 1845 as a fundamental problem for Christian believers, James gave it classic expression in 1899, and Taylor now provides a full-blown cultural analysis in his major 2007 work explaining why so many people today, young people and their parents in particular, have a difficult time relating to the Church, its teachings and rituals. This trend is often described today as those individuals who are "spiritual but not religious" or "believe but don't belong." What William James wrote approvingly of over one-hundred years ago is now becoming a growing movement, especially among younger Americans.

---

7. William James, *The Varieties of Religious Experience* (Hammondsworth, Middlesex, England: Penguin Books, 1982), pp. 334–335. Already in the middle of the nineteenth century, the brilliant religious thinker and convert to Catholicism, John Henry Newman, had put his finger on individualism as an anti-church phenomenon and described it as the fundamental problem facing Christians (though instead of "individualism," he referred to it as "liberalism" and an "anti-dogmatic principle"). He wrote that liberalism teaches "…that truth and falsehood in religion are but matters of opinion; that one doctrine is as good as another; that the Governor of the world does not intend that we should gain the truth; that there is not truth; that we are not more acceptable to God by believing this than by believing that; that no one is answerable for his opinions; that they are a matter of necessity or accident; that it is enough if we sincerely hold what we profess; that our merit lies in seeking, not in possessing…" (*An Essay on the Development of Christian Doctrine* [Notre Dame Indiana; University of Notre Dame Press, 1989], pp. 357–358). Contemporary sociologists such as Robert Wuthnow and Robert Bellah have documented how profoundly Newman's "liberalism" characterizes the practice of religion in the United States today.

8. Taylor, *Varieties*, p. 24.

Before Vatican II, however, Catholics, especially those who lived in the Northeast and Midwest, were able to stay connected to the regular practice of Catholic rituals and typically affirmed Catholic doctrines. They tended to live in neighborhoods where the larger increasingly secular culture made fewer inroads. During that period, they maintained a more coherent religious subculture than now, one that embodied identifiable religious practices performed by the whole community. These practices, including eating no meat on Fridays, clearly distinguished them from many of their mainline Protestant neighbors who, until the 1960s, were nearly indistinguishable from the dominant American culture.[9] However, Catholics were not alone in stressing, against the dominant culture, a sense of community. More conservative Christians, including Lutherans, Dutch Calvinists, and certainly Mennonites and the Amish, also set themselves apart from the dominant culture with its increasing materialism and secularism.

The community of the Catholic subculture has pretty much dissolved (except for new immigrant Catholics—mainly Latino and Asian). Most boomers and Generation Xers have been absorbed into the cultural mainstream. The communications and entertainment industries (TV, film, DVDs, cell phones, computers, iPods, and the newest "indispensable" personal electronic gadgets that hit the market regularly) have created a highly stimulating audio-visual culture, especially for youth who have grown up surrounded by these inventions. Typically suspicious of the authority of normative institutions (government, church and military), today's young Catholics seem to have particular difficulty recognizing the value of traditional authority and religious rituals done in community.

Recent Studies on Youth: Sharpening the Focus

In recent years, a number of sociologists of religion have focused their attention on generational differences among American Catholics. They have distinguished between three generations: pre-Vatican II Catholics, the "baby boomers" or Vatican II Catholics (born between 1941 and 1960), and Generation X or post-Vatican II Catholics (born between 1961 and 1981).

They report that a new generation (Catholics born since 1982), often called the millennial generation, is now growing into adulthood. What do we know about youth who were born seventeen years after Vatican II, fourteen years after *Humanae vitae*, who have lived their whole lives under mainly one pope, who have always known the environment to be in crisis, and have been warned

9. For a sophisticated argument in favor of restoring symbolically distinctive communal practices, such as fasting and the Friday abstinence, see Eamon Duffy, *Faith of Our Fathers* (Continuum, 2004), pp. 180–187.

repeatedly since 2001 that the United States is at war with people who want to destroy the American way of life? These millennials are being formed in the social and religious context of the United States in the 1990s and the first decade of the twenty-first century. They are now in high school and college. Who are they and how do they think?

Millennials, researchers report, are highly skeptical about social institutions such as government, business, marriage, education, and religion. This skepticism is strengthened by their focus on individual personal experiences and the authority of their conscience (over against societal rules and regulations). Their attitudes influence the way they think about the world they live in, the church in which they are being raised, and the schools they attend. The oldest of these millennials are now in their mid twenties. Many of them have graduated from college, and have several years of experience in the labor force. These older millennials are nearing the end of their most formative years and, therefore, are on the leading edge of their generation. Younger millennials are in the nation's colleges and high schools—still in the generational incubator and very much in the formative process. Exactly what they will be like as adults remains to be seen.

However, many parents, church leaders, and Catholic educators have asked what really can be known and predicted about this millennial generation. They seem especially interested in knowing whether millennials will be an extension of Generation X or will be markedly different. They want to know how best to present the Catholic tradition to Catholic high school students. There is much data to examine and evaluate. It is worth looking at these studies on youth and evaluating their findings. Then, in the light of these studies, it can be asked what Catholic educators need to do to pass on the faith more effectively to young people.

Current Research on Generations

Recent research on generations[10] shows that the biggest difference, by far, between the generations is between the pre-Vatican II Catholics and the succeeding two generations. Clearly, the cultural revolution of the 1960s, especially the dissolution of Catholic subculture and the Second Vatican Council combined to produce significant social and religious differences between Catholics who were born and raised before the 1960s, and those who came during and after that momentous period.

10. I am referring to studies such as *Laity: American and Catholic* (by William V. D'Antonio et al, 1996); *The Search for Common Ground: What Unites and Divides Catholic Americans* (by James D. Davidson et al, 1997); *American Catholics: Gender, Generation and Commitment* (by Willaim V. D"Antonio et al, 2001); and *Young Adult Catholics* (by Dean Hoge et al, 2001).

One reason why the gap is smaller between the Vatican II and post-Vatican II generations has to do with the choices that members of the Vatican II generation made. When faced with the choice of embracing the religious ethos of the pre-Vatican II Church and the ethos of the post-Vatican II Church, the majority of baby boomers chose the latter. While a minority of boomers hold on to or want to return to the faith of their parents' generation, most do not. On the other hand, there is a small but highly committed group of young people who seem to be very interested in a more traditionalist form of Catholicism. The majority of boomers, however, remain committed to core church teachings (e.g., Trinity, incarnation, resurrection, real presence, and Mary as the mother of God), but on other matters, they clearly favor the "new Church" over the "old Church."

Members of the Vatican II generation have transmitted this preference to most of their children, who can best be seen as extensions of their parents, not as radical departures from them. Still, given the even more individualistic world that Gen Xers have grown up in, they are even more autonomous in their thinking than their boomer parents. Most Gen Xers do not feel as obligated or committed to the institutional Church, as evidenced by the lower rates of Mass attendance and their frequent departures from official Church teachings on a number of ecclesiastical and moral issues, especially on sexual morality. They no longer enjoy the support of a strong Catholic community as they grow up.

How, then, do Gen X Catholics compare with the next generation of millennials? Research on the millennial generation is in its infancy. It will be a number of years until we have much of a sense of how different millennials will be from their Gen X parents and their baby boomer grandparents. One early study of millennials, conducted by Thomas P. Walters during the fall of 1999 and winter of 2000, included a survey of over 6,000 thirteen- and fifteen-year-olds in Catholic high schools and parish religious education programs. Walters reported seven "facts" about millennials. According to Walters, millennials: (1) are not thinking about becoming priests or religious; (2) are quite optimistic; (3) consider themselves religious; (4) are in danger of being theologically illiterate; (5) are "tele-literate"; (6) trust their parents; and (7) think they get mixed messages from the Church. Reading further in Walters' analysis, we find that the students he surveyed do not have a real connection to the Church or their parish. In a now familiar phrase, they "believe but don't belong." While they trust their parents, they are not encouraged by them to think of priesthood or religious life—something that doesn't even occur to them, even though they believe they are quite religious. Being "quite religious" seems to mean that they approach religion quite pragmatically (much like their parents), looking for what "works for them," and associating religion mainly with pleasing and affirming experiences.[11] It does not seem to mean that they understand well and commit themselves firmly to being Catholic Christians.

Walters' study is only one study of the millennial generation and makes no claims of being a representative sample of millennial Catholics (it includes an over-representation of Catholic school students). And, while it suggests that millennials might be different in some respects (i.e., more optimistic, more trusting of their parents), it also suggests that in many other respects millennials are likely to be natural extensions of, rather than radical departures from, their parents' generation.

Walter's interpretation rests on three findings related to their parents' beliefs and practices. First, members of the post-Vatican II generation, especially if they are college graduates, frequently identify themselves as "spiritual but not religious." James Davidson and his colleagues have reported that the vast majority of Gen X Catholics believe God has answered their prayers and has helped them in times of need, but 40 percent are not registered in a parish and only 33 percent attend Mass on a weekly basis.[12] Hoge and his colleagues report that 90 percent of Catholic young adults are "spiritual but not religious," while only 10 percent are "core Catholics," that is, can be said to be both spiritual and religious. We will return later to this phrase, "spiritual but not religious." These findings are echoed in Walters' findings that millennials "believe but don't belong" and are not thinking about becoming priests or religious.

Second, many Generation Xers lack the social networks and relationships that would make their faith a more explicit part of their lives. Although 72 percent say their mothers went to church weekly, only half say their fathers did. While 75 percent were close to their mothers while growing up, only half were close to their fathers. Seventy-one percent say their current social network includes a Catholic whom they admire, but only half say that person is active in the Church, and only one-third describe that person as a traditional Catholic. Gen X Catholics also are less likely to marry a Catholic than their grandparents and parents were. Only 60 percent of married Gen X Catholics are married to a

11. Thomas P. Walters, "Millennial Youth: Facts, Figures and Priestly Vocations," in T. P. Walters & B. Crawford, eds., *The Millennial Generation: Hearing God's Call* (St. Meinrad, IN: Abbey Press, 2001), pp. 15–25.

12. James Davidson, et al, *The Search for Common Ground: What Unites and Divides American Catholics* (Huntington IN: Our Sunday Visitor, 1997). Sociologists have designed research that is able to document a significant gap between what people report as their frequency of Church attendance and the actually frequency which is considerably lower (see Hadaway, Y. and P. Marler, and M. Chaves, "What the Polls Don't Show: A Closer Look at Church Attendance," in *American Sociological Review* Vol. 58, No. 6, [1993]) pp. 741–752.

Catholic. There is nothing in Walters' data, or in any other research, that indicates a reversal of these patterns. Thus, most millennials (keep in mind that a minority of young Catholics are very committed to traditionalist forms of Catholicism) are also not likely to have the "thick" Catholic networks that their grandparents and great-grandparents had.

This conclusion is important because significant social relationships obviously affect people's religious beliefs and practices. People are most likely to be active in the Church and most likely to embrace its teachings if their parents are religious, if they are close to their parents, if their friendships include other people who are active Catholics, and if they marry a Catholic. Young Catholics without these social networks are less connected with the Church and less inclined to embrace its teachings.

Third, young adults are critical of the religious education they have received in parishes and parochial schools. It would be most interesting if entering into some sort of time machine we were able to do a survey that would report the opinions of young people from the last 150 years. Perhaps we would discover that most youth never liked any of their religious education. When Davidson and his colleagues interviewed post-Vatican II Catholics, they asked them to describe their experience of religious education. The respondents consistently complained about the over-emphasis on process and the lack of substance. They often referred to the banners and collages they were told to create. Moreover, they said they learned little or nothing about major religious events such as Pentecost. Hoge and his colleagues document the same dissatisfaction, in even more graphic detail.[13] In personal conversations with college freshmen and sophomores, I find that members of the millennial generation continue to express dissatisfaction with their experiences of religious education. Certainly there are many gifted religious educators, and many catechists who teach solid content, but it does not appear that these teachers dominate the field of religious education. Given Walters' finding that millennials are on the verge of religious illiteracy, it would appear that the newest generation is also an extension of its parents' generation in this respect.[14]

---

13. D. Hoge et al., *Young Adult Catholics: Religion in the Culture of Choice* (Notre Dame, IN: Notre Dame Press, 2001).

14. Studies of English youth corroborate these findings. They document patterns of increased autonomy of young Catholics from the teachings and practices of the Church. Only 15 percent of teenage girls and 13 percent of teenage boys go to Church regularly. Though only 41 percent believe in God (!), 78 percent want to get married in Church and over half want their children to be baptized; 65 percent do not believe they are worth much as a person, 52 percent often feel depressed, and 27 percent have seriously considered suicide. See *The Tablet*, June 23, 2001, p. 924, as well as the books by Leslie Francis and W. K. Kay, *Teenage Religion and Values* (UK: Gracewing, Limited, 1995) and a later book, *Drift From the Churches: Attitude Toward Christianity During Childhood and Adolescence* (Cardiff, Wales: University of Wales Press, 1996).

Two Recent National Studies on Youth and Religion

There are several other studies on teenagers that educators should know about. The first is a major Lilly-funded research project on adolescents led by sociologist Christian Smith, whose conclusions about Catholic youth were mentioned at the beginning of this chapter; and second, there are several studies from the rapidly developing field of neuroscience on the cognitive capacities of adolescents.

The Lilly Endowment has funded the most extensive current source of information on the religious attitudes of US adolescents. Their sample included Catholics but did not focus on them. An executive summary of the findings compiled by Smith tells us some things we already know: all youth can't be put in the same bag (though many drift, some are very devout); the majority of teens don't see religion as that important (except for Walter's study), especially when it competes with time for school, television and other media; most youth, like their parents, are very individualistic; they are inarticulate about their faith; they view religion mainly as an instrument to help them become what they want to be; they try very hard to "make nice," especially when discussing religion with others in public; and they think religion helps them be good, but isn't necessary for being good. Perhaps more surprising are some other characteristics of adolescents found by Smith: that significant numbers of youth are exposed to religion and are personally and actively religious; that most are conventional in their religious identities and practices, that is, most teens follow the faith of their families without much questioning; very few think of themselves as "spiritual but not religious" (though other studies, especially of college students, show they do think of themselves this way); and the family continues to be the biggest factor in teenagers' lives connecting them to religious traditions and strengthening their faith.[15]

Smith devotes an entire chapter to Catholic teenagers. The first half of that chapter narrates lengthy interviews with three Catholic teenagers, none of whom attends a Catholic high school; the second half offers an analysis of the overall findings on Catholic teens. The results are not encouraging for anyone dedicated to Catholic education. Moreover, Catholic teenagers do not compare favorably with the teenagers of other Christian traditions, especially evangelical Christians and Mormans.

Smith's study is important and deserves close attention. While I have no empirical data other than my own experience with young Catholics over the last four decades, I wonder whether in fact the vast majority of high school youth today are "conventional in their religious identity and practices." And even though few teens think of themselves as "spiritual but not religious," might it not

15. Smith and Denton, *Soul Searching*, pp. 68–71.

be the case that they think that way since they've never heard that description of themselves—a description and an approved attitude that is much more often actually taught to them at colleges and universities where the particular is often seen as the enemy of the universal? That is to say, a widespread assumption among faculty at most universities is that strong particular religious identities are dangerous, since such identities make it easier for "true" believers to be intolerant and narrow in their views. Typical of this point of view are the ways in which Lawrence Kohlberg described the stages of moral development. He claimed that to reach the highest level of moral development, one had to transcend "institutional" (i.e., a specific religious tradition) religious identities. Only then could people be considered mature and truly universal in their faith.

I do believe, however, that Smith has put his finger on a dominant form of adolescent (and adult) religion in the United States when he describes it as "moral therapeutic deism." Most young people think of religion primarily in terms of rules—morality. They tend to place a very high value on feeling good about themselves, and they tend to be deistic—that is, they, especially Catholic youth, speak more about "God" than they do about "Jesus," and rarely think of reading Scripture or receiving the Sacraments as encounters with Jesus. Youth typically are, in this sense, "sub-Trinitarian." When I have asked Catholic high school and college students for reasons why the Catholic Church opposes remarriage after divorce, they give all sorts of reasons, but almost never mention that the teachings of Jesus as recorded in the New Testament might have something to do with the Church's position. Nor do most of them seem to link receiving the Eucharist with a "personal relationship" with Jesus; they tend rather to think of it as becoming closer to God, if they think much about the Eucharist at all. When some students tell me that they get nothing out of going to Mass, I often ask them if they believe in the real presence. When they say they do, I ask them how they can then say they get nothing out of going to Mass, and remind them that there, at mass, they receive Jesus Christ, the Son of God at Mass. But again, the culture refers only to "God" in general, a benign being (or as Smith describes their view of God, "a cosmic butler" waiting for orders as to how to help) who doesn't give too many specific orders about how to live and what to believe.

Few teenagers, Smith documents, talk about the difference between spirituality and religion, but they nonetheless often feel indifferent to doctrines and disengaged from the practices of their churches. By the time they get to college, many of them will be told that religions are human constructs. They will hear pejorative references to "institutional religion" and "organized religion"—surprising phrases since it is impossible to think of religions continuing to exist without at least some organization and institutional structures. Those who advocate "spirituality" tend to leave out those aspects of religion that they do not like, especially communally required beliefs and practices. "Spirituality" lends itself to being tailored according to the preferences of the individual.

Of course, churches and parishes may themselves contribute to these perceptions. The liturgical practices of religion at the local level can be perfunctory and lifeless. Explanations of doctrine may have little connection with life as it is actually lived and be presented without any understanding of the meaning and importance of the doctrine for living the Christian life. Religions should be schools of spirituality, places where individual spirituality is nourished and fed by a stream broader and deeper than any individual might try to create on his or her own. In their own ways, Catholic schools also need to be schools of spirituality, places where students absorb more than individualistic messages that the larger culture constantly feeds them. Smith's study may not have found much "spiritual but not religious" talk among the teenagers he interviewed, but the culture they breathe promotes that very split to the detriment of Christian life.

Smith wonders why most Catholic teens are so inarticulate, so individualistic and deistic, descriptors that, in his judgment, account for teens' distance from any robust form of Catholic belief and practice. At least part of the answer to his questions can be found, I think, in the culture of entertainment and consumerism that separates spirituality from religion. Smith himself suggests two possible answers: one, the breakdown of the family (he makes it clear that the depth of religious devotion and practice of the parents directly affects the religious identity of the teenager); and second, in line with what I am arguing, the overall influence of the larger secular culture, which influence is, in turn, greatly enhanced by the breakdown of the family. The consequences of these combined reasons can be disastrous—too many of our young people don't even reach the level of spirituality—at least the spirituality that is described in Chapter 2 in such glowing terms by the editor of *Tikkun*. Those who read the first half of Smith's chapter on Catholic youth may find themselves wishing that among the three students he interviewed at least one of them had been a graduate of a Catholic high school. And even if there had been, that would be no assurance that we would find students whose religious lives are vibrant.

The findings of the Lilly research and especially the chapter in Smith's book on Catholic teenagers were sobering enough to provoke an immediate response from the National Federation for Catholic Youth Ministry (NFCYM). In essence, the document, titled *National Study of Youth and Religion: Analysis of the Population of Catholic Teenagers and their Parents*, dated 2004,[16] analyzed Smith's earlier findings

16. The primary authors of the document are Charlotte McCorquodale, Victoria Shepp and Leigh Sterten.

on Catholic youth. Smith interviewed a total of 816 Catholic teenagers and their parents, though many more were surveyed. In a few instances, the wording of the questions posed by the Lilly survey may have made the conclusions about Catholic teens more negative than they would have been otherwise. For example, several of the survey questions used "evangelical" language that would be strange for Catholics. If, for example, Catholics are asked, "Have you accepted Jesus as your Lord and Savior?" Most would likely answer either "I don't know," or "I think I have," or "What do you mean?" Evangelicals, however, would answer yes and might even be able to tell you when they did so. In the Lilly survey, the following questions are asked: "How often do you read from the Bible alone?" This question almost sounds like one that Martin Luther would have asked. Another question, "Does your church feel like a welcoming place?" Protestant churches are typically smaller (except for the recent mega churches) than Catholic Churches; it is likely that members of large urban parishes would not be answering yes to this question. The survey also speaks of "youth ministers" and "youth groups," not the typical vocabulary used in Catholic Churches. Crucial for evangelical Christianity is evangelizing, or sharing the faith with others, an activity that—despite the repeated call of John Paul II for Catholics to launch a "new evangelization"—few Catholics understand, much less heed. One question asked if the person has shared his or her faith publicly and done so with someone of a different faith; most Catholics, unfortunately, shrink from such activity. A case could be made, then, that if the survey phrased some of their questions in a way more familiar to Catholics, a more encouraging set of responses may have been obtained. But even if this were done, I fear that the answers given by most Catholic teens would give us little reason to boast.

The study commissioned by the NFCYM, however, also included somewhat encouraging news for those committed to making Catholic schools effective. For example, 66 percent of Catholic school students report that when alone they read the Bible, compared with 51 percent of non-Catholic students. And 72 percent of Catholic school students have been to confession in the previous year, compared to 44 percent of Catholics in non-Catholic schools. Concerning at-risk behaviors, however, Catholic school students drink more alcohol than students in public schools. On the other hand, only 21 percent of Catholic school students had engaged in sexual intercourse compared to 61 percent of the public school counter parts. But then again, 65 percent of the Catholic school students have had oral sex, compared to 56 percent of public school students.

While it is surely the case that many Catholic students are "incredibly inarticulate" about matters religious, I wonder whether they are more inarticulate than the general population is about religion. I ask myself too whether Smith gave sufficient attention to both peer and cultural pressures that tell people, especially teens, to keep their religion to themselves. And there is some evidence from developmental psychology that only in adolescence do most young people begin to develop a personal interest in God. These questions on my part suggest that further research should be done before we conclude that adolescents are "incredibly inarticulate" (compared to whom?) about their religion.

From Sociology to Neuroscience: Youth "Hard-Wired" for Religion

One of the themes of this book is that communities with a strong tradition and supportive culture are able to form their young people effectively. Moreover, the presence of adults who care about their students and model the faith for them can be more important than having the students only study the faith. Studies in the emerging field of neuroscience support this thesis. For example, in 2003 a group of thirty-three professionals (doctors, scientists and professionals who work with youth) published a report from the Commission on Children at Risk titled *Hardwired to Connect.* This report, sponsored by the YMCA, the Dartmouth Medical School, and the Institute for American Values, provides statistical evidence of the dramatic declines in the well-being of adolescents over the last fifty years. They conclude that when adolescents are integrated into what the report calls "authoritative communities"—that is, religious institutions, intact families and other civic institutions serving children (such as the YMCA)—those adolescents are much more likely to believe that life is worth living. In the words of one of the members of the commission, W. Bradford Wilcox, a sociologist at the University of Virginia:

> These communities provide adolescents with a sense of belonging and with moral and spiritual meaning that lends their lives purpose and hope. When adolescents have no ties, or only attenuated ties, to authoritative communities, they lose hope and become vulnerable to a range of social and psychological pathologies, including suicide.[17]

One of the more intriguing assertions of this report is that adolescents are hard-wired to connect not only with other people, but also with moral and spiritual meaning. In other words, biologists and neurologists argue that human connections to family and God are rooted "not only in enduring social needs but also in the biological makeup of the human person."[18] For example, the report points out that adolescent girls who live with their biological fathers enter puberty

---

17. Bradford W. Wilcox, "Children at Risk," in *First Things* (February 2004), p. 12.

18. Wilcox, p. 14.

later than girls who live with adult males to whom they are not related, such as their mother's boyfriend or even a stepfather. Girls who live with their fathers are more likely to postpone sex than girls who live with a male to whom they are unrelated. There is then not only biological and sociological value for a family that includes both biological parents, but also moral value for the young woman moving on to adulthood.

The report also links adolescents' capacity for religion with their biological development. The authors of the study report that "adolescence is a time when the brain seems most primed to address fundamental questions about life and death, ultimate meaning, and the supernatural." Most of the brain is fully developed by late adolescence; however, the prefrontal cortex—the part of the brain that neuroscientists link to religious experiences—actually develops rather strikingly during adolescence. If during this time of change adolescents are able to connect with God, they are also more likely than their peers who report no such connection to find hope and meaning in life. Adolescents without an active religious life and a supportive religious community are not only "much more likely" to engage in deviant behavior, such as drugs and alcohol, but also to commit suicide.[19]

A more popular report of some of the findings of recent neurological studies on adolescent development may be found in a cover story of *Time* magazine, "What Makes Teens Tick." Not surprisingly, the *Time*'s article did not draw out any of the religious ramifications of adolescents' neurological development. The authors of the article, however, do say something important about the brain's gradual development. For example, concerning the aforementioned prefrontal cortex, they explain that it is one of the last areas of the brain to undergo significant development, an area that exercises "executive functions—planning, setting priorities, organizing thoughts, suppressing impulses, weighing the consequences of one's actions."[20] To expect adolescents to perform such functions well without a moral and religious framework would likely be much more difficult than if they had a moral and religious foundation guiding their thinking and behavior.

I find these studies helpful. However, their conclusions should not automatically provide the foundations of Catholic education. Caution should be exercised when citing the results of empirical studies about brain functions and positive thinking. Studies, for example, that argue that we will live longer if we pray and keep a positive attitude might suggest that the basic reason for prayer is to prolong life on earth. The truth is, rather, that we ought to pray first because that is

---

19. This summary of the study has been drawn primarily from Wilcox's article.

20. *Time,* May 10, 2004, p. 61.

our duty as creatures of God. If Christians prayed only to live longer, they'd make an art of avoiding martyrdom. Basing one's commitment to the practice of religion on demonstrable (scientific), positive effects might amount to nothing more than building one's house on sand. The conclusions of science often change with the passage of time and sometimes radically. The foundation of Catholic education and the source of its mission are built upon solid theological truths and moral practices: people are creatures of God redeemed by the death and resurrection of Jesus, and that through prayer and penance they learn how to love and become disciples of Jesus. That having been affirmed, the recent tentative results of some studies in the neurosciences offer a few additional, but not fundamental, reasons for educators to focus more clearly on what they may need to do to strengthen their schools' Catholic mission and identity.

Catholic educators should know about this recent research on adolescents. The research adds to the understanding of the religious development of youth. The research also highlights the substantial influence that the overall culture has not only on adolescents, but also on their parents, not to mention also those who lead and staff Catholic schools. In the light of some of the conclusions of this research, Catholic high schools with a strong sense of their distinctive religious mission coupled with a palpable and supportive community where adults and young people interact in a positive way can make a timely and immensely positive impact on the growth of adolescents into adult members of the faith.

Catholic Schools Work

As mentioned in Chapter 1 of this book, researchers on Catholic schools have for decades been reporting their extraordinary achievements. Already in the late 1960s and early 1970s, when many religious were giving up on the schools they had led and staffed so well for decades, the priest-scholar Fr. Andrew Greeley repeated produced studies that demonstrated the importance and benefits of parochial schools, especially the distinctive religious outcomes of Catholic schools. Greeley pleaded with the hierarchy and the members of the religious communities to remain committed to the education of the young. In *Minority Students in Catholic Secondary Schools,* he showed that not only did minority students in Catholic schools perform better than their peers in public schools, but that the most disadvantaged students enjoyed the greatest degree of achievement.[21] No Catholic researcher has produced as many solid studies on Catholic

21. Andrew Greeley, *Minority Students in Catholic Secondary Schools* (Washington, D.C: National Center for Education Statistics, 1981).

schools, nor stressed their importance, and defended their mission as fervently as Andrew Greeley.

I have been stressing in this book the importance of a community of support—a network of relationships that re-enforce the mission of Catholic schools. Part of what contributes to this community of support is the organization of a Catholic school. Already in the 1980s, James Coleman, a non-Catholic sociologist at the University of Chicago, focused his attention on the distinctive organization of Catholic schools and the consequent academic achievement of their students. Coleman and others showed that students at Catholic schools were academically more successful, experienced more consistent discipline, studied a more structured curriculum, benefited from a greater sense of community among faculty and students, and experienced themselves as more of a community than did their counterparts in public schools. In 1982, Coleman used the concept of "social capital," that is, the power of social relationships in Catholic schools (e.g., parental support, teacher commitment and availability outside of the classroom), to help explain the benefits of Catholic education.[22]

Culture powerfully shapes people. I have explained earlier that contemporary secular culture profoundly influences the personalities and religious beliefs of adolescents. Catholic high schools provide a distinctive and formative culture for the effective passing on of the Christian faith. In Chapter 2, I summarized the key findings of the widely discussed book by Bryk, Lee and Holland, *Catholic Schools and the Common Good.* Their research singled out the transformative power of the culture of Catholic high schools as the main reason that their students achieved more consistently at a higher level than their public counterparts.[23] That culture drew upon the core curriculum (not a large number of electives), the expectation that all students could and should attend college, and the emphasis on a moral basis of the school's sense of community. Their study showed that such achievement did not depend on the dismissal of problem students, nor upon families willing to pay the tuition.[24] In short, Bryk's book shows that the more

---

22. John Coleman, T. Hoffer, and S. Kilgore, *High School Achievement: Public, Catholic and Private Schools Compared* (New York: Basic Books, 1982).

23. Anthony Byrk, Valerie Lee, P. Holland, *Catholic Schools and the Common Good* (Cambridge, MA; Harvard University Press, 1993).

24. Helpful summaries of these studies and other related research are provided by John Convey's *Catholic Schools Make a Difference: Twenty-Five Years of Research* (Washington, D.C: National Catholic Education Association, 1992), and more recently James Younis and Jeffrey McLellan, eds., *The Catholic Character of Catholic Schools* (Notre Dame IN: University of Notre Dame Press, 2000). Another valuable resource is the *Handbook of Research on Catholic Education* (Westport CT: Greenwood Press, 2001), edited by Thomas Hunt, Ellis Joseph and Ronald Nuzzi.

coherent culture of a Catholic school helps adolescents grow in self-confidence, a sense of achievement, and in their faith.

This research should make Catholic educators proud of the achievements of students in Catholic schools. Given the lack of a coherent Christian subculture, students today need more from educational institutions than students in the past to make up for that missing subculture. Keeping in mind the theological foundations of Catholic schools, I wish to make, by way of conclusion and in the light of this research and building on it, some suggestions that I believe will improve the formative impact that Catholic schools can have on adolescents.

The Formation of Millennials: Three Recommendations

I have spent considerable time in this chapter trying to understand today's adolescents. Assuming that the larger culture is secular and hyper-sexualized, that the Catholic subculture in which young people have grown up is weak, and that clarifying the Catholic mission of the schools remains especially challenging today, then it may be asked on what should Catholic educators concentrate? While other recommendations might be made, I am most confident of the following three.

First, as I stated at the end of the last chapter, Catholic educators need to strengthen the substance and quality of the religious education and formation of their students. Religion teachers need to be the best educators in the school. Of course, good teachers are learners themselves. That is, they themselves love to learn. In the schedule of courses, religion courses should enjoy a prominent place—be taught every day, and not be seen as less important than science courses or the athletic program. If students need remedial religious education, they should receive it, even if that instruction takes place before or after the ordinary school day.

Besides religion courses, school liturgies should be well done, readers well coached, musicians well practiced and the environment conducive to prayer. Good liturgy requires skill in music, art and drama. Sometimes it is also important to celebrate a prayer service that non-Catholic Christian students can participate in as fully as Catholic students. Retreat programs tend to be more powerful when they include more faculty than just those who teach religion. It is helpful on such retreats when students give talks and witness their faith to one another, but students also need to hear witness talks from adults as well, especially their teachers. The cumulative effect of acting on these recommendations can profoundly shape the culture of the school.

Still it may be asked, why do so many students complain about their religious education? Are such complaints limited only to the courses without content or to the collage poster boards that have diluted many religious education programs after the Council? Is it not the case that a number of students are complacent, even bored "customers" as they are called now in some management literature—customers who are always "right?" Are students so mesmerized by action films and video games that a talking head in front of the classroom is inevitably so s-l-o-w that student attention flags?

> TV favors a mentality in which certain things no longer matter particularly: skills like the ability to enjoy a complex argument, for instance, or to perceive nuances, or to keep in mind large amounts of significant information, or to remember today what someone said last month, or to consider strong and carefully argued opinions in defiance of what is conventionally called "balance." Its content lurches between violence of action, emotional hyperbole and blandness of opinion. And it never, never stops. It is always trying to give us something interesting. Not interesting for long; just for now. Commercial TV teaches people to scorn complexity and to feel, not to think.[25]

Certainly, TV, video games, and the Internet are part of the problem. It will rightly be pointed out, however, that not all TV is corrupting. There are, after all, some documentaries that are well done, PBS can usually be counted on to provide informative specials, and some channels show classic films. True enough. My experience with adolescents, however, suggests that they rarely watch such programs.

To compete with and even replace, at least in part, the ordinary media diet of adolescents, individual religion classes need solid content and effective presentation. The overall curriculum needs to be well-organized and logically sequenced, taking into consideration the maturity level of the students. Retreat programs, sodalities groups, and opportunities to lead and serve support the content of religion classes. Certainly all teachers need to be competent, but those who teach religion need in a special way to be pedagogically effective. Science and math

---

25. Robert Hughes, "Why Watch It, Anyway?" *The New York Review of Books* (February 16, 1995), p. 38. Thomas Merton adamantly opposed television. He thought it posed a great danger for anyone interested in being contemplative: "The life of a television-watcher is a kind of caricature of contemplation. Passivity, uncritical absorption, receptivity, inertia." Watching TV is the opposite of contemplation: "for true contemplation is precisely the fruit of a most active and intransigent rupture with all that captivates the senses, the emotions, and the will on a material or temporal level" ("Inner Experience: Problems of the Contemplative Life (VII)," in *Cistercian Studies Quarterly* 19:4 [1984], pp. 269–270.) Merton had to have written those words sometime before his death in 1968; what would he have written had he been exposed today to commercial TV, video games and cable networks? Both the Hughes and Merton quotations may be found in Michael Casey's *Strangers to the City* (Paraclete Press, 2005), pp. 42–43.

courses obviously build on each other, and introduce material often completely new to students. When a religion curriculum is not well-organized and teachers teach mainly what they want to teach, repetition of material produces student yawns and the lack of curricular organization diminishes student learning. Teachers of religion need special support and regular opportunities to develop themselves professionally. Since the religion course is the one subject that will not be found in a public school, and since it is an important means for handing on the religious tradition, it ought to be among the best organized, taught and supported in the school.

My second recommendation has to do with the relationship between intellectual and moral formation. Charles Taylor noted, as we have seen, that although our own culture "tends to multiply somewhat shallow and undemanding spiritual options," there is a great cost to forced conformity—namely, "hypocrisy, spiritual stultification" and "the confusion of faith and power."[26] True as these observations may be, for teachers dedicated explicitly to passing on the Catholic tradition to high school students, the choice need not be either "shallow and undemanding spiritual options" on the one hand or "hypocrisy and spiritual stultification" on the other. There are vibrant alternatives to both the shallow and the stultified presentations of the faith.

Most studies on schools in the last two decades referred to the transformative force of the "culture" of the school. Leaders of institutions know how to build up to a "tipping point" in their institutions; that is, they know how to go about gradually changing the culture in such a way that the religious mission of the school becomes central to the education of the students.[27] Of course, as mentioned earlier in this chapter, the larger culture is also within all of us and typically shapes our presuppositions. Our students are more or less formed within that culture. Put simply, culture forms the way people think about things and influences how they act. Middle-class people take affluence for granted until they live among the materially poor. They remain largely unaware of their individualism until they live in, and not just visit, a truly traditional culture.

Earlier in this chapter, I noted the tendency, especially among young adults and college students, to separate consciously the spiritual from the religious. On the positive side, as has been noted, when Gen Xers and millennial Catholics say they are "spiritual," they may be indicating that they have chosen to be on a spiritual journey, albeit an individualistic one. It may mean that they more or less consciously reject materialism and consumerism. To the extent that being

26. Taylor, *Varieties*, p. 114.

27. See Malcolm Gladwell, *The Tipping Point: How Little Things Can Make a Big Difference* (Little, Brown and Company, 2000), especially chapter 8.

"spiritual but not religious" means these things, such persons may well be more mature than some of their peers who seek satisfaction in "shallow and undemanding" weekly connections with the faith. Moreover, if their only exposure to "religion" is attending a mass that neither strengthens community nor nourishes spirituality, then young peoples' rejection of "religion" could be a positive first step toward a more authentic religious life.

Rituals and practices that require reflection wed moral formation to intellectual growth. Schools should ensure that communal rituals be an integral part of the student's experience together. I have already alluded to secular rituals like sports and proms. I recommend three communal rituals: liturgical celebrations, plays, and leadership training. I have already stressed that liturgical celebrations need to be done frequently and well. Students should be invited to help plan liturgies, but need guidance so that the liturgies do not become performances or exercises in self-expression. The time taken to teach students how to read in public, how to perform liturgical dance (special encouragement is needed in this practice for male students), and how to sing well together, and even in harmony, is time well spent. Celebrants need, of course, to have a sense of the community and the particulars of the celebration, otherwise, their presence may seem almost accidental, or even foreign. In my experience, not enough time is devoted to preparing students to celebrate the liturgy. If the school places this much importance on the prayerful and carefully prepared celebration of the Eucharist, students will benefit greatly if outside of school their parents celebrate the Eucharist at the local parish as well. The parish and the high school can reinforce each other, but not without committed parents. Needless to say, it is more difficult for Catholic schools to be effective if parishes are not vital.

Second, high school plays frequently do more to strengthen young peoples' self confidence than any number of pep talks on self-esteem. Finding one's voice on stage, enunciating words carefully, being mindful of the appropriate phrasing of sentences, and developing a rapport with an audience have indelibly marked the lives of many high school students and affected the choices they have made concerning their careers. Plays require individuals to work together as a community and to present by a definite date a creative communal work. When the curtain comes down on the last performance, students spontaneously exchange hugs, cry easily and joyfully, and continue long afterward the friendships they developed through the play. Though not every play has such an effect, many do.

Creating opportunities for students to learn how to lead is still another way to join intellectual and moral education. Research indicates that, by comparison to public high schools, Catholic schools tend to provide more opportunities for leadership because of the many activities the school sponsors and how their teachers are involved as moderators for these co-curricular activities. I recommend that each semester a school devote a full day to helping students learn how to think about the needs of others and how to take responsibility for the direction of a group of their peers. Especially in high schools, student council activities and student clubs offer excellent opportunities for leadership training. Seniors and juniors should mentor and work with freshmen. The natural shyness of most adolescents prevents them from recognizing the impact they already have on their peers. Education in the forms of Christian leadership will help create a sense of responsibility for the larger community. Liturgical and dramatic rituals will provide students with experiences impossible to generate on their own. Indeed, religious rituals that form community can become a key dimension of the students' communal journey to maturity. For a generation of students (and their parents) who already tend to be individualistic and preoccupied with personal choices, communal rituals and practices can be a powerful counter-cultural formative agent in their lives.

My third and final recommendation has to do directly with the problem of the dissolution of the Catholic subculture. It is sociologically difficult to recreate that subculture. The conditions that fostered that subculture have changed dramatically, and Vatican II has pointed the Church in some new directions. But certain elements of the "old Church" subculture need to be recovered.

Catholic high schools should provide students with a language that helps them understand their faith. Solid religion programs help adolescents overcome the inarticulacy highlighted by the Lilly study. Years ago, I worked long and hard on a sermon for Christmas day. I preached to my own religious community of thirty-five brothers and priests that day, a daunting task to be sure. After the festive dinner that followed the Eucharist, I asked a confrere whose opinion I very much respected what he thought of the sermon. He was known for his intelligence, but also for his directness and honesty. I braced myself for his response. After a pause that seemed interminable, he said, "You treated the subject." Dismayed, I replied, "Treated the subject? Is that all you can say?" He then said, "That is a very high compliment; very few homilists treat the subject!" In a later conversation, he explained how few people know how to preach about doctrine so that it connects with the congregation. I think he was right. Too much of religion teaching is reduced to ethics, or to dry information about the Bible. Few sermons are devoted to the central doctrines of the faith: for example, creation, incarnation, Trinity, and redemption.

I have already given some additional reasons, perhaps even extenuating cultural circumstances, why youth are inarticulate about their faith. Nonetheless, it must be admitted that for most Catholics, boomers and their children alike, the God-language they use sounds more like deism than Christianity. Many Catholic youth have a difficult time talking about Jesus. They seem, as Christian Smith has written, functionally "sub-Trinitarian." Careful presentation of doctrines, and finding ways to spell out their ramifications for Christian living, would go a long way toward overcoming inarticulacy in religious matters.

Adolescents need more than clear and meaningful presentations of doctrine. They also need structured opportunities to explore and share their faith. In the pre-Vatican II Church, many high schools had sodalities that met weekly to discuss some aspect of the Christian life. Those sodalities often encouraged what today are called "service projects." Not all students were drawn to these groups. However, if student leaders, and not just the popular students, are active in such faith-sharing groups, the impact on the culture of the entire school can be significant. Teachers from many subject areas who moderate such groups can deepen what both they and their students learn. Catholic high schools would make a tragic mistake if they did not provide multiple opportunities for their students and faculty to deepen and nourish their Catholic faith.

Conclusion

I have argued that the emerging generation of millennial Catholics is likely to reflect many of the same social and religious tendencies that have been found among post-Vatican II, or Generation X, Catholics. Chief among these tendencies are to view themselves as spiritual without being religious (whether high school students use that language or not), to be involved in social networks that do not support Catholicism's communal and sacramental culture, and to lack the religious literacy they need to grow in their faith. While these tendencies are not entirely bad, they do pose many challenges, especially for faculty and administrators in Catholic schools. Having reflected on these trends and the challenges they present, I made three recommendations to strengthen the culture of Catholic schools: more effective teaching of religion, overcoming the gap between spirituality and religion, and building social networks that increase the strength of Catholicism's distinctive culture.

Having explored the history of Catholic schools in the United States, their mission and the culture in which they exist, discussed the challenges of leading such institutions, and provided descriptions of the students who attend them, a very important group now deserves some focused attention: the teachers.

8

Teachers: Calling and Response

Ambivalence About the Teaching Profession

"Teaching is not a lost art," Jacques Barzun once observed, "but the regard for it is a lost tradition."[1] In the introduction to this book, I wrote about the ambivalence that parents and pastors have about the value of Catholic schools. The ambivalence goes deeper and wider: it is located in today's culture. Teachers are not held in high regard: Teaching is "honored and disdained, praised as 'dedicated service,' lampooned as 'easy work.' ... Teaching from its inception in America has occupied a special but shadowed social standing... *Real* regard shown for those who taught has never matched *professed* regard."[2]

The United States is a nation that in many ways prizes doing over thinking. The saying, "those who can't do, teach," may be said in jest, but it still causes those who teach to wince with pain. This culture also tends to link intelligence with wealth, as in the old saying, "If you're so smart, why ain't you rich?" Gilbert Highet's 1950 classic, *The Art of Teaching*, sounds a familiar theme when he wrote, "The teacher's chief difficulty is poverty. He or she belongs to a badly paid profession."[3] As mentioned in an earlier chapter, the turnover rate among teachers in Catholic high schools is high: one quarter leave after only two years, and nearly half leave between three and five years. Even principals, who are the best paid, stay in office only five or fewer years.

Recruitment to the profession is one more problem. The most gifted students do not flock to the profession. Studies that reach back over seventy years document that the standardized test scores of education majors remain lower than

1. Quoted by Andrew Lam, "When Teaching Becomes Scutwork," in *National Catholic Reporter* (January 11, 2008), p. 31.

2. Quoting Professor of Sociology Dan Lortie, in Ernest Boyer, *High School: A Report on Secondary Education in America* (Harper & Row, New York; 1983), p. 154.

3. Gilbert Highet, *The Art of Teaching* (Vintage Books, 1989), p. 9. The 2007 NCEA document, *Dollars & $ense*, reports (p. 14) that the median salary of the Catholic high school teacher rose 50 percent from 1993 to 2006, compared to a 38 percent increase in the salary of public school teacher. Still, Catholic teachers are paid $10,500 less than their public counterparts.

most other majors.[4] It is not just a question of less gifted students entering the profession, but also that those who leave the profession for better paying work are often the better teachers whom the school can least afford to lose. Especially young male teachers who begin families worry whether they can afford to stay in a Catholic school, even though they may love teaching there.

Given all these problems, many of which stem from the culture but also some that rise from within the teaching profession itself, what can be said that will realistically provide encouragement and support for those who choose to teach in Catholic high schools today? What can be done to staunch the bleeding of the personnel who can do the best job of forming the next generation of students? In the face of all these sobering statistics and the lack of support in our culture for the teaching profession, I argue that teaching is the most important of all the professions. Most people seek the services of doctors only when they are sick and lawyers only when they are in legal trouble. Such visits are expensive. But people return to good teachers, however, all their lives, and do so without any cost. Indeed, none of the good doctors and lawyers would be doctors or lawyers were it not for the hundreds of teachers who have taught them how to be good doctors and lawyers. Teaching, I argue, is the most important of all the professions.

In this chapter, I will make the case for this argument by describing how teachers, and not just administrators, are leaders in a special way. Moreover, becoming a good teacher can be learned through developing good pedagogical habits. Teaching in a Catholic high school allows every teacher the privilege of passing on the faith, first by example, and then by word. The best teachers are perpetual students themselves, and are students not only of what they teach, but also the culture. They have developed the habit of study, which at bottom is really a spiritual practice. I conclude this chapter with several recommendations to strengthen the teaching profession, which, as I believe, is the most important of all the professions. One of the central arguments of this book is that for Catholic high schools to be successful, students need teachers, witnesses and exemplars of the Christian life, who help them understand, appreciate and criticize the cultural trends that continues to shape them.

Democratizing Leadership

In two of the earlier chapters, I focused on the theological and moral dimensions of leadership. I focused then on the roles of the principals of Catholic high

---

4. Boyer, *High School*, p. 171. Boyer's book was published in 1983. Since then, there have been a number of national efforts to recruit better students to the profession and reform teacher education. I am not aware of any recent studies, however, that show that this problem has been solved.

schools. I may have inadvertently misled the reader into thinking that only principals are called to leadership. Teachers, as I now hope to make clear, are also called to be leaders, and in a special way. None of the five Christian themes developed in Chapter 5, and none of the four cardinal virtues discussed in Chapter 6, are to be exercised only by people in official positions of leadership. What teacher does not need to be prudent, control her temper with students, be fair in grading, and persevere in good spirits to the end of the academic year? What teacher should not draw strength from knowing he is a member of a larger community, that there are many ways to be a good teacher, and that his students need to develop good habits, beginning with the habit of study? Everyone in the school needs to develop these virtues. In fact, everybody everywhere needs them.

It is commonly assumed that leaders are born, not made. This is not the case. If being a leader presupposes the possession of the virtues, then those who have developed these virtues are able to exercise leadership in whatever position they hold. The tragedy is that many people do not exercise the discipline to develop virtues. Instead, they give in to sensuality, lack perseverance and are unable to focus. Many never really think about what they are called to do with their lives. Often, they were raised in families where there was little discipline, where unlimited access to the Internet and TV replaced reading and reflection, and where they ate unhealthy food and rarely exercised.

Leadership virtues, like all virtues, are developed through practice. A virtue is not acquired through one act; it is acquired through repeated acts, just the way someone who wants to become a skilled tennis player works at it, day in and day out. From medieval philosophy, following the lead of Aristotle, we also have the important concept of a "habit." In today's culture, the word "discipline" sounds more conscious and active, while "habit" sounds more automatic, even simply rote. However, in its rich philosophical context, "habit" means a conscious repetition that makes doing what one ought to do consistently easier to do. Two very different examples should make this clear. Michael Jordan, one of my all-time favorite basketball stars, practiced the basics daily—dribbling, jump shots, foul shots, even rebounding—again, and again, and again. When I and millions of others watched him play with what appeared to be effortless and graceful ease, we may not have realized the day-to-day discipline it required for him to reach that level of athletic excellence.

Let me offer a second example. I recently had the privilege of sitting in a concert hall just a few rows away from the stage on which Itzak Perlman, perhaps the world's greatest living violinist, performed. It is hard for me to describe how taken I was, not only with his artistry with the violin, but also with simply watching his facial expressions and his bodily movements, both of which communicated total concentration and joy. The violin is one of the most difficult instruments to play well. To play as Perlman does required years of discipline and practice, beginning, I presume, with the scales. In short, he has developed the "habit" of playing the violin.

The habits needed for leadership are not to be found only among those who are formally educated. For most of history, very few people had access to schools. People were educated at home and in the fields by their parents and extended families. Mass formal education is very recent. My parents, only one of whom had a high school education, were virtuous people. My grandparents, none of whom finished grade school, raised my mother and father very well. Since both my grandfathers passed away before I was born, I knew only my grandmothers. I loved talking to them, especially my mother's mother, whom I had the privilege of knowing until I was eighteen, when she died at the age of nearly eighty. My grandparents were wise and virtuous people. None of them, as far as I know, studied the faith formally but always seemed to understand it well and live it, and they did so in ways I can only hope to do in my own life.

I do not want to be misunderstood. I do not intend to dismiss the value of study, especially the habit of study, about which I will have more to say later. But at this point I want to emphasize that leadership is best associated with virtue, the practice of which builds character. Personally, I think that the deep faith of the members of my family would have been strengthened if they had the opportunity to study it. That opportunity would have helped them develop a more articulate grasp of it. The faith would then have become, I believe, an even greater joy and support for them. Teachers who have acquired an articulate grasp of the faith have an extraordinary opportunity: they can help students develop habits that will bring them great competence in writing and speaking and thinking about the faith.

William Johnson Cory, a master at Eton, an excellent boarding school in England, described the purpose of education. Addressing a group of privileged students in 1861, Cory told them that education forms their minds and teaches them how to think critically:

> You are not engaged so much in acquiring knowledge as in making mental efforts under criticism. A certain amount of knowledge you can indeed with average faculties acquire so as to retain; nor need you regret the hours you have spent on much that is forgotten, for the shadow of lost knowledge at least protects you from many illusions. But you go to a great school, not for knowledge so much as for arts and habits; for the habit of attention, for the art of expression, for the art of assuming at a moment's notice a new intellectual posture, for the art of entering quickly into another person's thoughts, for the habit of submitting to censure

> and refutation, and for the art of indicating assent or dissent in graduated terms, for the habit of regarding minute points of accuracy, for the habit of working out what is possible in a given time, for taste, for discrimination, for mental courage and mental soberness. Above all, you go to a great school for self-knowledge.[5]

Eton was then and remains to this day an elite boarding school. Few principals of Catholic high schools in the United States would give such an address to their students, and certainly not on the first day of school. And while there is a highly cognitive (as opposed to affective) tone to Cory's remarks, he does well to underscore the importance of students acquiring habits and "arts"—that is, habitual ways of handling questions and responding to situations. To have the formation of habits as the object of education (as I will discuss later in this chapter when stressing the importance of study as a spiritual habit) is more important than memorizing answers to pass standardized examinations. And when Cory adds that one goes to school for self-knowledge, a Catholic educator will not only concur, but add as well that along with that self-knowledge, and essential to it, is the knowledge and love of God. As Augustine frequently reminded his congregation, the purpose of life is to know oneself and to know God.

When I refer to democratizing leadership, I am making the point that every Christian—indeed everyone, teachers and students—has the responsibility to develop good habits, which is how one acquires the virtues described in earlier chapters. Developing the virtues through good habits makes it possible for all Christians to grow in their call to holiness, a call that the Second Vatican Council made explicit. Just as it is not only those in official leadership roles who are called to be leaders, neither is it the case that only priests because of their ordination or religious vows are called to holiness. In the Christian life, baptism is the basis for the call to holiness. Holiness, it might then be said, has been democratized.

Catholics can learn something in this regard from the Protestants. The Catholic philosopher Charles Taylor believes that modern identity took a step forward at the time of the Reformation when through the influence of the Protestant reformers, especially Martin Luther, "ordinary life" was affirmed as the location where all people are to grow in virtue and holiness.[6] By "ordinary life," Taylor means "those aspects of human life concerned with production and

---

5. Cited in Henry Rosovski, *The University: An Owner's Manual* (Harvard University Press; 1991), p. 108.

6. See his magisterial study of the history of Western thought, *Sources of the Self: The Making of Modern Identity* (Harvard University Press, 1989), especially the chapter entitled, "God Loveth Adverbs."

reproduction, that is, with labor, the making of things needed for life, and our life as sexual beings, including marriage and the family."[7] It has taken Catholics longer to affirm that holiness should be a characteristic of "ordinary life" as well.

If all human beings are called to develop the virtues, the basis of holiness, what might be said more specifically about teachers and their special way of exercising the virtues that form the solid basis for all forms of leadership? Teachers are dedicated to passing on a tradition of learning to others. They are also called to embody what they teach, lest their personal example undercut what they say. An extraordinary question in the *Summa theologia* of St. Thomas will help make clearer the unique way teachers exercise leadership as they pass on that tradition.

Teaching: Up Front and Personal

If teaching is the greatest of all the professions, what should be said more specifically of the call to be teachers in a Catholic school? All teachers in a Catholic school bear a certain responsibility, some directly and others indirectly, for the passing on of the faith in word and deed. St. Paul lists teachers along with apostles and prophets, making it clear that handing on the faith to others is an extraordinary privilege; some commentators even interpret Paul as saying that administration and speaking in tongues are lower gifts than teaching (1 Cor. 12:28). Whatever the proper ordering of such gifts, Christians over the centuries have written about the importance of the ministry of handing on the faith. Nearly forty years ago, I heard a wonderful sermon based on an article from the *Summa* of St. Thomas Aquinas (1225–1274). It was about passing on the faith. Indirectly, it was also about one of the most important aspects of teaching: personal witness.

In the third part of the *Summa*, in the fourth article of question 42, Thomas asks whether Christ should have written down what he taught.[8] Should Christ have written any books? What an interesting question! Even more interesting, is the way Thomas goes about answering it. Each question in the *Summa* is asked and answered within a predictable structure: First Thomas gives several reasons why whatever the question he poses should be answered in the positive; then he gives his personal position; and finally, he loops back and responds, in the light of his stated position, to the questions he posed at the beginning.

Thomas begins by presenting three reasons why Christ should have written down His doctrine. First, since Christ said that his doctrine is supposed to last till

7. Taylor, *Sources*, p. 211.

8. I am indebted to Basilian priest and scripture scholar, William Irwin, C.S.B., who, in the spring of 1973, based one of his sermons on this question from the *Summa*.

the end of time, it would have been fitting for him to put it in writing so that it might more easily and more accurately be handed down to posterity. Second, since the old law was written in stone by God (as described in the Exodus story about engraving the Ten Commandments in stone), it seems then that Christ should also have put his doctrine in writing. And third, since Christ was concerned that the truth be taught, writing it down would help eliminate occasions when his teachings could be distorted by others who came after him. In fact, Thomas mentions that some people suspect that Jesus' disciples made him out to be more than he actually was. These people, the argument goes, would have believed what Christ himself wrote.

Next, Thomas sets forth his own position by explaining that there are three reasons why it was best that Christ did not write down his doctrine. First, the more excellent the teacher, the less appropriate it is that he or she should spend time writing. Why? Because excellent teachers imprint their lessons directly on the hearts of the listeners, just as did Pythagoras and Socrates who, because they were excellent teachers, were unwilling to write anything.

Second, because of the excellence of what Christ had to teach, it is impossible that it would be captured adequately in words. Here Thomas cites John (21:25): "There are still many other things that Jesus did, yet if they were written about in detail, I doubt there would be room enough in the entire world to hold the books to record them." Thomas explains this is not because of a space problem, but because those who would attempt to write these books would only skim the surface and be unable to penetrate the depth of what Jesus did and taught. At best, their words would be able only to point to that depth, never capture it.

Third, it is best that Jesus did not commit his teaching to books, because if he had, then passing on his teaching would not require the active involvement of others. Just as he personally taught his disciples, so he prefers that his disciples do the same—that is, they personally teach others, who will then personally pass on the faith as well. If, however, Christ had written books containing his teaching, all that would be necessary would be to distribute those books, and invite people to read them by themselves.

Finally, Thomas responds briefly to the three reasons that he gave at the beginning of the question that suggest Jesus should have committed his doctrine to writing. He explains that, first of all, we should remember that Christ is the head and all believers are members of his body. It is not quite true, then, to say that Jesus did not put his teaching into writing. Why? Because Jesus moved some of his disciples to write down, as much as they were capable, what he did and taught. Thomas writes: "For at his command they [the disciples], as it were, wrote whatever he wishes us to read concerning his deeds and words." Second, the old law was given in the form of sensible signs, but the new law, the doctrine of Christ, in which is contained the Spirit of life, should be written not in ink, but with the Spirit of the living God, not on tablets of stone, but in the human heart. And finally, concerning those who claimed that they would accept what Christ himself had written, Thomas wryly observes that anyone unwilling to believe what the disciples have written would have also refused to believe what Christ Himself would have written.

I have summarized at some length this question of the *Summa* because I think it contains some precious insights into the great privilege of being called to pass on the faith. I believe that the way that Thomas discusses the matter is very helpful for understanding the role of teachers in Catholic schools as a true calling. I shall limit myself to three of those insights—ones that bear directly on the need for teachers to witness to a profound mystery of faith, to be skilled pedagogues, and to recognize that since they are part of a community, they need not assume sole responsibility for handing on the tradition.

First, it is evident from what Thomas wrote that at its core a Catholic school explores the deepest mystery of love known to humankind. The fact that there is no fully adequate way to put the mystery of God's love neatly into words, and much less into tidy definitions—or even in *Summa* questions and answers—should make us all pause in awe at what we are trying to do as teachers in Catholic schools. No formula exists that says it all, nor is there some definition that will define it perfectly, or some retreat program that will make the Gospel irresistibly compelling. People who embody the faith are the best visible representations of it. They witness to the truth of what they say or, to put it colloquially, they walk the talk. A picture, the Chinese say, is worth a thousand words. In the school setting, this means that who teachers are as persons will always have a far deeper impact on their students than what they actually teach, whatever the subject. Adults remember the personalities of the teachers they had in grade and high school much longer than they remember anything they might have been taught.

Second, besides being virtuous people, teachers need also to be competent teachers. They need to be able to organize and present their material in a thoughtful and lively way. Moreover, they need to understand their students, whom I described in the last chapter. Teachers are not mere impersonal conveyors of knowledge. It is not sufficient for them to pass out books and distribute lecture notes. Nor is it enough to teach students how to construct clever arguments.[9]

---

9. The Greek philosophers, beginning with Socrates warned against teaching clever arguments to youth, since they, once they learn how to argue cleverly, too easily argue for amusement rather than for discovering the truth (on the role of "dialectical reasoning" in theology and the development of the scholastic *Questio*, see Yves Congar, *The History of Theology* [New York: Doubleday & Company, 1968], pp. 69–84.

If teachers are to educate in the full sense of the word (both to teach and to form students), then they themselves need first to be transformed in and through the very process of handing on the faith tradition on which the school has been founded, and then develop the practices of good teaching. What teachers in a Catholic school should seek is not just that their students memorize texts (though memorization too has its place), but ultimately that they be touched personally by the Word within a community attentive to words about the Word—just as St. Thomas explained in his treatment of how the disciples of Jesus both wrote about and witnessed to the truth of the Gospel.

Third, Thomas makes it clear that in the entire process of handing on the faith, believers are not alone. Not only is the Spirit of Jesus within them, but they are members of the body of Christ. The first of the theological themes developed in chapter five is the realization that no one who understands Christianity is alone; all are members of a community that has been shaping them long before they were ever aware of being shaped. Traditional theology also speaks about a person as a being in the state of grace. Given the great responsibility that teachers assume upon entering a classroom,[10] they can and should be confident that God assists those who undertake the ministry of teaching in the Christian community. There are reasons, therefore, to believe that teachers can rely on the Holy Spirit who will gently strengthen their efforts to hand on the tradition in the best ways they know.

A Passion for Teaching

Some of my own students who have gone on to become fine teachers confided to me that they never realized how demanding it is to teach well. The virtue of fortitude, or courage, helps every teacher continue on with the task, which despite periods of delight, can be a bit of a slog as well. One of the reasons some people have remained teachers all their lives is that they have felt "called" to the profession. What does it mean to speak of a calling? Parker Palmer, a Quaker and spiritual writer, offers some insightful thoughts about one's calling (though he uses the word vocation):

---

10. Highet devotes a long chapter of his book to descriptions of great teachers, some of whose students have nonetheless turned later in life to doing evil deeds. This leads Highet to stress the serious responsibility every teacher has: "Real teaching is not simply handing out packages of information. It culminates in a conversion, an actual change of the pupil's mind.... It is a serious thing to interfere with another man's life. It is hard enough to guide one's own. Yet people are easily influenced for good or evil, particularly when they are young or when their teacher speaks with authority. The effects of bad teaching, of glib and shallow advice... are quite incalculable" (*The Art of Teaching*), p. 249.

> Vocation means a calling that I hear. Before I can tell my life what I want to do with it, I must listen to my life telling me who I am. I must listen for the truths and values at the heart of my own identity, not the standards by which I must live—but the standards by which I cannot help but live if I am living my own life.

Parker's reflection clarifies an important characteristic of a calling: it is something that comes from deep within. The voice a person seeks to hear has an authority that one's own superficial preferences do not. And still, that calling is deeply imbedded within the person. It touches what is at the true center of a person. Teaching becomes a passion.

Unfortunately, Palmer's way of describing the search for one's calling makes it seem as though, through a process of detecting what is deepest inside of them, people may simply be calling themselves. It is their own inner life that tells them what to do and to be. To avoid what might turn out to be only a conversation only with themselves ("Am I comfortable with this choice of mine," or "Does this choice make me feel better about myself"), people should realize that a calling is actually issued by someone other than themselves. To speak of life as a gift suggests that someone has been "gifted" by someone else. As another Quaker once remarked, the question "Who am I?" inevitably leads to an even more important question, "Whose am I?" I would add that the answer to the second question (to whom do I belong?) sheds the clearest light on the first question (who am I?).

Frederick Buechner, a Presbyterian pastor and widely read religious writer, offers a somewhat different understanding of a calling. He emphasizes that a calling is an invitation to do something extraordinary. He understands a calling as the work that God calls a person to do. The problem is that there are many different and sometimes conflicting voices. To decide what is one's authentic calling, Buechner believes that it will be the work that a person most needs to do and that the world most needs to have done. Enjoying your work is not a sufficient sign by itself that one has found one's calling. After all, notes Buechner, one might enjoy writing deodorant commercials. On the other hand, even if a person's work is important—he gives the example of being a doctor for a leper colony—but the person doing that work is bored or depressed by it, then that person has yet to find her calling. To find one's true calling, Buechner concludes that "neither the hair shirt nor the soft berth will do: *The place God calls you to is the place where your deep gladness and the world's deep hunger meet.*"[11]

---

11. See Frederick Buechner, *Wishful Thinking: A Theological ABC* (New York: Harper and Row, 1984), p. 95.

Like Palmer, Buechner also makes a very important but somewhat different point: accepting your call from God doesn't mean being glum and sad. There is real joy to be found in discovering and accepting one's vocation. Sometimes, when situations are very bad and impossible to change, well-meaning people might say, "You'll just have to accept it; it is God's will." Such exhortations too easily lead people who are suffering and trapped to hate "God's will," especially since God's will has been identified with everything that persons wouldn't choose but are now told they have to accept. Rather, as Buechner suggests, God's will, or one's vocation, should be a source of deep joy, and therefore not be resisted, feared or imposed.

Buechner also says that to have a true calling people need to be doing significant work, work that the world most needs to have done. This is a very challenging statement. It is also problematic. It is challenging for the simple reason that there are many things the world badly needs to have done, and many of them are very hard to do. Some people seem to have the requisite talents and gifts to undertake some of these very challenging tasks. Buechner expects people with a real calling to give themselves to extraordinary tasks. Today, more and more individuals have choices—the possibility of taking up one of several possible tasks. Unfortunately, some people choose to dedicate themselves, often simply for reasons of financial gain, to work people really don't need—for example, the lucrative pornography industry or, as Buechner suggests, creating deodorant commercials.

In earlier decades, however, not everyone enjoyed the luxury of many possible choices, as do people with a good education in a good economy. My father, a wonderful man all his life and devout Methodist most of his life, had only an eighth-grade education. As a recently married man with a newborn baby, he and my mother left the family farm in central Ohio in 1936, right in the midst of the Great Depression, to take a job at a Cook Coffee roasting plant and warehouse in the Cleveland flats. He worked there for twenty-six years, and for the last fifteen of those years served as the manager of the place, supervising over thirty workers. In defense of my father's choice, some might playfully suggest that he indeed devoted his life to meeting one of the world's deepest hunger—coffee. But in the larger scheme of things, my father, who did his work devotedly and lovingly as did my mother (in order to support my four siblings and me), fulfilled his calling. I believe that any good work embraced with faith and generosity, gives glory to God and becomes a genuine means of holiness.

Vocation meant one thing decades ago for a generation of Americans who were emerging from the working classes in the years after the Depression and the Second World War. Working in a coffee plant, my father made it possible for me eventually to obtain a doctorate, my three sisters to become nurses, and my brother a commercial pilot. Teachers today can think of where their students are in this story of assimilation and upward migration. Some will be working in immigrant communities where, if their students become plant managers, it will be a great triumph. Those working with the privileged children of the Catholic middle and upper classes, precisely the ones who have benefitted from the early generation's hard work, might need to prod the privileged to think about the world's deep needs, rather than their own shallow ones.[12]

Some forty-five years after my father left the farm and moved to Cleveland, John Paul II stressed the dignity of ordinary work in his encyclical, *Laborem exercens* (1981). He wrote that work had three purposes: (1) to make a living (a living wage is understood to be enough to support the whole family, including one's spouse); (2) to find self-expression and personal fulfillment; and (3) to make a contribution to society. These three purposes are not pitted against each other. When the pope asked himself how work acquired its dignity, he did not point to it meeting the world's deepest need. Instead, he distinguished between the subjective and objective dimensions of work. The objective dimensions of work are the various fields of economic activity, such as agriculture, industry, and government. The subjective dimension of work, however, is independent of whatever one is doing, assuming that a person is not robbing banks. Rather, the subjective dimension emphasizes *who* is doing the work. The person doing the work is created in God's image and likeness and is called to realize oneself, and to be given the opportunity to contribute. What a person does, the objective dimension, is not as important as the subjective dimension. In promoting the dignity of the worker regardless of the work, the pope subverts the idea of classes of people, though teachers do well to take into consideration where their students are in the class system of the United States. All persons have dignity, whatever their work. At the same time, teachers need to help students think about seeking, to the extent that they have a choice, meaningful work that contributes to human flourishing. My dad, who I think knew that his work had dignity, would have liked to have read John Paul II's encyclical, even if it had been written by a Catholic—and a pope to boot.[13]

I do not speak of teaching as a career, which makes it sound as though teaching is a "professional" role one assumes as only a part, albeit an important part, of one's life. I am thinking rather of those people who are called to be teachers. This distinction helps us understand the difference between saying "I teach" and "I am a teacher." The former is an activity; the latter is a statement of who a person is. When I speak of teaching as a calling, I mean that a person who has a calling to

12. I am indebted to Professor Una Cadegan for making this point clear to me.

13. See Dennis Doyle, *The Church Emerging from Vatican II* (Twenty-Third Publications, 2nd ed., 2004), pp. 131–135.

be a teacher *must* teach. While I am talking about teachers in classrooms, I realize that my father, in some important ways, taught the workers he supervised, just as my mother, along with my father, initiated me and my siblings in practices that we repeated, not knowing then that my parents were helping us form habits, the foundation of virtuous living.

Confronting Moralistic Therapeutic Deism

Earlier in this chapter, I discussed that wonderful text from Thomas Aquinas in order to make it clear that in passing on the faith, the witness of believers is more important than handing out books. The discussion on teaching as a vocation stressed the importance of a calling to the profession, which in turn helps teachers to stay in the classroom when they might be tempted to leave the profession altogether.

In Chapter 3, I presented a five-point description of the dominant culture in the United States. I started with its over-emphasis on the individual and then the continuing tug-of-war between the secularists and religionists. Then I focused on three cultural powers that I believe have a direct impact on young people: the media, the emphasis on the therapeutic, and the "spiritual but not religious" movement. In the previous chapter on students, I devoted considerable space to a discussion of the findings of a significant study of the religious lives of teenagers conducted by Christian Smith, a sociologist at the University of Notre Dame. Though I raised some questions about the appropriateness of the way he phrased his survey questions for Catholics, I think his study gives us the most profound and far-reaching insight into where most young people are today when it comes to their faith. Smith describes teenagers' overall view of God, their "*de facto* creed," as moralistic therapeutic deism (MTD), which he believes is displacing the traditional faiths of Protestants, Catholics and Jews. He describes the five characteristics of MTD as follows:

1. A God exists who created and orders the world and watches over human life on earth.
2. God wants people to be good, nice, and fair to each other, as taught in the Bible and by most world religions.
3. The central goal of life is to be happy and to feel good about oneself.
4. God does not need to be particularly involved in one's life except when God is needed to resolve a problem.
5. Good people go to heaven when the die.[14]

---

14. *Soul Searching*, pp. 162–163. Smith is aware that a deistic God never intervenes in human affairs, but sticks with the word "deism" since, for most teens, God is inactive except, as he notes, when called upon to fix a problem.

What worries Smith, and should worry teachers and parents as well, is that most teenagers believe that nothing influences them to think the way teenagers do; teenagers believe that they are autonomous and independent individuals. In other words, they totally discount the power of the culture to shape their attitudes and desires. Even though most teachers, especially young ones, have been shaped by the same culture that has shaped their students, they still need to do their best to understand, appreciate and criticize that culture, and take note of the profound influence it has on them and their students.

Part of cultural criticism involves the continuous and difficult task of distinguishing between ideas and practices that flow from a committed Christian life and those that oppose it, often not by a frontal and obvious attack, but rather by subtly undermining it in the way that much of TV and the film industry does by the products they produce for mass consumption. If teachers do not take seriously a critical evaluation of the culture, they may, when they encourage their students to embrace the "freedom of the children of God," actually end up promoting irresponsibility. Or, to offer another example, when teachers set out to build communities of faith, they may find that, given the therapeutic propensity of our culture, they actually end up fostering groups characterized more by narcissism than by agape, more by their desire to feel affirmed and accepted than by their willingness to sacrifice for others. Students who have received years of religious education cannot be assumed to have internalized the Gospel, especially if that education has not been supported by the family and made habitual through repeated religious practices.

In the light of Catholic teachers' calling to pass on the tradition, it becomes evident why they sometimes must confront and criticize their students, given the culture they unconsciously absorb. The Gospels provide many examples of Jesus who frequently confronted not only his disciples, but also the religious leaders of his day. In fact, his harshest words were directed to religious leaders. He also found it necessary on numerous occasions to confront his hand-picked disciples who kept looking for a political messiah, and who abandoned him in his hour of greatest need. If Jesus confronted his disciples, why should teachers presume that they would not need also to confront their students? Jesus loved his disciples but did not hesitate to confront them. In fact, he confronted them precisely because he loved them. Loving students does not mean coddling them, especially if they have itching ears and closed minds. As one high school graduate said some years after his graduation, "I wish more of my religion teachers had been willing to 'interfere' with my life."

One important way that teachers should confront their students is to teach. To say this may seem obvious, but some educational experts today discourage teaching.[15] The author of Deuteronomy told the Israelites, "Take to heart these words which I enjoin on you today. Drill them into your children. Speak of them at home and abroad, whether you are busy or at rest. Bind them at your wrist as a sign and let them be as a pendant on your forehead. Write them on the doorposts of your houses and on your gates" (6: 4–9). The author of Deuteronomy recommends the use of various pedagogies to pass on the tradition: repetition, visual aids, material objects that restate the lesson, and parental example and support. It is not enough to talk about the tradition—it needs to be "drilled" into the children to become ubiquitous and habitual.

Nor is it enough for teachers to encourage students to express themselves. The proponents of "values clarification" claimed, as I explained in an earlier chapter, that helping students clarify their existing values was the key to moral formation. While teachers can help students recognize what their values are, they should help them do something even more important than that: they should help their students sort out which of their values are ones they should retain and which they should change, especially in the light of the Christian faith. "Drilling" the tradition into students doesn't mean impersonal and robotic repetition; it should mean a persistent and thoughtful effort on the part of teachers to help students understand and live a great religious tradition. In many ways that tradition, taught well, confronts and critiques the dominant culture and, in that endless process, shapes the minds and hearts of both teachers and students. To give just one example, the culture bombards students with messages about what it means to be successful and attractive. Teachers need to explain in compelling ways that success for the Christian is laying down one's life for others, and attractiveness is measured primarily in terms of one's ability to love.

Teachers as "drillers" is, admittedly, not the most student-friendly and caring approach now featured in so much of the literature used to promote Catholic education. A more positive way to describe this same effort is for the teacher to concentrate on filling the students' imaginations with engaging stories about virtuous people or honest stories about evil people, and flooding their imaginations with images, visual and literary, that lift them above the culture they typically inhabit—a culture of individualism, consumerism and entertainment.

In the early 1940s, C. S. Lewis gave three lectures on education, especially the teaching of English. He was provoked by the authors of a textbook who decided that the best protection against propaganda was to teach students that their

15. In the age of the computer, some educational experts have stated that there must now be a "paradigm shift," from the "sage on the stage" to the "coach on the sidelines." If in some complete way that shift were to be made, it would spell the end of "teaching."

emotions were inappropriate in the evaluation of works of literature. Since youth were prone to "sentimentality," the authors stressed that purely rational analysis was the only reliable basis for unbiased interpretation of literature, since emotion can easily lead a person astray. Lewis saw things differently. Instead of fearing emotional distortions of reality, he recommended that since emotions are an essential part of what it means to be a human being, that they be educated in such a way that students would develop not false but appropriate sentiments.

> For every one pupil who needs to be guarded from a weak excess of sensibility there are three who need to be awakened from the slumber of cold vulgarity. The task of the modern educator is not to cut down jungles but to irrigate deserts. The right defense against false sentiments is to inculcate just sentiments.[16]

Today's media deserts include action films in which "good guys" (usually a single good guy, the authentic American individualist) brutally slaughters with amazing ease dozens of bad guys, or video games in which the player himself (not as often herself) gets to execute bad guys with the push of a button. The pornography industry addicts many young people who can easily access visual images in the privacy of their own rooms where, after watching people who have allowed themselves to be objectified in "cold vulgarity," they begin to objectify others, including themselves, as objects only of sexual pleasure. As Lewis says, the best way to help adolescents defend themselves against such debasement of their emotional life is to expose them to good literature and genuine beauty, helping them get to the point where their education protects them from becoming easy prey to vendors of trashy novels and vulgar films.

Christian Smith uses the word "therapeutic" to describe teenagers' view of God. God is there to make them feel better about themselves. Therapeutic personalities are self-absorbed; their religion is all about them, not about God. I've already suggested earlier in this book that educating students for leadership as service to others is one effective way to break young people out of their self-enveloping bubble. Another, also mentioned earlier, is to orient them to the recognition of God and their need to praise God—through prayer and especially liturgies that are well done, that is, are prayerful and aesthetically rich. Finally, another practice which can help students think beyond themselves is silence, either for study or for prayer. Before television, before radio, and before the movies, there were other forms of entertainment—vaudeville, minstrels, bear-baiting and dog-

---

16. C. S. Lewis, *The Abolition of Man* (Geoffrey Bles; London, 1943), p. 14.

fighting, to say nothing of cock-fighting and eye-gouging. Neither TV nor bear-baiting encouraged silent reflection and reading. Today, a media fast that allows persons to be alone can paradoxically lead them out of themselves into more substantial relationships with others. Periods of silence in the classroom, during which teachers ask students to think about something and jot down their thoughts, are all too rare.

Already sensing the destructive consequences of excessive exposure to modern media, C. S. Lewis wrote that the modern age is starved for solitude and friendship.[17] Young people are preoccupied about relationships, about having a best friend and being included in the group, but they seldom seek solitude, or see in the practice of silence a way to deepen their relationships. But solitude and friendship are intimately related. Someone who must always be on the go, stimulated and entertained by media, rarely slows down enough just to be with others. How can a friendship deepen without two people spending time together? And how can there be any depth at all if there is no sense of one's own self, brought about both by being comfortable with being alone, and by being with others who are honest and tell you what they think? And how can one study if one can't be alone? Of course, it is possible to learn much in groups. But just as praying in a group does not replace personal prayer, neither can discussions with others be a substitute for silence, individual reflection and study.

The Habit of Study: A Spiritual Discipline

If teachers are to motivate their students to study, they need themselves to develop the habit of study. It is difficult to pass on to another person what one does not embody in the first place. Studying as way to enhance one's living is not widely understood. Students seldom grasp the relationship; that is not surprising. That many teachers do not understand that relationship is part of the problem. Given the tempo and pressure of the typical academic year, many teachers scramble, especially if they have several preparations, just to have materials ready for the next day's classes. Unless continuing education is a requirement for continuing certification in one's profession, many teachers never really study again for their own enrichment. Rather, they forage for digestible materials that they can use in the classroom. In general, people still read newspapers, magazines and stuff on the Internet. But serious study usually ends after their last academic examination.

After all, Americans are not known for their intellectual bent; rather, they are a pragmatic people busy with many things, more like Marthas than Marys. For

17. Ibid., essay entitled, "Membership," p. 31.

every intellectual, there are thousands of generous but over-extended activists. This is true of teachers as well. High school teachers often have to spend their summers in other employment so that they can supplement their school salaries just to make ends meet. Some dioceses have found it necessary to *require* teachers to update themselves on a regular basis or lose their accreditation.

Religious Jews seem to have joined study and devotion more intimately than Christians. To be a Christian, some seem to think, requires that believers just accept and live what Christ taught—it is a matter of being and doing, not also studying. Christ never said, "Your learning has saved you" or "He who has studied much will be forgiven much." What degrees did he ever earn? Did he ever publish a book, an article, or even a short review? Didn't Aquinas state that Jesus preferred to transform people rather than write books? So, just how necessary is it for a Christian, a follower of Jesus, to study?

To get beyond activism, it may help to think of study as a spiritual discipline. One of the most striking essays I have ever read on study as a spiritual discipline was written by the French intellectual Simone Weil, who died in 1943 in England at the age of thirty-four, probably of starvation—she did not wish to be enjoying better meals and living conditions than her fellow Jews incarcerated in the Nazi death camps across the English channel. She was an extraordinary intellectual, a gifted mathematician and philosopher who was attracted to Christianity and drawn to the Jesus of the Gospels, but could not bring herself to be baptized.[18] A year before she died, she wrote an essay entitled "Reflections on the Right Use of School Studies with a View to the Love of God." She explains that nothing contributes more to a deep prayer life than the ability to study and to study hard. She lays out her argument in the first few sentences of her essay:

> The key to a Christian conception of studies is the realization that prayer consists of attention. It is the orientation of all the attention of which the soul is capable towards God. The quality of the attention counts for much in the quality of prayer. Warmth of heart cannot make up for it.[19]

Using mathematics as an example, Weil explains that it does not matter whether a person finds the answer to a problem or achieves an understanding of a proof.

---

18. Along with Blaise Pascal (1623–1662), the brilliant French mathematician, scientist and religious thinker and George Bernanos (1888–1948), the French novelist, dramatist and essayist, Pope Paul VI included Simone Weil among the three most important influences on his thinking.

19. Simone Weil, *Waiting on God: The Essence of Her Thinking* (Fontana Books, sixth edition, 1971), p. 66.

The most important thing is that they make a genuine effort to do so. "The useless efforts made by the Cure d'Ars for long and painful years," she continues, "in his attempt to learn Latin bore fruit in the marvelous discernment which enabled him to see the very souls of his penitents behind their words and even their silences."[20] In the view of Weil, students should not seek good grades or try to win honors; rather, she says, they should study equally diligently all their different subjects regardless of their natural talent for them. If students fail to do a problem right or make a mistake in grammar, they should seek to understand why they failed and proceed to correct themselves. The type of attention she recommends "consists of suspending our thought, leaving it detached, empty and ready to be penetrated by the object."[21] She concludes her essay by drawing on the New Testament parable of the pearl of great price: "Academic work is one of those fields which contain a pearl so precious that it is worthwhile to sell all our possessions, keeping nothing for ourselves, in order to be able to acquire it."[22]

Though Weil's essay is aimed at students in whom she wishes to create a love of the discipline of study, it can easily be applied to teachers as well. Teachers might be tempted to assign to themselves in some exclusive sense the role of teaching and to their students that of learning. Yet, teachers need to become disciplined students of their own subject, which they need to know well enough to be able to teach it effectively. Obviously, good teachers also *listen* carefully to their students. Students need to know that their teachers care about what they, as students, think and do. Good teachers learn from their students—not necessarily about the subject they teach, but often about how best to teach that subject.

The habit of study that I am recommending includes, but is not limited to, reading books. It also draws upon the power to read and understand, as Jesus did, the "human heart" (John 2:25). Buddhists speak of "mindfulness," being aware of one's surroundings, of oneself, of what is being said and how one feels about what is being said. Egotistical people rarely understand what others are feeling. Until their first heart attack, most professionally driven people rarely slow down enough to examine the career path they have been traveling. If teachers develop the habit of study, they develop at the same time the attentiveness of Simone Weil wrote about, and for that matter, a capacity for prayer as well.

In Chapter 4 I cited St. Bernard of Clairvaux (1090–1153) who stressed that above all, great teachers love their subjects (both their academic subject and their subjects, that is, their students). St. Bernard thought that learning helped people

---

20. Weil, pp. 68–69.

21. Weil, p. 72.

22. Weil, p. 76.

love more than if they did not learn. The road from learning to loving is no more automatic than the road from knowledge to virtue, as there are too many learned people who don't love and too many knowledgeable people who are not virtuous. Teachers can pervert their calling in many ways. Some may abuse study by using what they learn to dominate their students. Less reprehensible are those who teach only to earn a living—a modest one at that. Still others might study so that with their knowledge they might impress others.[23] Like their colleagues in other professions, teachers who study for good reasons open themselves not only to knowledge, but also to strengthening gradually their skills for loving and praying.

Support for the Teaching Profession

At the beginning of this chapter, I set myself a difficult challenge: to make a compelling case for being a teacher in a Catholic high school. I reviewed the ambivalence that many people in our culture have about the teaching profession, whether at public or private and religiously affiliated schools. I mentioned the involuntary almost universal reluctant acceptance of the relative poverty that nearly all teachers are forced to accept and how many of them, especially the most talented, remain in the profession only briefly. And finally I mentioned the problem of recruitment, both recruiting talented students to the field of education, and the time that should be spent on recruiting teachers to Catholic schools.

What will help teachers stay in their profession, embrace the mission of Catholic education and dedicate themselves to study and continual professional development? Thomas Aquinas suggested that the essence of teaching is personal witness. I've argued that teachers need to experience their lives and work as a calling, to develop a passion for teaching, be willing to confront the culture, and be students themselves, both of their subject and their students. It is very unlikely that most teachers will be able to do and be these things without more support than they have been receiving. Four practical initiatives will provide at least some of that support.

First, the process of *recruiting* people to the profession of teaching needs improvement. Most students go to college to be better prepared to land a good-paying job. Teaching, as I have already noted, doesn't pay well. How to go against the larger culture is not at all easy. One recent innovative effort recruits students,

23. C. S. Lewis wrote disapprovingly of those teachers who delight more in their knowing than in the thing known, not in the exercise of their talents, but in the fact that those talents are theirs. See "Learning in War-Time," in *The Weight of Glory* (Eerdmans, 1974), p. 50.

most of whom are not education majors, to teach in the underserved schools in America, either inner city or rural schools. These students are not required to have degrees in education or teaching certificates. Some exceptionally talented students join these programs. It is also the case that some high school students are so inspired by some of their own teachers that they decide to enter that profession. Not a few Catholic high schools number on their faculty former graduates of their school. Good teachers are the best recruiters to the profession. That encouragement should not be left implicit; it needs to be made explicit, so that the best and most well-disposed students might begin to think about becoming teachers. Years ago, Catholic high schools used to sponsor co-curricular clubs for future teachers. They should continue to do that.

Catholic high schools need to be more attentive than before to how they go about recruiting faculty. I noted in Chapter 1 that pastors (and here I am speaking mainly of pastors of parishes with Catholic grade schools), ranked the recruitment and retention of faculty nearly last, but enrollment and budget as their major concern. This seems to me short-sighted. Surely an urgent issue, enrollment is not the most important issue: rather, it is the quality of the education being offered. I also mentioned the incredible energy and intensity that college basketball coaches devote to the recruitment of their athletes. Coaches know their jobs depend on recruiting excellent athletes. In my many years teaching and administering at the university level, I saw over and over again that the best departments actively recruited faculty; they never simply posted a job description in appropriate journals and waited to see who applied. The best departments were constantly recruiting, even when they had no position to fill. Recruiting the best faculty is an active and around the clock activity. The quality of the faculty exercises profound influence on the mission and atmosphere of the entire school.

My second recommendation has to do with the *ongoing formation* of the faculty. In an earlier chapter, I suggested that religious orders should set aside some of their money to create endowments that support the preparation and formation of lay leaders of Catholic high schools. I have already made the point in this chapter that leadership in the school is not limited to the administration. In fact, it is the faculty who are on the front lines, who have direct contact with the students. Those of us who decided to dedicate our lives to the vocation of teaching were usually not inspired by the principals of our schools, persons with whom we had little contact, but rather by the dedicated teachers we met daily in classrooms and in co-curricular activities. Teachers need professional support. Endowments, therefore, should be created to support all faculty, especially lay persons, so that they might take mini-sabbaticals, attend extended professional training programs, opportunities for paid study leaves, do graduate studies and, in general, be enabled to develop a habit of study that I have stressed in this chapter.

A third suggestion has to do with increasing the salaries of teachers. Teachers in Catholic high schools should be paid at least the equivalent of what their counterparts in the public schools are paid. The 2007 NCEA study, *Dollars & $ense,* as I noted earlier, reports that over a thirteen year period the average salary of Catholic high school teachers rose more than that of their public school counterpart (a 50 percent increase compared to 38 percent). Even if the faculty in Catholic schools were to catch up to the public school salaries, they will simply have achieved the same level of low compensation that the culture is content to assign to the profession. In the public system, unions have helped to increase the salary of teachers. Yet, I remain ambivalent about teachers' unions, for the simple reason that many of them have so focused on the needs of teachers that the needs of the students are largely eclipsed. Fifty years ago most of the salaries were paid to religious brothers and sisters, who then had to cover only room and board. Since then, the increased amount needed to meet the needs of lay teachers has been huge. The difficulty of achieving equity with the public schools should not be underestimated. On the other hand, equity must remain the goal.

My fourth suggestion builds on one of the strengths of Catholic high schools—the sense of community based on its unique mission. Teachers, especially those who are just beginning in the profession, can feel quite lonely, even intimidated, as they enter the classroom for the first time. The find themselves isolated there, equipped with only a textbook and a list of students, and are expected from that point on to control and inspire their students, some of whom may not be at all interested in either being controlled or inspired. It is precisely at this point that structures are needed that allow teachers to learn from each other. Enthusiasm and skills for teaching increase when teachers take the time to talk to each other about what they are doing—about what seems to be working and not working in their classes. Collaborating on preparations, presentations, and special projects such as retreats, strengthens the commitment to the profession. The English word *community* comes from the Latin verb *munire*, which means "to build" and the prefix *cum* means "with." Thus community comes from building something with others. It takes time, effort, and a common purpose to guide a common effort. The real key to building a sense of community among teachers is to involve them in working at becoming better teachers together. School administrators, therefore, need to find ways to structure such periods of sharing and support among their teachers.

These four recommendations, if implemented, would go a long way to strengthening faculty at Catholic high schools. Setting up endowments is not that difficult, materially speaking. As I explained earlier, most members of orders who worked as teachers and administrators in these schools are not recruiting new members now, and therefore are property rich and personnel poor. The annual bishops' collection taken up to support retired religious has helped the poorer orders, especially some women's orders, to meet the health costs of their retirees. But many orders are in decent financial shape. Once they are able to cover their retirement expenses, it would be possible for them to set up substantial endowments for the support and formation of teachers in Catholic schools. The only thing that would prevent this from happening is ambivalence about the value of Catholic schools—an ambivalence in those very orders which had in earlier decades served in and sustained them.

Besides my four recommendations, Ernest Boyer, writing on behalf of faculty in public schools, adds a few more that would improve the immediate working condition of teachers. He recommends that teachers be assigned no more than four formal class meetings a day, be allotted at least an hour of class preparation time every day, be rescued from monitoring hallways and lunchrooms, and be supported in creating a more intellectually stimulating climate in the school.[24] Noting that teachers suffer from a lack of recognition, he recommends that they be given various awards, including one that would be quite easy to implement. Boyer describes how Fr. Timothy Healy, S.J., the then president of Georgetown University, would convene fifteen Georgetown students who had come from the same high school and ask them who their best high school teacher was. At each Georgetown graduation, Healy would then mention the name of the teacher at the spring commencement exercises: "I would like to introduce a candidate for an honorary degree. She teaches at _____ high school and is one of the great educators who has made Georgetown possible." Why could not Catholic colleges and universities do the same? Boyer also recommends increasing the salaries of teachers and reforming teacher education programs. He concludes his chapter on teachers with the succinct statement, "We cannot expect students to shine unless we brighten the prospects for teachers."[25]

While I think all of Boyer's suggestions could be implemented in Catholic high schools (with the possible exception of only four classes a day), I wish to comment on two of his suggestions. Giving awards to excellent teachers often meets resistance from those who fear the creation of divisions and jealousy among faculty. The practice of merit pay meets with similar objections. On the other hand, the dangers of treating every teacher the same, regardless of his or her

24. Boyer, *High School*, p. 159–160. To strengthen the intellectual climate, Boyer recommends the practice of rewarding good ideas, establishing a "Teacher Excellence Fund" that supports ideas for the improvement of teaching and ongoing education of the faculty.

25. Boyer, p. 185.

performance, are greater than recognizing and rewarding excellence. If the administrators of the school can offer the support and encouragement to all their teachers will help them to become better, administrators will make it more difficult for faculty who might object to awards, be they financial and reputational. Even though the financial award is likely to be small, it would be valued by dedicated teachers.

Conclusion

Earlier in this chapter, Simone Weil directly linked the development of the powers of attention through dedicated study and the practice of prayer. Both study and prayer strengthen a person's ability to be attentive. Although she did not refer to Jean LeClerq's classic, *The Love of Learning and the Desire for God: A Study of Monastic Culture*,[26] her thinking flows in the same great river as the great monastic tradition that linked the library and the chapel. Leaders in Catholic high schools—administrators and teachers alike—are able to draw explicitly on this rich and explicitly theological confluence of study and prayer, on attentiveness and the ability to love. One does not have to be a psychologist to know that anyone's ability to love is deeply influenced by their own experience of love. To put it in a nutshell: people love with the love with which they have been loved. Or to paraphrase the title of LeClerq's book, learning about love as a Christian leads to a deeper understanding of how God loves everyone first. Despite initial appearances, God takes the lead and only gradually, through attentiveness, do people of faith come to recognize that love and respond with gratitude.

Elie Wiesel, a survivor of the Nazi death camps and Nobel Prize winner for literature, described the central passion of his life as an educator and writer:

> It is the realization that what I receive I must pass on to others. The knowledge that I have acquired must not remain imprisoned in my brain. I owe it to many men and women to do something with it. I feel the need to pay back what was given to me. Call it gratitude.[27]

I have argued in this chapter that despite all its problems—its lack of status and financial rewards—teaching is the greatest of the professions. I wish to end this chapter on a personal note. As a junior in college, I had the opportunity to play the role of Thomas More as developed by playwright Robert Bolt in *A Man for*

26. Fordham University Press, New York, 1982.

27. *Parade Magazine*, May 24, 1992, p. 4.

All Seasons. In that play, More has many great lines, including one about teaching that has stayed with me all my life. Richard Rich, an ambitious and unscrupulous young man seeking political power, visits More at his home and complains about his lack of success in securing a position of prominence and power. More, fully aware of the treacheries and reversals of political life, suggests that he consider being a teacher: "Why not be a teacher? You'd be a fine teacher. Perhaps even a great one." Seeing little fame and power in such an occupation, Rich replies, "And if I was, who would know it?" "Your pupils," answers More, "your friends, God. Not a bad public, that...."[28] Indeed! And not only one's students and one's friends, but the students' parents, as well as those students who become teachers, perhaps even great teachers.

---

28. Robert Bolt, *A Man for All Seasons* (Vintage Books, 1960), p. 6.

9

New Models and More Money

Introduction

In this chapter I discuss two threats to the survival of Catholic high schools: the charter school movement and the ever-rising cost of going to a Catholic school. I also examine some new models for Catholic education, especially the Cristo Rey model, and new ways to raise money.

In recent years, observers of Catholic education have said that charter schools create the greatest threat to the survival of Catholic education. Why? Because charter schools allow for greater local leadership, more demanding academic curricula, tax-dollar support, and even, in some cases, focus on character education. While this combination of improvements over typical public schools makes charter schools more attractive to many parents, these same improvements can and should move Catholic education to focus more clearly what they alone can do: offer an education that is rooted in the Gospel of Jesus Christ, form students both religiously and morally, and draw upon an international and two-thousand-year-old tradition of wisdom about life.

Early on in this book, I stated that "money follows vision." That vision comes from clear-headed and committed leadership for Catholic schools. Vision and commitment are more important than money. In fact, a lot of money (a reality among many suburban and affluent Catholics) can corrupt a Gospel vision. Placing vision above money, however, should not tempt leaders of Catholic schools to be naive about how hard they must work to contain costs and raise money. Rather, their challenge remains learning how to access greater financial resources than are presently tapped and, at the same time, to reduce costs where possible without affecting the quality of education they offer or reducing the salaries they pay.

Charter Schools

A new development in public education has been the creation of charter schools, which compete against public schools, especially those which are failing. They also pose a threat to Catholic schools. As mentioned in an earlier chapter, Fr. Ron Nuzzi, the director of the Alliance for Catholic Education leadership program at the University of Notre Dame, thinks that the charter movement poses the greatest current threat to Catholic schools in the inner city.[1] As one of the most important efforts to reform public schools, charter schools are run by private management but supported by tax dollars. Charter schools are free of the bureaucracy of most public schools and hire the teachers they want (the leaders of charter schools typically oppose teacher unions). They also set higher academic standards than the public schools, build better data systems, and require students to wear uniforms. It is not surprising that many parents living in urban areas find them an attractive alternative to the local public school. Over the past ten years, the number of charter schools has rapidly increased.

President Obama's Secretary of Education currently wields a four billion dollar fund to pressure states to lift the limits they have placed on the number of charter schools they allow. At the time of this writing, Tennessee had recently upped the number of its charter schools from 50 to 90, Illinois doubled its number to 120, Louisiana passed a law that simply eliminated any cap on the number of its charter schools, and the governor of Massachusetts had proposed legislation that more than tripled the number of slots for students in charter schools.[2] And against the strong opposition of the teachers union in the large LA public school system, its board of directors recently voted to allow 20 percent of its schools to become charter schools.

Critics of the charter school movement argue that charter schools take away from the public schools, especially struggling inner-city schools, the most important resources that contribute to the improvement of those very schools: the best students, the most effective teachers, and taxpayer dollars. Those who defend them believe that greater local control and more rigorous accountability will, in the long run, show the way to reform public schools.[3]

However, some charter schools perform better than others, evoking from the current Secretary of Education, Arne Duncan, the remark: "I am not a fan of charters. I'm a fan of *good* charters. Bad charters are part of the problem."[4] The actual academic performance of charter schools has been mixed, sometimes better, sometimes worse,

---

1. Peter Meyer, "Can Catholic Schools be Saved?" in *Education Next*, Spring 2007, p. 17. Meyer cites a RAND Corporation study that determined that private schools in Michigan were losing as many students as public schools to charter schools.

2. Anne Marie Chaker, "Expanding the Charter Option," *The Wall Street Journal*, August 13, 2009, D1–D2.

3. Bruce Fuller, "A Gamble: Can Charter Schools Fix Public Education?" *Commonweal* (March 26, 2010), p. 16.

4. Fuller, p. 15.

and sometimes about the same as public schools.[5] In any event, the leaders of inner-city Catholic high schools feel threatened by the proliferation of charter schools: a good inner-city public school at little to no cost will, they fear, draw parents away from sending their children to the more expensive Catholic school.

New Catholic Initiatives

In response to these challenges, Catholic educators dedicated to the survival of Catholic schools have pursued two important initiatives to support their schools. The first is vouchers, government support given to families, especially in the inner city, where many school districts have failing schools. The plea for government support for private Catholic schools is hardly new. In 1841 Archbishop John Hughes (1797–1864) gave a talk at Carroll Hall in New York City in which he denounced "the injustice of employing the funds raised by taxing all for the benefit of a portion of Society, and to the exclusion of one entire class." The beneficiaries were Protestants whose common schools, as we have seen, taught generic Protestantism. Many Catholic parents felt in conscience that their children needed a Catholic education—but resented having to pay twice: first to pay for what in essence was a Protestant education for Protestant children, and then also to pay for their own Catholic schools. Hughes said he would be satisfied if "the tax so imposed that each denomination might receive the benefits of its own quota," but, unfortunately, that was not to be. In an ironic twist, it was Hughes' objection as well as that of other Catholic leaders to the Protestantism of the public schools that contributed to the eventual secularization of public education.[6]

One hundred and forty years later, the Harvard educated Catholic Senator from New York, Daniel Patrick Moynihan (1927–2003), wrote that due to the

---

5. Fuller cites the research of Stanford economist Margaret Raymond who documents the uneven results of charter schools in different states, concluding that "in the aggregate there are no discernible achievement differences" (p. 17). Diane Ravitch, a historian of education at New York University, thinks that the educational policy of the Obama administration simply prolongs that of the Bush administration: "This whole fund [the 4 billion dollar plus fund] is being used to lure or bribe or implore or compel states and school districts to do things that we don't actually know are going to make things better" (*Time*, September 14, 2009, p. 29). She has recently published a book-length criticism of both the Bush and Obama initiatives, as well as challenged the assumptions that shape the education funding priorities of the Bill & Melinda Gates Foundation, which recently contributed $60 million to the LA charter movement. Diane Ravitch, *The Death and Life of the Great American School System* (Basic Books, 2010). Her basic argument is that teachers need to be treated as professionals, instead of being constantly forced to teach to a test.

6. See the *Complete Works of the Most Rev. John Hughes, D.D., Archbishop of New York, Comprising his Sermons, Letters, Lectures, Speeches, etc.,* Compiled and edited by Lawrence Kehoe, Vol. 1, 2nd ed., revised and corrected (New York: for the Compiler, 1865), pp. 275–284.

Catholic-Protestant antagonisms of the nineteenth century, the United States was the only democracy in the world "that does not routinely provide aid to nonpublic schools as a part of its educational system." He went on to state that the Supreme Court was simply wrong to tell state legislatures that they could not provide aid to Catholic schools because of the First and Fourteenth amendments.[7] Within a decade of Moynihan's article, leaders concerned about the education of inner-city children in Milwaukee and Cleveland created proposals for vouchers that passed legal scrutiny and withstood subsequent legal challenges. The key for the legality of these programs was directing the voucher not to schools, but to low-income parents so that they could choose which school to send their child. The vouchers also allowed for a "freedom of conscience" clause that allows students to opt out of religious instruction if they have enrolled in a school with a religious tradition not their own. Catholic proponents of voucher programs have stressed that they wanted success not just for Catholic schools, but also for public schools in which, they added, nearly 90 percent of Catholics students enroll.[8]

One of the most prolific and sophisticated proponents of school choice has been John E. Coons, an emeritus professor of law at the University of California Berkeley. His argument for choice does not focus on support for private religious schools. Rather, he aims at the state monopoly on education that takes away the choice that the family, and especially the poor, should have. At the risk of over-simplification, his argument can be summarized in the following points.[9] First, in

---

7. See his "What the Congress Can Do When the Court is Wrong," in *Private Schools and the Public Good: Policy Alternatives for the Eighties,* ed. Edward McGlynn Gaffney, Jr (Notre Dame Press, 1981), pp. 79–84. Citing the studies of Coleman and Greeley, Moynihan dismisses the "silly notion" that Catholic schools are elitist and racism, and stresses that now Catholic schools offer an excellent education, causing the opponents to aid for Catholic schools now to "argue that if everybody had the slightest opportunity to enter them, there would be no public school system left." Some opponents to the growth of charter schools now say similar things. Both Moynihan and Hughes' texts are reproduced in *Creative Fidelity: American Catholic Intellectual Traditions,* edited by R. Scott Appleby, Patricia Byrne, and William L. Portier (Orbis Books, 2004).

8. In support of a state referendum on vouchers scheduled for November of 2000, the bishops of California stated that they "consistently sought to support our public schools, which the majority of our Catholic children attend. We greatly appreciate the countless men and women—many of them Catholic parishoners—who provide dedicated service and leadership to society through their efforts in public education. We are also convinced that no single model of education is appropriate to the needs of all persons" ("Proposition 38: School Vouchers," in *Origins*, Vol. 30. No. 7, October 5, 2000, p. 284.

9. Coons has written a great deal on this subject. Take for example, his article in *America* magazine (August 13–20, 2001) pp. 7–10, "Rescuing School Choice from Its Friends," or more recently, "Private Wealth and Public Schools," in the *Stanford Journal of Civil Rights and Civil Liberties*, Vol. 4, Issue 2 (October 2008) pp. 245–281. Full disclosure: I serve as an associate for The American Center for School Choice, an organization that John Coons chairs.

the United States, there is no real system of public education, since certain public schools (in wealthy suburbs) are simply inaccessible to poor inner-city families—a "balkanization of education by family wealth."[10] Therefore, Coons likes to refer to "government" rather than "public" schools. Moreover, even though states prescribe a minimum level of content, the interpretation of that content, especially its moral meaning, is highly conflicted in the public schools. Government schools have no way of settling fundamental questions of human value, such as the morality of sexual behavior, gender roles, and the religious and moral significance of scientific theories such as evolution. If the moral dimensions of what the local school decides to teach are offensive to the wealthy, they can simply remove their children from the school and send them elsewhere. The poor have no such freedom. And even if teachers and administrators in a government school system could agree on moral issues, they would be unable to base their agreements on any transcendent warrant, since in the public system they are not allowed to base any moral teachings on God's authority. In the light of these conditions, Coons concludes that "imposing any one of these conflicting notions [e.g., social contract or natural law] about ethical foundations upon the captive family makes education lawless, arbitrary and morally random."[11]

Finally, Coons turns to deeply held American values to promote his argument: the freedom of speech (poor peoples' voices, he notes, are rarely heard), a greater freedom for individuals facing the "education market," and the rights of parents to chose the education they want for their children. Coons' approach embraces all families, not just the poor. In sum, Coons would turn all government schools into charter schools, a direction in which the Obama administration seems to be moving. For those private religious schools that choose to be part of this parental choice program, Coons recommends that the religious courses be mandatory (mastery of content required of all students, but not religious expression of belief), and that they would control locally the curriculum and the hiring of faculty.[12]

One of the obvious advantages that Catholic high schools would have under the arrangement proposed by Coons is not just the freedom to teach about moral issues that are becoming more and more contentious in modern society,[13] but also

---

10. Coons, "Rescuing Schools" p. 8.

11. Ibid., p. 9.

12. Coons, "Private Wealth and Public Schools," p. 278, note 77.

13. Charles L. Glenn, *The Ambiguous Embrace: Government and Faith-based Schools and Social Agencies*, (Princeton University Press; Princeton New Jersey: 2000), pp. 19–20, who points out that the supposed neutrality of the state-run schools on moral issues is impossible to attain: "The myth that secularism is a neutral position between belief and unbelief is widely accepted, despite its inherent absurdity."

to teach the religious foundations of their morality. The Enlightenment, as I explained in Chapter 2, sought without complete success to find a rational basis for morality, one that would not require an appeal to religious authority as morality's ultimate foundation. The continued existence of religious schools suggests that more than a rational basis alone is needed for a robust moral formation. Religious schools have the freedom not only to teach morality, but to explore openly and fully the religious foundations of the morality they teach. People are not only rational animals, they are also, as one author recently titled his book, *Moral, Believing Animals*.[14]

Vouchers or parental choice programs affect only a very small percentage of students. Coons' proposal would affect all students and, for that reason, will not likely be accepted in the near future, however congenial it would be for Catholic schools. Nevertheless, still other potentially transformative possibilities, though affecting again only a few students, exist and should be seriously considered. For example, Catholic educators have created schools which depend on student work/study programs for financial support. One of the best known of these programs on the high school level is the Cristo Rey schools, of which there are now 24 that enroll 6,000 students. The first such school was founded in Chicago by the Jesuits in 1996. After demonstrating its effectiveness (over 90 percent of its graduates go on to college), 23 more schools have been founded since 2001.[15] The children of families that can afford a private high school education are excluded from these schools (in 2008, the average income of families with sons and daughters in Cristo Rey schools was $33,000).

How are poor families able to pay private high school tuition? The students themselves earn money that goes directly to the school. For all four years of high school, students, boys with ties and girls in dresses, form a team and work one day a week at a business which sponsors them so that they can earn what most schools hope will be 75 percent of their tuition, the rest being paid by the family and covered by donations. All students attend a three-week training program before beginning their first year so that they can learn the basics of business behavior, including how to shake hands, maintain eye contact, answer the phone, and

---

14. Christian Smith, *Moral, Believing Animals: Human Personhood and Culture* (Oxford, 2003). I highly recommend this book, which I recently used as one of several texts for an undergraduate course I taught at the University of Southern California. Smith is a social scientist who recognizes that the religious dimension is not only important, but also enriches and sustains the moral dimension.

15. See www.cristoreynetwork.org for further information. The expansion of these schools would not have been possible without generous philanthropy, including a $12 million gift from B. J. Cassin and two grants totaling nearly $16 million from the Bill & Melinda Gates Foundation.

prepare for entry level jobs. Fr. John Foley, S.J., the founder of the first Cristo Rey high school, explains that the students benefit not only from the school, but also from their experience in the businesses that sponsor them. "Imagine them," he says, "going to the Sears Tower, to the 60th floor, and finding they have a desk there."[16]

The Cristo Rey model poses considerable administrative challenges: the work arrangements make for complicated academic schedules, and sometimes the business mentors of the students, especially the first year students, find it difficult to adjust to fourteen year olds and to find them meaningful work. The number of these high schools that can be in a single city is limited, especially given the large number of corporate sponsors that need to be found. And while these schools do great things for students who otherwise would be condemned to failing public schools, they reach only a small fraction of the students who desperately need such an institution.[17] And when we look at the number of students who benefit from school vouchers, we learn that only 150,000 of the nation's fifty million public school students—that's less than 0.003 percent—are able to access tax dollars to attend private schools.[18]

These numerically small but bold new models of Catholic education demand vision and sacrifice on the part of teachers, students and their families. They educate, however, only a very few students.[19] We need to ask, therefore, whether there are initiatives that would provide financial support for all students in Catholic schools.

Financing Private Education

All of these Catholic inner-city innovations—efforts to secure vouchers and expand the Cristo Rey movement—underscore the critical importance of finding the finances needed to pay faculties who now are predominantly lay people. If

---

16. Barbara Kantrowitz and Karen Springen, "The Rev. John Foley: Education," in *Newsweek*, January 28, 2009, at www.newsweek.com/id/44248/output.

17. Besides the Jesuits, the De La Salle Brothers, the Christian Brothers, the Sisters of Notre Dame, the Sisters of the Holy Child Jesus and other religious communities are founding such schools. For a moving and candid description of a successful Christian Brother school in Harlem, see Patrick J. McCloskey's *The Street Stops Here: A Year at a Catholic High School in Harlem* (University of California Press, 2008). At the level of innovative Catholic grade school initiatives in the inner city, see also the NativityMiguel schools, which now number 64 and enroll 6,000 students: www.nativitymiguelnetwork.org.

18. McCloskey, *The Street Stops Here*, p. 411.

19. It is estimated that about two million children—about 4 percent of the total primary and secondary school population and nearly as many children as are now in Catholic schools—are homeschooled. See Tristana Moore, "Give Me Your Tired, Your Poor, Your Huddled Masses Yearning to Homeschool," *Time*, March 8, 2010, p. 48.

money is uppermost in most peoples' minds, then Patrick McCloskey makes a compelling case for public support of at least all inner-city Catholic high schools. He documents that voucher systems, which sometimes cover the entire cost of tuition for Catholic high schools, are less expensive than what it costs to run public schools. He cites a recent study (covering the years 1990–2006) that state budgets saved $22 million and local public school districts $442 million. Those savings, McCloskey adds, could have been poured back into the public schools.[20] For another stunning statistic, if all students currently enrolled in Catholic schools attended public schools, it would cost the taxpayers and additional $20 billion.[21]

However, once the relationship between dollars spent on education and student achievement is carefully examined, it becomes clear that increasing the amount of money spent for each student is not the factor that best ensures learning. Years ago, James Coleman found that "social capital" is the major factor that contributes to improved learning. Studying high schools with a clear religiously based mission, Tony Bryk and his colleagues concluded that the most important factor in the success of Catholic schools was the sense of community among teachers and students:

> Schools organized as communities exhibit a set of common understandings among the members of the organization. These include tenets about the purpose of the school, about what students should learn, about how teachers and students should behave, and—most important—about the kind of people students are and are capable of becoming.[22]

---

20. McCloskey, p. 409. His statistics are drawn from an article by Susan L. Aud, "Education by the Numbers: The Fiscal Effect of School Choice Programs, 1990–2006" (in Milton and Rose D. Friedman Foundation, April 2007), available at www.friedmanfoundation.org/friedman/downloadFile.do?id=243.

21. Again, McCloskey, gets this figure by taking the national average cost of educating students (2,320,651 of them) at Catholic schools over against what it costs to educate students at public schools. However, not all agree on the comparative costs of Catholic and public education. For example, in an article, "Catholic vs. Public Schools: Myth and Reality," *National Catholic Reporter*, March 30, 2001, p. 44, Joseph Claude Harris, the chief financial officer for the Society of St. Vincent de Paul in Seattle, argues that once public school expenses that include overhead costs (to support superintendant offices), special education, transportation, remedial programs and food services are factored in, the overall difference between the cost of educating a student in a Catholic vs. a public school is less. Harris suggests that instead of 40 percent less, as claimed by an article Harris critiques, the difference is more like 8 percent. For another analysis, one which includes the cost of religious schools sponsored by a variety of Christian denominations, see Michael Guerra, "Mission and Money: Religious Schools and Their Finances," in Thomas Hunt and James C. Cooper, eds., *Religion and Schooling in Contemporary America* (New York: Garland Publishing: 1997).

22. Bryk et al., *Catholic Schools and the Common Good*, (Harvard University Press, Cambridge Massachusetts; 1993), p. 277.

We have already explained how difficult it is for faculty at public schools to come to any consensus on the many contested moral issues that divide people today. It remains difficult, therefore, for faculty at public schools to agree on how students, and how, indeed, they as teachers should behave. It is easier to come to such an agreement when the faculty accepts a religious tradition, which grounds expectations of how they and their students should behave. Concerning the moral authority that Catholic high schools have, Bryk and his associates write:

> [A] voluntary community enjoys a base of moral authority. Such authority depends on the consent of those influenced by it, and it is made possible by the commitment from both teachers and students to a particular school. The presence of moral authority is important because much of what happens in schools involves discretionary action. Great effort may be required within public bureaucracies to secure basic agreements on issues that are intrinsically matters of judgment. In a voluntary community...many potentially contentious issues never develop into conflicts, because communal norms define a broader reality of 'what is appropriate here.'[23]

While Bryk may be overestimating how much of one mind faculty at Catholic high schools are today, he is surely right that families that choose at great personal cost to send their children to a Catholic school where the teachers really want to be teaching—that such schools have social capital. And as argued above, such schools, even if they benefited from great financial resources, would not for that reason alone enjoy strong social capital. There is, therefore, something to be said for a school that is guided by a religiously based mission embraced by both parents and teachers—a mission whose basic purposes need not be constantly renegotiated.[24]

Even though I argue that adequate financial support is not *the* most important factor in sustaining Catholic schools, the leaders of Catholic schools need to be more forward thinking about increasing their sources of financial support. They can learn a lesson from Catholic colleges and universities. It was only in the 1950s that a handful of Catholic colleges and universities began to create a "development mentality." That is, they began to understand that if they were to realize their aspirations to become excellent educational institutions, they needed to reduce the number of courses and students that faculty were expected to teach, increase the library funding, offer competitive financial aid, and improve their

23. Ibid., p. 314.

24. Glenn, *The Ambiguous Embrace*, p. 262,

facilities. If they did not find the money to do such things, they realized that they would continue to be unable to compete with secular institutions that offered to students all these advantages at a reduced cost.

As recently as 1960, most Catholic colleges and universities had no professional development staffs. They did not keep track of their most successful alums, and they had no organized approach to foundations which they could approach to support their educational mission. Some Catholic colleges still don't do these basic fund-raising tasks well, and as a result are often living on the edge of bankruptcy. Once lay boards of trustees were established in the late 1960s and the large numbers of religious who founded, staffed and ran these institutions left these institutions, many colleges and universities realized that they had to build professional fund-raising staffs. But even at that moment of clarity, they lagged nearly a century behind prestigious private universities in fund-raising practices. And to this day, a sizeable proportion of the existing 220 or so Catholic colleges and universities in the United States are almost completely tuition driven. As a result, they annually suffer anxieties over whether they will meet their enrollment targets.

Catholic high schools without lay boards of trustees need to establish them. They also need to invest in professional fund-raising. It takes time, money and expertise to raise money. Effective fund-raising efforts can't be done well on the cheap. The regular faculty and staff, who are already over-extended, should not be expected to take on additional fund-raising duties. I devoted two chapters to the importance of leadership in Catholic schools. That leadership needs to focus not only on keeping the mission clear and on recruiting and forming faculty, they also need to think creatively about the financial health and future of their school. Sister Dale McDonald, the director of public policy for the National Catholic Education Association, believes that Catholic schools which thrive do so because of leadership: "What we've seen in some of these places that would have all the elements for failure is that success comes from dynamic and creative leadership at the diocesan and school level—people who know how to create partnerships and get things done. They turn things around."[25] In particular, Sister McDonald had in mind building partnerships with people in the business world, often grateful alums of Catholic schools who are prepared to "give back" if invited.

The authors of the University of Notre Dame's 2008 study, *Faith, Finances, and the Future*, made a variety of suggestions for improving the finances of Catholic schools, beginning with some cost-saving mechanisms, such as having dioceses work with other dioceses to create better and less costly health care insurance. Currently, every diocese negotiates its own plan. Suppose, for a

25. Cited by Vincent Gragnani, "Getting Catholic Schools Off the Dole," in *America*, February 13, 2006, p. 12.

moment, that Catholic dioceses throughout the country worked together to secure one major health care plan—great savings could be found. Moreover, similar diocesan, state and even national cooperation in buying technology, various educational supplies, and electricity and heating could again save millions of dollars.[26] The first White House "faith czar" appointed in George W. Bush's first term, John DiIulio, reminded Catholics that state governments have loaned textbooks to parochial schools for free, allowed parents with children in parochial schools to deduct payments on state income tax returns, and have paid for computers and a deaf child's sign language interpreter at religious schools.[27] Taking these suggestions to heart means that leaders in Catholic high schools should seek all forms of financial support, including monies that are available through foundations, state and federal government programs.

Besides limiting cost, the authors of the Notre Dame study suggest that the leaders of Catholic high schools can increase revenues in a variety of ways, including capital campaigns, annual giving opportunities, keeping close track of their alums, writing grants and approaching foundations, and organizing an office that handles bequests and wills. A number of Catholic colleges and universities now have well-trained staff who do these things, and who could be very helpful advising those high schools that wish now to do them as well. In recent years the number of Catholic high schools that have hired professionals to do public relations and development work has increased. As of 2007, however, still only about 40 percent of Catholic high schools had such people in place.[28]

Besides innovative high schools (the Cristo Rey model) and programs that allow for parental choice and vouchers and professional fund-raising, a few bishops have shown creative leadership in finding financial support for their schools. Consider, for example, the success of Indiana's Archbishop Daniel Buechlein, O.S.B., who in the mid 1990s launched a $20 million campaign to rebuild two inner-city schools. The Indianapolis-based Lilly Endowment contributed $5 million of the $20 million, and several years later, impressed by Buechlein's leadership, offered an additional $10 million grant if the diocese could raise an additional $5 million. The bishop accepted and met the challenge by going mainly to business leaders. He devoted additional money to recruiting and forming excellent teachers, and helping Hispanic students.[29] Consider also

---

26. R. Nuzzi, J. Frabutt and A. Holter, *Faith, Finances and the Future* (Alliance for Catholic Education at the University of Notre Dame, Notre Dame Indiana, 2008), pp. 47–48.

27. John I. DiIulio, *Godly Republic* (University of California Press, 2007), pp. 65–66.

28. *Dollars & $ense,* (National Catholic Education Association, Washington DC; 2007), p. 10.

29. Gragnani, p. 14.

that Catholic schools in Wichita are free to all Catholics, and lower tuition is available to poor non-Catholic families in their inner-city schools.[30] Also, through its High School Equalization Fund, the archdiocese of Cincinnati was able in 2008 to distribute nearly a million dollars to sixteen of its high schools—not a great amount, but at least something.

Some other bishops, for example, have also led creative initiatives, such as the bishops of Memphis and New York City. However, exemplary Episcopal leadership seems to be the exception rather than the rule. The rule sadly seems to be that more and more inner-city Catholic schools close for lack of leadership and finances. The shift to lay leadership in Catholic schools is widespread and increasing very rapidly. I have explained how demographic trends have contributed to the closing of Catholic schools. A recent study on Catholic grade schools done by the Center for Applied Research in the Apostolate identified the most critical factor in school closings is demographic shifts: "people moved and the schools didn't." Over the five-year period studied (2000–2005), the number of Catholic grade schools declined by 339, a 5 percent drop. Most of the schools that closed were in the eastern and the upper-Midwestern United States; however, in the Sun Belt area, newer schools in suburban areas and the Southeast often have waiting lists. For parents, especially those in cities and Rust Belt areas, tuition assistance in some form is the single factor that best predicts the likelihood of enrolling their children in Catholic elementary schools. Unfortunately, only 15 percent of Catholic elementary schools are located in areas where some form of publicly funded aid (vouchers, tax credits, or scholarship programs) is available.[31] These demographic shifts have affected Catholic high schools as well.

Even a voucher program was not enough to keep schools solvent in Washington, D.C., where, for example, Cardinal Donald Wuerl had to turn seven inner-city Catholic grade schools into charter schools (therefore supported by tax dollars). He explained that while he believed that charter schools were not alternatives to Catholic schools, they would provide a better education for the children than public schools.[32] The superintendant of Catholic schools for the

---

30. McCloskey, *The Street Stops Here*, p. 437, n. 11.

31. CARA: Special Report (Spring 2006). For a recent report on the state of the inner-city Catholic schools in Boston, see Joseph O'Keefe, "How to Save Catholic Schools: Let the Revitalization Begin," *Commonweal*, March 25, 2005. O'Keefe makes a researched plea for greater dedication on the part of bishops, religious and laity to inner-city Catholic schools. In 2005, the diocese of Brooklyn announced that it would close twenty-two elementary schools (see Chapter 1 where it is reported that in 2009 the diocese stated that it would have to merge or close fourteen more schools) and shortly afterward the archdiocese of Chicago said it would close twenty-three elementary schools.

32. www.washingtonpost.com/wp-dyn/content/article/2008/06/16/AR2008061602933_p.

D.C. archdiocese, Patricia Wietzel-O'Neill, assured parents that these seven former Catholic schools would be "values-based" charter schools "where they can continue to talk about those [values] that make you a good person."[33] In both an earlier chapter and this one, however, I have described the difficulty that public schools have in teaching morality. Still, it can surely be hoped with the Cardinal that the D.C. charter schools will provide a better education than the students might receive in the public alternative.

Finally, if Catholic schools need to create "development mentalities," Catholics themselves need to develop a "giving mentality." After carefully examining the best existing data on Catholic philanthropy, Mary Jo Bane, a social scientist at Harvard, poses a question: how is it that American Catholics who now occupy in socioeconomic terms the nation's middle- and upper-middle class, whose religious teaching tells them that "faith without works" is empty and that helping the poor is a priority—why do these Catholics by every measure "lag behind other large religious groups, and are only just ahead of citizens who profess no faith at all, in their average levels of volunteering and giving"?[34] A partial response to Bane's question is that many leaders of Catholic institutions have yet to learn how to make a compelling case to their fellow Catholics to give.

Catholic Schools Internationally: Some Insights

I have limited myself in this book to the topic of Catholic high schools in the United States—a topic that still is bigger and more complex than can be handled in a single book. Nevertheless, Senator Moynihan recommended that in addressing any serious issue it is worth examining what the state of the question is in other industrial democracies.[35] Therefore, a few brief observations about the situation of Catholic schools in other parts of the world add some interesting perspectives to our own situation in the United States.

---

33. www.catholic.org/printer_friendly.php?id=25883§ion=Cathcom.

34. Cited by DiIulio, *Godly Republic*, pp. 167–168. DiIulio also cites George Weigel, a conservative Catholic and author of a biography of John Paul II: "Catholics are among the worst givers in the country.... One-third of the registered members of a parish give constantly and generously, one-third give occasionally, and one-third give essentially nothing.... The question of how to instill a greater sense of responsible generosity in U.S. Catholics has thus become a significant issue for the twenty-first century Church, whose vast network of parishes, schools, social welfare and health care institutions can no longer rely on the inexpensive labor of priests, brothers, and sisters" (Weigel, "The Problem with Religious Philanthropy: Catholic Giving," *Philanthropy*, May/June 2005), p. 28.

35. "What the Congress Can Do When the Court is Wrong," in *Private Schools and the Public Good*, ed. Edward McGlynn Gaffney, Jr. (University of Notre Dame Press, 1981), p. 79.

In Canada, six of the ten provinces currently have some form of public funding for faith-based schools. In Ontario, government funding covers all primary and secondary Catholic education—but not the schools of other faith-based groups. Both public and Catholic schools, however, are required to follow the same core curriculum standards established by the province's Department of Education, and both must hire province-certified teachers. In 2007 a heated debate exploded over proposals to extend funding to other faith-based schools (which enroll only 2 percent of the students in the province). Some argued that it was only fair to extend tax support to all faith-based schools; others argued that no faith-based schools should receive public support. In one poll, only 23 percent of the voters found the status quo acceptable. Many Catholics felt that the funding that their schools had enjoyed since 1984 was in danger, recalling, perhaps, that less than ten years before Newfoundland, where sexual abuse in the schools was extensive and highly reported, ended its support for all Catholic and Protestant schools.[36]

In the Province of Quebec, Cardinal Marc Ouellet of Montreal has persistently criticized a new "Ethics and Religion Culture Programme" required by the province in the fall of 2008 for all public, Protestant and Catholic schools. Ouellet says the course "is conducted at the expense of the religious freedom of the citizen, especially [that] of the Catholic majority."[37] Even Cardinal Grocholewski, the prefect of the Vatican's Congregation for Education, weighed in on the debate, stating that "talking in the same way about all religions is almost like an anti-Catholic education, because this creates a certain relativism." A Jesuit high school in Montreal sued the province when their request for an exemption for the Programme was denied. The Jesuits claimed that the Programme was "contrary to its faith mission."[38]

Since 1944 in England, all costs, including salaries, have been covered by the government—except for building construction and maintenance, for which the Churches contribute only 10 percent of the cost. The Catholic and Anglican schools have been allowed to retain control of the religion curriculum, protect the religious atmosphere of their schools and place clergy on their boards. Church schools enroll 25 percent of all students in the country. But again, controversy has

36. Peter Kavanagh, "Faith Schools in the Firing Line," *The Tablet*, October 6, 2007, p. S8.

37. Peter Kavanagh, "Vatican Attacks Quebec's Compulsory RE Course," *The Tablet*, February 28, 2009, p. 30.

38. Also in Kavanagh. In Spain, a similar battle is being fought where compulsory courses in civics introduce issues such as gay rights and stem cell research. Though thousands of students have boycotted these classes, Spain's Supreme Court ruled that students were not free to opt out of them.

hit the Catholic schools, which have been criticized recently for being sectarian. A quarter of the students who enroll in Catholic schools are not Catholic, and in a few schools the majority of the students are Muslims. In some Catholic schools, the principals insist that Catholic schools are meant for Catholics, and where Muslim students outnumber Catholics, Catholic parents sometimes take their children out of these schools. Recently, a government proposal argued that at least 25 percent of students in Catholic schools should not be Catholic. Even though on average about 25 percent of students in Catholic schools are not Catholic, the leaders of the Catholic schools vigorously objected to the proposal, which eventually failed to pass in Parliament. Another charge being leveled at Catholic schools, one that has often been raised by secularists in the United States as well, is that they benefit only themselves and not the common good. Opponents of Catholic schools argue that admitting only Catholics and teaching a specific religion in a school which is supported by the state is not defensible. As one critic put it, Catholic schools should focus on "influencing the community rather than educating Catholics."[39]

In Australia, where over a third of the population is Catholic, fewer than half the Catholic children are in Catholic schools; nevertheless, 20 percent of all students in Australia are enrolled in Catholic schools. In the United States, less than 10 percent of Catholics are enrolled in Catholic schools. Proportionate to the overall population of Australia, the size of the Catholic school system is immense—in fact, the Catholic Church in Australia is the country's largest single employer.[40] All teachers in Catholic schools receive from the government the same salary as their counterparts in the public schools. One Australian educational researcher concluded soberly, "Without this government support, the schools would close tomorrow."[41]

Conclusion

What lessons might the leaders of Catholic high schools draw from this rapid survey of the situation of Catholic schools in other countries that provide partial and sometimes full financial support to private faith-based schools? One lesson should be quite clear: receiving government support does not assure that this financial support will not be challenged. Second, unless clearly defined

39. Nicolas Kennedy, "For Whom the School Bell Tolls," *The Tablet*, August 8, 2009, p. 4.

40. Michael Furtado, "Where the Good News is a Class Act," *The Tablet*, October 25, 2008, p. S4.

41. Jeffrey Dorman, "Some Determinants of Classroom Psychosocial Environment in Australian Catholic High Schools," in *Catholic Education: A Journal of Inquiry and Practice*, Vol. 13, No. 1, (September 2009), p. 8.

forms of autonomy permit Catholic schools to determine their own curriculum, their student body and their faculty, the government will inevitably try to exert various forms of control. At present, the only successful voucher programs are those that give money not to schools but directly to families. And even with such autonomy, still others who in principle oppose faith-based schools as sectarian will attack them for a variety of reasons. The rapidly growing number of charter schools in the United States have steered clear of teaching any religion. As believers in the United States become more pluralistic, public schools find it to be nearly impossible to deal with any religious topics without controversy. Third, receiving money from the government does not prevent a continuing set of challenges for Catholic schools, sometimes posed by other religious groups, sometimes by government officials wanting to exert more control, and sometimes by secularists wanting to end all such funding. And finally, to the extent that the claim is true that all Australian Catholics schools would immediately shut down without government support, it is all the more amazing that as many Catholic schools in the United States which enjoy next to no government support remain open.

Without sufficient financial resources, no organization, and certain no Catholic schools, can continue to exist. Moreover, as our brief international survey of various funding arrangements for Catholic schools shows, having sufficient funds does not meet all the challenges that seemingly never stop being thrown at Catholic education. Money is important, but not the most important factor in ensuring the vibrancy and future of Catholic education. This, then, is the time to reiterate what is most important for Catholic education to flourish.

10

The Future of Catholic High Schools

Introduction

I began this book claiming that for Catholic high schools to flourish, three things had to be achieved: clarity about their distinctive mission, care in the recruitment and formation of lay leadership and faculty, and a critique of modern culture. It is time now as I approach the conclusion of this book, to restate and re-emphasize the importance of these conditions for vibrant Catholic high schools.

I believe that the most important factor for the future of Catholic high schools is a clear vision of their mission—a mission fully embraced by the faculty. In the fourth chapter, I stressed that Catholic schools had an important advantage over public high schools: they can draw explicitly on a theological foundation for the moral formation of their students. When a transcendent foundation is missing, one of two things tends to happen: either disagreements, especially over the morality of certain sexual issues, polarize the school community, or the faculty simply avoids addressing moral issues. The leaders of Catholics schools are obliged to form their students intellectually, morally, religiously and intellectually, and do so by drawing on the Catholic theological tradition and practice, especially the Eucharist, and, it should be added, by being excellent teachers in all subjects.

Mission Slippage

In recent years, however, some of those who have the responsibility for leading these important educational institutions have not shown sufficient clarity about the distinctive mission of their schools. Moreover, contemporary culture has deeply influenced even the best of Catholic families, most of which can no longer count on strong Catholic subcultures to support their understanding and practice of the faith. Middle- and upper-middle class Catholics who live in suburbs with good public schools often chose them over Catholic schools, even though they could afford to send their children to the latter. In inner cities, a rapidly increasing number of charter schools are providing an alternative to the public schools and a low-cost alternative to Catholic schools. Add to these threats the ambivalence of key people (some religious, bishops, and parents), who otherwise could be counted on to lead and support Catholic education, and we get a fuller picture of the great challenge that faces the leaders of Catholic education today. What is most needed is a shift among these key Catholics away from ambivalence about the value of Catholic education to a clearer vision of their mission and significance.

Without intending it, too many Catholic schools have suffered from a "mission slippage." In an important book on faith-based schools and secular governments, Charles Glenn, a professor of comparative education at Boston University, concludes that while government control ever remains a danger to faith-based schools, an even greater threat to faith-based schools is the "loss of conviction" that robs such schools of their unique value.[1] I have argued that much of contemporary culture is not friendly to Christian faith, and that the culture's influence on Catholics is more pervasive than it was decades ago. But having said that, it is also true that dedicated lay leadership, properly formed in the Catholic tradition and in its distinctive vision of education, can challenge that culture best by running first-rate Catholic high schools.

Clarity About the Mission

In an otherwise superb and widely read study of Catholic schools, Stanford Professor of Education and Catholic Tony Bryk and his co-authors claimed that "the spirit of Vatican II has softened Catholic claims to universal truth with a call for continuing dialogue. . . ." Bryk and his co-authors went on to explain with approval how instead of the pre-Vatican II "emphasis on indoctrination in the 'mind of the Church,' contemporary religion classes now emphasize dialogue and encounter."[2] If Catholic schools remove their distinctive theological foundations, Bryk writes, it follows that the "creation of secular schools espousing a similar set of humanistic beliefs and social principles" could create as well the kind of social organization that contributes to the success of Catholic schools.[3] I am not as confident as Bryk that what is distinctive about Catholic schools, shorn of Catholicism's dogmatic and religious basis, could be successfully transformed into a humanism robust enough to generate the same degree or type of social capital excellent Catholic schools enjoy. And while I believe that the ability to teach the tradition well benefits from dialogue and encounter, and that indoctrination in any form should have no place in a Catholic school, I also believe that

1. Charles L. Glenn, *The Ambiguous Embrace: Government and Faith-Based Schools and Social Agencies* (Princeton University Press, 2000), p. 265.

2. Bryk et al., *Catholic Schools and the Common Good*, (Harvard University Press, Cambridge Massachusetts; 1993), p. 302.

3. Bryk et al., pp. 250–251.

the doctrinal foundations of Catholicism make clear who Catholics are and how they might fruitfully proceed in dialogue.

When proponents of Catholic schools defend themselves against the charge of being sectarian or indoctrinators, they may again be tempted to play down their distinctive theological foundation. They sometimes respond to such charges by emphasizing the contribution that Catholic schools make to the common good, but do so in ways that masks their distinctive foundation. Commenting on the mission of Catholic schools, Monsignor Dennis Murphy, who served as the secretary general of the Canadian Conference of Catholic Bishops and founder of the Institute for Catholic Education, described the Catholic contribution to the common good, its "value added" if you will, in this way:

> In a society that struggles with moral values, few would question the value of schools that speak the biblical message of young people honouring their parents and of parents honouring their children; of a seamless life ethic encouraging them to see the relationship between concern for all the dispossessed and the elderly and for people and whole countries that live at the side of the road; of opting for the protection of life at all stages, which includes everything from the wrongness of bullying to supporting the need for just social structures; of avoiding the folly of war, and so on.[4]

Nothing in Murphy's description of the way that Catholic teachings contribute to public life is wrong; but by itself, without the addition of the distinctive theological underpinnings of the Catholic moral vision, it could be read, especially by those Catholics who stress the distinctive moral teachings (especially those having to do with sexuality), as simply another form of "Catholic lite." At the same time, however, Monsignor Murphy's appeal to the "seamless life ethics" is anything but lite, as it challenges the way in which, in the United States at least, the political parties have divided up the "social issues," that is, the morality of homosexual marriages and abortion on the one hand, and social justice (especially as it relates to the economy), war, capital punishment and immigration on the other. Informed Catholics need to keep their focus on the relationship that exists among all these matters, rather than stressing one and ignoring the other.

Leaders of Catholic high schools need, therefore, a very important skill: the ability to link theological truths, beginning with the doctrines of creation, the incarnation, and the Trinity, with the moral teachings that flow from them. Christians revere creation because it is a gift from God. They treasure the incarna-

---

4. Dennis Murphy, "Values Added," *University of St. Michael's College in the University of Toronto Alumni Magazine*, Vol. 47, No. 1 (Spring 2008), p. 4.

tion since both human and divine Christ makes it possible to link the love of God and neighbor in a way never thought possible before. And the doctrine of the Trinity anchors in the very nature of the Godhead profound insights into the dynamics of Christian community—dynamics that wisely navigate between individualism on the one hand and collectivism on the other.[5] It is the intimate relationship between theological and moral teachings that is most likely to be separated in today's pluralistic society.

Perhaps some leaders of Catholic schools hesitate to emphasize their Catholic distinctiveness because they will appear to be "conservative." Labels such as "conservative" and "liberal," widely bandied about today in the religious culture wars, tell us little about the nature of Catholicism. Rather, being distinctively Catholic, whether as a liberal or a conservative, requires that every Catholic be committed, for example, to both ecumenical and interreligious dialogue. Vatican II's document, *Nostra aetate*, the Church's statement on its relation to other religions, states that the Catholic Church "rejects nothing of what is true and holy" in other religions.[6] Along with Benedict XVI, I worry about moral and doctrinal relativism. But the antidote to relativism is not absolutism. The antidote is a thoughtful and appreciative appropriation of the Catholic tradition, its history and its doctrines, and a generous understanding of its relation to other religions. I also worry about indoctrination. And the antidote to indoctrination is not ignoring doctrine, but rather to teach doctrine in a thoughtful and open way, that makes it possible for students (and faculty) to question and explore, and in the process, learn in appropriate freedom the doctrinal foundations of Christianity.

Careful Recruitment of Faculty

The second most important factor for the flourishing of Catholic high schools is the recruitment and formation of faculty. At the university level, capable leaders recruit and retain good faculty. When such leadership is lacking, the best faculty

5. Leaders of Catholic high schools who make the case for the contribution that their graduates make to the common good might find some support in the recent research of Harvard sociologist Robert Putnam who completed a study that shows that persons who are involved in religious life and practices are likely to be more involved than their secular counterparts in the larger community. Putnam also draws attention to the growing number of young Americans who are vastly more secular than their older counterparts. Students in Catholic high schools should be among those young whose religious lives will be deepened and, as a consequence, their involvement in their local communities increased (see *Gatherings: A Publication of the Department of Small Christian Communities, Archdiocese of Hartford, Connecticut*, Vol. 21, No. 1 [Spring 2006], pp. 1, 4–5.)

6. *Vatican Council II*, ed. Austin Flannery, O.P., *Nostra aetate*, par. 2, pp. 570–571.

find better places to go, but the less talented are unable to leave; they can't compete with better candidates who also apply to other universities. During the 1970s, we who remained Marianists used to repeat a clever but sober saying, "The intelligent leave, the good die young, and here we are!" To recruit and retain the best possible faculty, the leadership of the school has to send a credible signal that the school is moving in a positive direction, and the faculty need to feel supported in their teaching and service, and need to enjoy working together. As mentioned in a previous chapter, this support for faculty concretely means a modest teaching load, not too many class preparations, decent compensation, and opportunities for regular ongoing education.

For a Catholic high school that has been drifting or suffering "mission slippage," it can take years for able leadership to establish clarity about its mission and create positive institutional momentum. It is unlikely that any time soon Catholic schools will cease closing, especially in the inner city. However, those schools which are able to develop a distinctive Catholic culture, recruit an excellent faculty and staff, and maintain close contact with grateful alums will survive. This can be done, and is being done in some places. Leaders in all Catholic schools need to do it as well.

In the hiring of faculty, administrators can not afford to ignore the religious commitments of the candidates they interview. All things being equal (though in reality they never are), preference should be given, as was mentioned in a previous chapter, to hiring competent Catholic faculty. At the same time, the contribution of faculty and staff who are not Catholic, but are still religious, is often equal and even, in some cases, superior to that of Catholic faculty. In the matter of hiring, administrators should never cut corners: they need to do due diligence, to check all references, and invite their own best faculty to interview candidates and invite them to teach a lesson.

Hiring excellent faculty is then a preoccupation. Still it is true that some candidates who appeared to be excellent when hired do not turn out to be excellent. The leaders of Catholic schools, therefore, need not only to "hire for mission," they also need to be able to "fire for mission." Of course, faculty who do not meet expectations should be given an opportunity to improve—if they don't, they should be fired. Legal advice is important when dismissing anyone. To avoid liability at this difficult juncture, administrators, at the point of hiring, should make clear to all candidates not only the mission of the school, but also what is expected of them as teachers. A detailed but accessible faculty handbook that outlines obligations and expectations is not only a protection for administrators, but also for faculty.

In the best Catholic high schools, the leadership of a school, including the faculty, maintain, as I noted earlier, a perpetual "recruitment mode"; they are always on the look out for the kind of teachers they most want to be part of their educational community.

Just as important as the careful recruitment of faculty is the formation of faculty once they are part of the school community. Richard Shields, a high school teacher and an adjunct professor of education at St. Michael's College in Toronto, explains that new faculty, even those who prefer to teach in Catholic schools, bring with them, for better and worse, much of the culture that shapes the students they will teach:

> They bring with them a mixed and uncertain understanding of the Catholic faith. They have grown up in an atmosphere of suspicion towards authority, uncertainty about institutions, and 'multicultural richness and religious homelessness.'[7]

The ongoing formation of faculty is, therefore, necessary. During my third and last year of teaching in a high school (1973–1974), I organized continuing-education programs for the faculty and administrators with whom I worked. The year before, I had just finished all the courses required for a doctorate in historical theology, and instead of proceeding directly to writing a dissertation, I had asked my religious superiors for a year "off" from the year-round intensity of four straight years of graduate and summer language studies. They assigned me to be the chaplain and religion teacher at a suburban high school with 1,000 students. I taught religion to the entire junior class and the senior honors class. Needless to say, it was a very busy year. It was hardly a year "off," but still turned out to be a very good year and a break from graduate school. Each month, after a slightly shortened school day, the entire faculty met, usually on a Monday afternoon. Some light refreshments were served first and then someone presented a talk which was followed by open discussion. The entire session ended by 4:00 P.M. in the afternoon. The principal was very supportive.

At first, some faculty grumbled; but by the end of that year, most looked forward to the next year's lineup of speakers and topics. The challenge, however, was to find speakers who could deliver.[8] We brought in some gifted teachers from other schools to talk about their approaches to teaching. I led four of these afternoons on issues related to the Catholic tradition. The week before we met, I passed out one or two short articles on the subject to be discussed. These monthly meetings were very well-received, cost next to nothing to organize, and

---

7. Richard Shields, "Nurturing Spirituality and Vocation: A Catholic Approach to New Teacher Induction," in *Catholic Education: A Journal of Inquiry and Practice*, Vol. 12, No. 2 (December 2008), p. 162.

8. Today, however, excellent programs for ongoing faculty formation can be had in the form of the many videos and CDs on Catholicism, its history and traditions, available for adult education.

sharpened the sense of the distinctive mission of the Catholic high school, both religious and educational. These sessions also created a stronger sense of community among the faculty, especially through some of the small discussion groups in which faculty talked about important issues with their peers, sometimes for the first time. I had planned to organize a full two-day orientation for the entire faculty at the beginning of the next academic year, but my religious superiors sent me back to full-time study to write my dissertation. I was hoping to spend the rest of my life working in high schools. Instead, they wanted me to work at the university level. In retrospect, as so often has been the case in my religious life, they were right.

Looking back on that year, it was already evident then that some of the faculty, even those who had been raised Catholic, had only a tenuous understanding of Catholic tradition, and its relevance for shaping the ethos of a Catholic high school. I suspect that the grasp of Catholicism by today's young teachers may be even more uncertain than it was for faculty in 1973, though there are many more educational resources today for learning about the faith. All the more reason now to sink significant resources—time, money and talent—in the recruitment and formation of teachers.

Confronting the Culture

The youth culture, including youth in their 20s and early 30s, have absorbed unconsciously many of the dominant images that media pumps out so energetically and with such psychological and visual savvy that only serious initiation in the Catholic culture will create enough distance and perspective to confront contemporary culture. To confront students where "they are at" requires that faculty learn how to critique the culture. While helpful, it is not enough for faculty to have a good grasp of Catholic doctrine alone. More is needed if the gap between doctrine and life is to be closed.

The art of teaching meets students where "they are at," but never leaves them there.[9] The final requirement for a flourishing Catholic high school flows directly from the first two: clarity about mission and the effective recruitment and formation of faculty and staff. I am referring now to the need for the leadership and faculty to understand and critique the dominant culture, using that social analysis as framework within which they teach their students.

The explicit character of this critique will vary greatly depending on what subject is being taught. For example, the choice of literature texts can elucidate,

---

9. See William J. O'Malley's article, "Faulty Guidance: A New Framework for High School Catechesis Fails to Persuade," in *America* (September 14–21, 2009), pp. 14–16.

expose and criticize any number of cultural trends, depending on the texts chosen. What is taught in physics or chemistry classes will not lend itself in the same way to cultural criticism as does a literature class. On the other hand, the very practice of science—forming a theory, testing it through carefully constructed experiments, and then, in the light of those experiments, reformulating, if necessary, the theory—this rigorous process can in itself be an education about the discipline doing good science demands from scientists. A music appreciation class can open students' understanding to a much wider repertoire of music than they would likely be listening to on their iPod. Social science classes, especially when taught historically, help students escape being merely contemporary. For more affluent schools, service trips that immerse students in different cultures can begin to open their eyes to all sort of things they take for granted at home.

If good teaching begins by meeting students "where they are at," it might then be asked, just where are students today? In Chapter 7 I provided a description of high school students based on a number of national studies. I gave special attention to the important study by Christian Smith and Melinda Lundquist Denton, *Soul Searching*, focusing in particular on what they wrote about the religious lives of Catholic teenagers and offering my own commentary on their findings.

Chapter 5 of their book, "American Adolescent Religion in Social Context," is just as important as their comments on Catholic teenagers. In some ways, it may be even more important than their chapter on Catholic adolescents, since in Chapter 5 they describe the cultural trends that shape today's adolescents in such powerful ways. Taken together, the description of those strong trends is daunting: therapeutic individualism, mass-consumer capitalism, the digital communication revolution, residual positivism and empiricism, the structural disconnect of teenagers from the world of adults, and the problems of adults that affect the religious life of students today. While the chapter makes for depressing reading, I believe that what they highlighted in their description of American culture is basically accurate. However, had they added some of the positive dimensions of today's culture, their description would not be as depressing. In Chapter 3 of this book, I too pointed out, as they do, a number of the same negative trends in the culture, but I also described some positive trends, such as the desire for freedom, support for human rights, demand for integrity, a growing respect for religious pluralism, and a hunger for religious experience. But even when those positive trends are added, the challenge that faces Christian educators of teenagers today remains formidable.

The Jesuit William O'Malley has been teaching religion to teenagers at Catholic high schools for over forty years. He wrote an article sharply criticizing the document *Doctrinal Elements of a Curriculum Framework for the Development of Catechetical Material for Young People of High School Age*, which the American bishops had approved in 2007. O'Malley believes the document is "pedagogically counterproductive," "the product of theorists and administrators," and along with the *Catechism of the Catholic Church*, is "utterly without persuasive force with young people." O'Malley argues that given where the students are, the "top-down" and abstract (no stories) approach of the bishops will not work. With a Celtic flare, O'Malley, drawing from his own extensive experience in the classroom, offers the following vivid description of just where he thinks students are today:

> By the time high school students come to the *Framework*, they will have spent unimaginably more hours in the grasp of TV, video games, iPods, the Internet and movies than they will spend before all the teachers they will ever have through graduate school. Few religion teachers will be as convincing as 'Survivor' ('To win you have to screw your teammates') and 'The Bachelor' ('If it feels good, why not?'). Their sex education courses, even in Catholic schools, thoroughly explain the mechanics, with little or no emphasis on the fact that human beings make the interchange much more than that.... The number of teenage drunken drivers caught yearly by police, and by death itself, shows that many teens are unfazed even by the law of cause and effect. The fear of hell that motivated my generation's virtue is nullified, and the thought of spiritual atrophy carries no sting. In role-playing moral dilemmas, their motives can be as relativistic and utilitarian as any atheist's. Yet the *Framework* makes bold to begin by idealizing a crucified felon who could have escaped if he had only shut up. Kids cannot fathom that.[10]

In that same issue of *America*, another religion teacher, Brad Rothrock, a veteran of only five years in the classroom, sounds a more hopeful note about teaching teenagers. But he too admits that effective teaching requires that the teacher be familiar "with a range of subjects seemingly unrelated to those covered in the religion textbooks." Why? Because he, like O'Malley, realizes that the students today "have already formed their own basis for belief and unbelief," and in both instances

10. O'Malley, "Faulty Guidance," p. 16. For a defense of the bishops' document, see Alfred McBride, "A Sturdy Framework," in *America* (September 28, 2009), pp. 16–18. In essence, McBride agrees with O'Malley's description of most adolescents today, but stresses that the document is only a doctrinal framework, not a pedagogical treatise. *How* to teach these doctrines effectively to adolescents, McBride explains, is the task of the publishers of religion textbooks, within the doctrinal framework provided by the bishops. I suspect that without the help of gifted and experienced teachers, such as O'Malley, even the publishers will mostly be at a loss to do what the bishops expect them to do.

their implicit "philosophies are cobbled together from some of the worst God-talk popular culture has to offer."[11]

Both O'Malley and Rothrock offer good pedagogical suggestions that bridge the huge gap between the important doctrinal basis of Christianity and the way that students, shaped so extensively by the dominant cultural tends, should understand their faith and live their lives. What these two religion teachers recommend is actually based on a keen cultural social analysis, the kind that every teacher in a Catholic high school, regardless of the subject he or she teaches, needs to develop. Both authors recommend broadening students' range of reason, so that they don't flip-flop between a narrow empiricism and mindless fideism (or accepting only what can be scientifically proven as reliable and wrongly equating faith with superstition, that is, believing something with no reasons for accepting it). O'Malley adds that teachers need to help students become personally familiar with prayer, understand the difference between absolute certitude and moral certitude, recognize the truth-bearing value of stories, become aware of how brainwashed they are by the media, and that Christian morality means more than being a decent human being.[12] As I have stressed throughout this book, educators in Catholic high schools must be able to confront the culture if they are to teach effectively, especially since at least some of what they teach will necessarily be in conflict with some of the culture. Both O'Malley and Rothrock do this well.

All teachers face students who often have a long way to go just to acquire the habit of study. Without that discipline, described so well by Simone Weil in Chapter 8, neither teachers nor students learn much. People who want to develop the discipline of study receive little support from a culture of immediate gratification, media that over-simplifies complex issues by stuffing their reports into snippets and sound bites, and music that pounds the eardrums and lyrics that vulgarizes the language. So, those dedicated individuals who set out to pass on the Christian tradition to the next generation should not underestimate the challenge that awaits them.

Conclusion

Coupling together these three imperatives—clarity of vision, recruitment and formation of faculty, confronting contemporary culture—will go a long way to

---

11. Brad Rothrock, "God and the Teenage Mind," in *America* (September 14–21, 2009), pp. 11–13.

12. O'Malley, "Faulty Guidance," p. 16.

ensuring that educators in Catholic high schools will make the distinctive contribution to society that is most needed. The ambivalence about the value of Catholic schools that weakens some people entrusted with their leadership can be overcome. Those administrators and faculty who develop a distinctive vision for the future of Catholic high schools will be able to pass on the faith in a coherent and supportive context of intellectual and moral formation. What is needed is the fiery resolve of Archbishop Hughes of New York who over 150 years ago exclaimed, "We shall have to build the schoolhouse first and the church afterward. In our age, the question of education is the question of the Church!"[13]

By itself, however, strong Episcopal leadership will not be enough. As we have seen, the first and most important educators are parents. How do today's Catholic parents understand their responsibility to educate their children as Catholics? How should leaders of Catholic education, bishops and laity, address Catholic parents? These final important questions are addressed in the epilogue which concludes this book.

---

13. McCloskey, *The Street Stops Here,* p. 416, citing Sol Stern, "How Dagger John Saved New York's Irish" (no further bibliographical information on Stern's article).

11

Epilogue: Post-Deferential Parents

The Loss of Institutional Authority

Although there may never have been a time when the actual practice of the laity in the Church could be summed up in the expectation of some bishops that they were simply to "pray, pay and obey," it certainly has been the case that for most of the history of the Church the hierarchy has assumed that it could command the faithful, sometimes under the pain of sin, and generally that they, the laity, would comply.

I refer in this epilogue to "post-deferential" parents. To defer to someone is to give them the benefit of the doubt, to place first what they think, and to do what they expect. Since the 1960s, however, with the huge baby-boomer generation growing into young adulthood, a series of profound cultural shifts left institutional commitments—including government, churches and marriage—honeycombed with reservations. Sociological surveys have documented how tenuous is the commitment that our youth today have with the Church as an institution. These same surveys have documented that while many Catholics today list as most important to them the Sacraments, helping the poor, the Virgin Mary and Jesus' resurrection from the dead, they also indicate that attendance at Sunday Mass is not that important and that they should be able to make up their own minds about matters of morality. That last expectation would not be so troubling if it were not coupled with a high degree of religious illiteracy among Catholics, especially, the boomers and their children.[1]

One of the major problems of the Church is clericalism, an assumption among many of the ordained that they are to be accorded special privileges. But it is important in a generally post-deferential culture to realize that clericalism may be found among many more groups than just priests and bishops. Academics can live in professional cocoons and presume that their knowledge entitles them to a status superior to the less educated. Lawyers and coaches

1. See, for example, D'Antonio, William V., James D. Davidson, Dean R. Hoge, and Mary L. Gautier, *American Catholics Today: New Realities of Their Faith and Their Church* (Lanham, MD: Rowman & Littlefield, 2007), especially pp. 173–183.

and police can also circle their professional wagons, forming a club that protects their own. We are used to reading in the press about rigid conservatives; well, there are also rigid liberals, or, as I prefer to describe them, authoritarian liberals. Some parish directors of religious education, to mention just one example, can arrogate to themselves more infallibility than does the pope. And then there is the familiar joke that goes: What is the difference between a terrorist and a liturgist? The answer: you can negotiate with a terrorist. In a post-deferential culture, then, not only parents but everyone needs to learn how to learn and how to lead without being authoritarian ("Lording it over others," which Jesus warned his disciples not to do) or indifferent (the "whatever" response).

Despite the challenges we face in a post-deferential culture, I have argued throughout this book that the laity can be, and now many of them often are, important leaders in the Catholic Church in America. Instead of commanding, the hierarchy more than ever must persuade the laity through their credibility, transparency and accountability. I also indicated in the first chapter that parents are one of the audiences for which this book has been written. Moreover, I have described in several chapters the key roles that parents play in the faith development of their adolescent children. Parents have enormous responsibility for the education of and formation of their children into adults. In this epilogue, an additional word needs to be said about the new reality of the laity in the American Catholic Church, especially as they relate to one another and the hierarchy.

With the possible exception of the Irish in Boston, where, throughout the nineteenth century, the Puritan elites exercised almost exclusive educational and cultural control and the bishops demonstrated only a weak commitment to building Catholic schools,[2] Catholic parents have been deeply concerned about the education of their children. So were most of their bishops. But how the bishops addressed this concern, how they understood the obligation of those parents with school-age children, how they addressed those parents, and indeed, how they understood their own responsibility to support and promote Catholic schools, has differed considerably. Some bishops zealously promoted the building of Catholic schools; others sought only to add religious instruction to the basic secular education provided by the public schools. Some bishops thought seriously about ordering parents, under pain of sin, to send their chil-

2. *Urban Catholic Education: Tales of Twelve American Cities,* edited by Thomas C. Hunt and Timothy Walch (University of Notre Dame: Alliance for Catholic Education Press, 2010), see Chapter 4, "Puritan City Catholicism: Catholic Education in Boston," by John J. White.

dren to Catholic schools; others realized many parents simply could not afford to do so. In all instances, at least in the nineteenth century and well into the twentieth century, few bishops recognized the gifts of the laity and rarely invited them to assume responsibility, as partners with them, for the education of the next generation. Rather, some of them spoke to the laity in the language of commands, even threats. By the last third of the twentieth century, however, the relationship between bishops and the laity had changed dramatically. By then, the post-deferential culture had arrived. But the seeds for a better approach to collaboration between the laity and the hierarchy were already being sown a century earlier by John Henry Newman, who was made a cardinal in the last decade of his life.

Newman and the Importance of the Laity

One of my favorite nineteenth-century theologians, John Henry Newman, once quipped that the Church would look foolish without the laity, forming as they do over 99 percent of the Church! As a historian and a theologian, Newman understood the critical role that the laity played in the life of the Church. He never reduced their role to "praying, paying and obeying." Newman thought it important that the laity not only produce children, populating the Church with future priests and religious, but also be consulted, even in matters of Church doctrine. In an article that he published in 1859, more than a decade after he converted from the Anglican to the Catholic Church, he argued that the laity played a crucial role in helping the hierarchy discern authentic teaching. Through his study of the early Church, he discovered that it was the faithful laity who helped the bishops understand that they should oppose Arianism, which was widespread, even among a number of the bishops. He understood that the faith of the whole Church formed the basis for the teaching authority of the bishops.

Not everyone agreed. Msgr. George Talbot, also a convert in 1840 from Anglicanism to the Catholic Church and then ordained a priest in 1846, and eventually, by the 1860s, a trusted advisor in the Vatican to Pope Pius IX and close friend of the English Catholic Cardinal Edward Manning, did not have the highest opinion of his fellow convert Newman. In a letter to Manning, commenting on Newman's 1859 article, "On Consulting the Faithful in Matters of Doctrine," and on the popularity of Newman after his 1864 *Apologia pro vita sua*, Talbot famously asked: "What is the province of the laity? To hunt, to shoot, to entertain. These matters they understand, but to meddle with ecclesiastical matters they have no right at all, and this affair of Newman is a matter purely ecclesiastical.... Dr. Newman is the most dangerous man in England, and you will see that he will make use of the laity against your Grace."[3] Pius IX himself once wrote that "the one duty of the multitude [the laity] is to be led, and like a docile flock to follow their pastors."[4]

Episcopal and Lay "Clericalisms"

Unlike the mid-nineteenth century Vatican, most US bishops, even in the nineteenth century, would be unlikely to refer to the laity in terms as dismissive as those used by Talbot. Surrounded by a dominantly Protestant population, American bishops often spoke about the responsibility of parents to educate their children. From 1829 on, they met every two years to discuss pastoral challenges they faced, a major one being the education of immigrant children. A number of families were sending their children to public schools. That same year, the bishops warned Catholic parents about the dangers of public schools:

> In placing [your children] at school, seek for those teachers who will cultivate the seeds which you have sown; for of what avail will it be, that you have done so much, if the germs which begin to put forth shall now be stifled or eradicated; and should tares be sown where you have reaped the soil?[5]

Once Horace Mann began to establish common schools suffused with their Protestant ethos, some lay Catholic apologists exhorted the rapidly growing number of Catholic parents to send their children to Catholic parish schools. None was more vocal than the Catholic novelist and short story writer, Mary Anne Madden Sadlier who, in her 1856 novel, *The Blakes and the Flanagans*, threatened damnation for Catholic parents who allowed their children to attend public schools:

> Ah, it would be well if Catholic parents would think more of these things than they do. If they would only consider that they are accountable to God and his Church for the precious gift of faith, and are bound under

3. John Henry Newman, *On Consulting the Faithful in Matters of Doctrine*, edited with an introduction by John Coulson (Sheed & Ward, 1961), pp. 41–42.

4. Paul Lakeland, *Church: Engaging Theology* (Liturgical Press: Collegeville, Minnesota, 2010), p. 141.

5. Timothy Walch, *Parish School: American Catholic Parochial Education from Colonial Times to the Present* (National Catholic Education Association, 2003), p. 30. Walch has written an excellent history of the parish school movement. I will cite him several times in this epilogue.

> the pain of deadly sin, to transmit it to their children pure and undefiled, they would not dare to send those children to godless schools, where they are sure to lose their precious inheritance, or having it so shorn of its splendor, so poor and feeble, that it is not longer worth having.[6]

Even more authoritarian than Sadlier was another member of the laity, James A. McMaster, editor of the *Freeman's Journal* in New York. He wanted the bishops to *force* Catholic parents to send their children only to Catholic schools. When the bishops did not support him, he wrote in early 1874 to Vatican officials who quickly responded to the American bishops with a series of question asking why Catholic parents were sending their children to public schools and whether the bishops should then deny them the Sacraments.[7] Several bishops responded to the Vatican officials explaining that though the public schools were obviously not Catholic, they were not anti-Catholic (actually, this was not quite true, as we saw in an earlier chapter), but taught secular knowledge, and therefore offered no religious education. They reported that in rural areas there were few Catholic schools, and that in many of the bigger cities the Catholic schools were inferior to the public schools. They also explained that they were not in favor of denying the Sacraments to parents who had not sent their children to Catholic Schools. Their response did not, however, end the debate. As we saw in Chapter 2, the establishment of parish schools became one of the major items on the agenda of the bishops gathered in 1884 for the 3rd Plenary Council in Baltimore. Even at that time, Archbishop John Ireland of St. Paul, along with a few other bishops, were not in support of establishing parish schools.

After World War II, when Catholics began to have big families and religious sisters and brothers were plentiful, a number of "builder bishops" pushed for the establishment of more Catholic grade and high schools. Among them, Cardinal Spellman of New York City built two hundred parochial schools in the 1950s. In 1954, Cardinal Stritch of Chicago told Catholic educators gathered at the NCEA convention that he was determined to find a place for every Catholic student who wanted to attend a Catholic school. John O'Hara of Philadelphia led the construction of 133 new parochial school buildings and twenty new diocesan high schools.[8]

Even though most religious orders experienced an extraordinary growth in membership after World War II, the tremendous expansion, then, of the number

6. Ibid., p. 56.

7. Ibid., pp. 58–59.

8. Ibid., pp. 170–172.

of schools forced bishops to hire more and more lay teachers. These teachers had to be paid more than the religious. They were often seen as inferior teachers compared to the religious. They were not appreciated. In 1960, O'Hara's superintendent of schools, Fr. Edward Reilly, wrote:

> The percentage of lay teachers is as heavy as we ever care to have it. In most cases the best lay teachers do not approach the average Religious in performance. Consequently, we feel strongly that the more lay teachers we have, the less effective will be our schools.[9]

The first Vatican word of encouragement and praise for lay teachers came some twenty years later when in 1982 the Sacred Congregation for Catholic Education issued a document acknowledging the major contribution that lay teachers made to Catholic schools. Even more, the Congregation underscored the importance of lay teachers receiving "an adequate salary, guaranteed by a well-defined contract and authentic responsibility."[10] Nevertheless, by the mid-1980s, the American bishops had turned their energies to writing two major pastoral letters, one on war and the other on the economy. For all practical purposes, the bishops no longer focused their attention and energy on Catholic schools in the way that a number of bishops in major cities did in the 1950s.

Parents and the Future of Catholic Education

One of the major arguments of this book is that lay teachers can and do deliver an excellent Catholic education. I am not making a virtue out of necessity. That is to say, I am not arguing this point now simply because the majority of teachers in the Catholic classrooms are now lay. Nor am I saying that either religious *or* lay teachers are better educators. I believe that a combination of both religious and lay teachers in high schools is best. And as already noted, the danger today is not that religious will once again outnumber laity, but that religious may disappear completely from the classroom. Together, well-formed and prepared, both religious and lay teachers can and do give a superior education in many Catholic schools.

9. Ibid., p. 173. With the same concern for finances and the same assumption that religious were superior to lay teachers, Cardinal Joseph Ritter of St. Louis stopped all building of Catholic schools in 1962 in order to keep in the classroom at least three religious for every lay teacher. Even though the bishops placed the value of religious in the classroom way above that of lay persons, most of them did nothing to finance their education or support their teacher certification programs.

10. See *America* magazine, "A Vatican Salute to Catholic Lay Teachers" (October 30, 1982), cited in Walch, p. 236.

In the conclusion of his history of Catholic grade schools in the United States, after noting that many of the currently existing Catholic schools do offer a quality education, Timothy Walch lists the reasons for the continuing dramatic decline in the number of Catholic grade schools: (1) the drastic drop in the number of religious; (2) the dramatic drop in the number of children Catholic couples have; (3) the materialism of American culture; (4) the quality of the facilities and cost of public schools; (5) and that public education is no longer seen as a threat to the faith. Walch concludes that many Catholic parents, especially those who live in the suburbs and who are affluent, "do not value the spiritual development of their children as highly as their career development."[11] Given this analysis, with which I largely agree, what then needs to be done to make it more likely that "post-deferential" parents will choose Catholic schools for their children? There is no simple answer. However, I will offer three observations.

First, if the only alternative to a Catholic school is a very poor public school, many parents, if they can afford it, will do what they can to get their children into a Catholic school. Where there is a good public alternative, parents will chose the public school unless the Catholic school is academically better. Parents should not have to choose between the spiritual and intellectual development of their children. In fact, a Catholic high school that offers the education that it should will not only provide spiritual development, it will also provide a *superior* education, precisely because it will integrate knowledge; attend to both the heads and the hearts of their students; engage parents more intimately in the education of their children; deepen their understanding and strengthen the practice of their faith; and prepare their graduates to enter thoughtfully a culture that offers opportunities and has needs, not just for technical skills, but even more for wisdom and generosity.

Second, given both the general religious illiteracy and the varieties of clericalism that afflict American Catholics, there is a greater need than ever for more effective religious education. I trust that the analyses, explanations and arguments of this book have made clearer the important role that Catholic high schools can make in overcoming some of this religious illiteracy. Various forms of adult education, primarily located in parishes, but also linked to Catholic schools for the parents of students, need a much greater commitment of resources and personnel. In this regard, Catholic colleges and universities (a topic that I hope to take up in a future book) could play a much more significant role than they currently do, not only with the religious and theological education they provide their students and the training of teachers for Catholic schools, but also by the assistance they

11. Walch, p. 243.

can and should be giving to parishes and Catholic primary and secondary schools.

Third, perhaps it is time to revisit the suggestion that the priest-sociologist Andrew Greeley made nearly forty years ago. On the basis of research done through the National Opinion Research Center at the University of Chicago, Greeley argued in a 1973 *New York Times Magazine* article that the cause of the decline of Catholics schools was weak leadership.

> The fundamental crisis in Catholic schools is neither financial nor organizational. It is theoretical.... Catholic schools will go out of existence mostly because Catholic educators no longer have enough confidence in what they are doing to sustain the momentum and sacrifice that built the world's largest private school system.[12]

Never the master of nuance, Greeley told the bishops in a 1976 book that they should get out of the Catholic education business and hand over the funding and administration to the laity.[13] In the late 1960s, this is precisely what the religious orders did who owned and operated over 90 percent of the 230 or so Catholic colleges and universities in the United States: they established lay boards of trustees with real fiduciary responsibility for the mission and financing of their schools. Working out the precise way in which these institutions remain Catholic has been an ongoing dialogue with the bishops. On the whole, this new arrangement for Catholic colleges and universities has secured for them not only more financial resources, but also a greater range of talent in thinking about educational, administrative and marketing issues.

Turning over Catholic high schools to lay boards of trustees has already been attempted in the case of several high schools founded and operated by religious orders. These efforts have met with varying degrees of success. But one thing is for sure: the more lay people, especially those who have developed a good sense of the distinctive mission of Catholic high schools, and who take personal responsibility for the leadership and support of Catholic high schools, the better those schools will be.

Greeley may have been wrong to place most of the blame for the decline in Catholic education at the feet of the bishops. There have been multiple reasons for their decline, as Walch noted. Whatever the reasons, I repeat that Catholic

12. "The Catholic Schools are Committing Suicide," *New York Times Magazine* (October 21, 1973), cited by Walch, p. 183.

13. Greeley, McCourt and McCready, *Catholic Schools in a Declining Church* (Kansas City Missouri, 1976), p. 325.

parents should not have to choose between the spiritual and intellectual development of their children. Money follows vision. Catholic high schools that have understood well their distinctive Catholic mission and who have found ways to foster lay leadership will not only survive, they will be the first choice of post-deferential parents as well.

Conclusion

It may surprise the reader if, at this point, I now conclude that the solution is for lay Catholics, though some may have not done so before, to pray, pay and obey. Prayer is crucial for the Christian life, for the animating vision of a Catholic high school will never be derived solely from management books, spreadsheets and better public relations. Paying is both necessary and possible. It is necessary since there is not much likelihood that the federal government will begin in any significant way to support Catholic schools. It is possible because, in the larger Catholic community in the United States, there is sufficient wealth to support Catholic education. And finally, the laity must obey, since all Christians, lay or clerical, must have, as their first priority, discovering, embracing and living out the will of God.

Bishops should realize that in a post-deferential age, issuing commands, demanding conformity, threatening the laity with various sanctions, rarely works if, indeed, it ever did. More than ever, laity and bishops need to pray and work together, drawing upon the special competencies of each other, forming and following their consciences, as they together seek to find the will of God at a time when the entire Christian community faces both continuing problems and new realities.[14] Bishops remain the official teachers of the faith; if that were not the case, there would be an even greater polarization in the Catholic community than we now sadly see. At the same time, parents are the first and most important teachers of their children, in faith and in life. In a post-deferential Church, bishops must continue to exercise their leadership, but do so in a way that invites the laity to think with them, so that together they might learn more about the long and deep tradition of the Church. Bishops, like all Christian believers, need

---

14. Again, to return to the wisdom of Cardinal Newman, at the end of a chapter on conscience, in a book commenting on the recently declared dogma of papal infallibility, he famously gives a toast: "Certainly, if I am obliged to bring religion into after-dinner toasts (which indeed does not seem quite the thing) I shall drink,—to the Pope, if you please,—still, to Conscience first, as to the Pope afterwards" (*The Vatican Decrees*, Notre Dame Press, 1962), p. 138. Newman could affirm the traditional Catholic doctrine of the primacy of an individual's conscience especially since he was hardly religiously illiterate. In our post-deferential age, however, there is a greater need to form consciences than simply to presume they are ready to be followed.

to be open to new learning without ever abandoning the ancient wisdom of the tradition. As paradoxical as it may seem, the bishop who at times is able to admit that he is not sure, or that he may not know how to address a particular issue, may well be the bishop who is most successful in enlisting the expertise, support and cooperation of the laity.

In September of 2000, when Fr. William Joseph Chaminade (1761–1850), the founder of my religious order, the Marianists, was beatified, along with Pope John XXIII, John Paul II described him as a great advocate for the formation of lay leadership in the Church. Like so many saints, Chaminade was ahead of his time. In early nineteenth century France, the Church was in shambles. The French Revolution had dealt a severe blow to the many institutions of the Church. The Church literally had to be rebuilt from the ground up. Chaminade clearly saw then that the most important thing for him to do was to build strong communities of faith among the laity. Rather than focus on individuals, he formed communities, and those communities shaped and led institutions. Without solid Christian institutions, Chaminade thought, the aggressively secular culture would gradually weaken the Christian faith of everyone.

We live today in a culture that gives little support to the religious life of its citizens. The great need and the great opportunity of the present time is for parents, indeed for all lay Catholics, to assume the responsibilities and leadership that is theirs by their baptism, and to do so especially by providing for the formation and education of the next generation, beginning with their own children.

Index

Most footnotes with content not already mentioned on the same page are indexed here, indicated with the suffix "n".